Training
The Sporting Dog

Training
The Sporting Dog

Donald Smith

Ervin E. Jones

American Hunting
Dog Club

This book is dedicated to the incommunicable memory of Peaches and Chuckles, and to Basel and all of the other dogs that endured the development of our training program and proved that it worked, and for the lifelong ease and joy of our future hunting companions.

Book Design by M.L. Flanagan, Clinton, Connecticut
Second Edition edited by J.M. Fink, Granby, Connecticut

Contents

Acknowledgments

No book is written without the help of many people and, in this case, with the help of many dogs.

Steve Babine, Joe Fink, Bill Pacitti, John Russell and others read through the various rough drafts with red pencils in hand and kept us on the right track. Their many suggestions and comments were of great help. We will always appreciatively remember one suggestion that stood head and shoulders above all others. A long paragraph was circled with a terse comment in the margin: "You can do better than this." The spirit embodied in that comment was shown by all.

Obtaining pictures that clearly demonstrate the points made in the text was a far more difficult task than expected. Fortunately, there were some dedicated amateur photographers who were willing to see most of their work scrapped, smile, reload their cameras and try again. The foremost among these was Rich Tapp. John Russell, Ed Saalfrank, Bill Stevenson and others all contributed. We thank them all.

The dogs had the most trying job of all. They had to endure the delays and repetitions required to get the picture just right. When the dogs handled the task flawlessly, we often missed the shot for various reasons. There are about nine sporting breeds represented here. Their ages range from three months to the very old pros. Amee, Ashley, Banner, Basel, Bill, Bonnie, Brandy, Brittany, Butch, Charlie, Coal, Cob, Ebon, Gert, Holly, Jessy, Maggie, Maverick, Mac, Mistress, Monty, Neil, Reba, and Sarah all contributed with great style

x   TRAINING THE SPORTING DOG

and endurance. Many more participated but the pictures were not usable. We also want to thank all the handlers for putting their dogs through this difficult routine.

A special thanks to June Damiano who had the agonizing task of deciphering our writing and producing the various rough drafts while we repeatedly tried to get things right.

Training
The Sporting Dog

Introduction

This book has but one purpose -- to help you train your sporting-type hunting dog to his maximum hunting potential. Sporting dogs are either spaniels, retrievers or pointers. Sporting dogs should be trained to produce game properly as specified by their breed and to retrieve all shot game. A dog properly trained to hunt is a good companion under all circumstances.

Anyone can train a dog provided that his willpower and mental toughness are stronger than those of the dog. This is not intended to imply that every person can train every dog since there is such a wide spectrum of each of these attributes in both people and dogs. If a true commitment is made to the task, most people can train most dogs in the sporting group. There are some dogs, fortunately very few, that cannot and should not be trained. These dogs are the excessively shy, the soft, the self-hunters and the uncooperative bolters; they are not worth your effort. These dogs are the dangerous fear-biters and overaggressive dogs; they should not be tolerated.

There are as many ways to train a dog as there are dog trainers. Few, if any experienced trainers, will agree on the method to use for every step in the training of the complete dog. This book presents one method that strives to show the details that will allow you to control each step and to recognize when the dog has learned that step. While it is possible to train a dog for very limited work by yourself, it is virtually impossible to train a complete hunting dog alone. A complete hunting dog is steady to wing, shot and fall and will retrieve all shot game, marked or blind, dead or crippled, on land, in the marsh or on open water. One pair of eyes, ears, hands and feet are just not enough to accomplish this task. The method presented herein is based on *training* -- correct repetitions with praise, not *breaking* -- punishment for either forced or allowed mistakes. The dog has an innate desire to please and to cooperate with man. Our training system utilizes this desire to produce a happy, eager, trained dog. To take advantage of the strongest possible influence in training -- praise -- every task must be broken down into basic elements that can be controlled, and correct repetitions must be ensured. As each successful element is taught, the previous element becomes the control that guarantees correct performance. When a particular command, such as **Whoa**, has been correctly taught and learned, it becomes the control for teaching another task, such as steadiness. You will find a detailed sequence for each element that itemizes what the handler and the dog must do to ensure a correct repetition. Each sequence is followed by a series of questions to help you analyze the performance of both you and your dog.

Before you start training your dog, read the book through completely. Give it some thought and then read it a second time. Get a good understanding of how the work progresses and how the various basics are used to produce the finished dog. Use the book to analyze and assess your dog's training. Then start with the basics that will be needed to produce a finished trained dog.

1 | Comments On Training

Training, as defined and used in this book, is the act of teaching the dog what you want him to do by getting him to correctly perform tasks repetitively. Training should be distinguished from breaking. Breaking is a method that allows or forces a dog to make a mistake in order to correct him through punishment. Training must be achieved through positive reinforcement, that is, correct repetition with praise.

Dogs of all ages should be taken afield (both land and water) on a regular basis. The duration of the field session and the activity performed will vary with the type, age and maturity of the dog. This time should not be used for basic table or yard work. It is time for the dog to develop his working instinct, get in condition, and explore the world. Pointing dogs should be allowed to run free and develop their natural working range and pace. Flushing dogs should be started on the fundamentals of quartering. Dogs should be allowed to learn about the water at their own pace -- not forced. By all means take your dog out for a good run and a swim as often as possible. It will be good for both of you. Just remember, do not use any command words that the dog has not learned thoroughly. Refer to Chapter 17, Going Afield, for details.

PRAISE

Praise is the most powerful training aid there is and yet it is the most under utilized. Virtually all dogs are born with the instinct to cooperate with and a desire to please man. Only praise in its many forms and phases can develop a dog to its full potential. The generous use of praise in training and handling a dog guarantees a happy, sparkling worker. Praise cannot be overdone when applied to a dog that is doing exactly what you want him to do.

If you expect a dog to believe the praise you give, every fiber of your body must be involved in the praise. Your eyes, voice, attitude and movements must convey your pleasure in his work. Remember, the dog can read you like an open book. If you hold back part of yourself, he will know it. Most dogs live for and thrive on praise.

It should be obvious to you when your dog is happy. While you may not be as demonstrative as your dog, it is equally apparent to him when you are pleased and happy. Likewise, the dog knows when you are displeased. He has a problem here, however, because he does not always know why you are displeased. Human body language for displeasure seems to be much stronger than body language for pleasure. You should be conscious of that. Silently praising the dog to yourself will help you with your body language.

The dog that has been trained on generous praise can be easily controlled by the tone of your voice. A negative attitude exhibited by the trainer, such as an aggressive negative growl, can cause a dramatic change in the dog's behavior, and cause him to react as if he has been whipped. This level of control is possible only because of the tremendous difference that the dog recognizes between the praise he desires and what he receives when he misbehaves. When a base of generous effusive praise has been well established, the dog perceives and responds to your disapproval of his behavior more readily. Therefore, any negative sound from you lets the dog know that what he is doing, or is about to do, is wrong.

On the other hand, the dog that hears only faint praise, no praise or predominantly condemnation, will rarely know when his efforts are pleasing you and cannot build on his innate cooperation and desire to please. Therefore, harsher means will be needed to show your disapproval of his actions and much of the potential rapport between dog and handler will never be realized.

Caution: Praise is not a release signal. Praise tells the dog that you are pleased with what he is doing and that he should continue to do it. The dog must learn that praise results from his successful efforts to please you. When you have convinced a dog that he has pleased you, he will come alive with joy and show it.

It is the trainer's responsibility to control the repetitions so that the dog cannot make a mistake while learning. However, it is impossible to do so at all times. The goal must be that both the dog and the trainer perform correct repetitions consistently. This requires that each training command be separated into its basic elements in such detail that you can control each step and insure its correct performance. A complex response consists of a sequence or chain of simple responses linked together. Training must be done in progressive steps so that each step and each command complement each other and become the basis for the next. There must be no steps trained out of proper sequence for temporary ease, convenience, or because the dog happens to do it well.

BODY LANGUAGE

The dog is a pack animal and, as such, can readily be taught his place in the order of things. If you do not establish that you are the leader, the dog will quickly assume that role. The degree of dominance in a dog will have little effect on training as long as you establish that you are the boss. This does not mean punishment. The dog reads your body language and his world is controlled by it. Your movements, attitude, and tone of voice tell him who is the boss. He will perceive whatever that body language tells him and you cannot mask it with a few words. You must also learn to read his body language since you cannot effectively train and handle him without this communication.

TEMPERAMENT

Temperament and mental toughness determines how intensively a properly bred dog can be trained, and dictates how long it will take to train him. A good understanding of the dog's basic temperament and your own personality is essential to effective training. A dog's true temperament is not always readily apparent, thus, you must be aware of dogs that appear soft but in reality are not. If you set a training pace that overwhelms the dog, the result is frustration for both the dog and the trainer. Frustration may severely damage the progress of the dog's training since some dogs will refuse to respond completely. To get good results, the trainer must fully accept and work at the pace dictated by the dog. A bold confident dog can be trained much quicker than a soft uncertain one. Once you start advanced training, the dog's temperament must be stable enough to withstand the contradictions the dog will encounter. For instance, leave a marked fall (dummy or game) and make a blind retrieve.

The trainer must have the disciplined will power to overcome stubbornness and other eccentricities of the dog. The bold dog needs only to be taught control, whereas, the soft uncertain dog may require considerable confidence building. The ideal dog is the self-confident dog that accepts your training willingly and readily. The bold or dominant dog will have to be continually reminded that you are the trainer. If you can train and control such a dog there is no limit to what he can accomplish. Do not waste your time with dogs that are shy, overly aggressive, fearful, or fearbiters. Such dogs will only let you down in tough situations and will never be honest, dependable, hunting dogs.

Dogs that deliberately bite birds have a weak temperament. While the incidents of biting may be reduced, biting cannot be completely cured since the trait is hereditary and will crop up from time to time. Biting birds is frequently associated with other forms of mishandling of game.

The weak temperament that allows gun-shyness to occur is also hereditary and falls in the same category as bird biting. A dog of sound temperament cannot be "accidently" made gun-shy by a single incident; it requires concerted effort. The effects of gun-shyness can be lessened but not cured, and the dog will never be a dependable worker under difficult hunting conditions. For instance, four shooters in a goose blind with 12-gauge magnums firing over the dog's head will likely cause it to quit hunting or even bolt.

COMMANDS

A command is an order delivered with authority by tone of voice, by hand, by whistle or other alternate means. A command is not a request, suggestion, question or plea. A command is given firmly in a normal speaking voice. Since instant obedience is expected you must demand it. The dog must be trained to obey all commands and to expect that a command will be given only once. Therefore, do not give a command that you are not capable of enforcing or that you are not prepared to enforce. Commands should be simple words or sounds given crisply which will carry well for the distance required. Do not use the dog's name in conjunction with, or ahead of, a command. It is convenient if a dog is taught that his name means **Fetch** in an obvious retrieving situation and should only be attempted after the dog is well trained. It does not matter what word you use for a given command. Just remember that you may have to use it when you are excited, so don't get too fancy. One word that may cause you a problem is "okay" since it is used so frequently in normal conversation.

The dog must instantly obey any command given and must be controlled or guided by that command until a countermanding order is given. The countermanding order for **Fetch** is **Out**, not **Heel** or any other command. A dog can be told to **Fetch** and when he has the object, instructed to **Heel**. He must continue to carry the object, no matter where you go, until the **Out** command is given. The **Heel** command does not supersede the **Fetch** command but is complementary. When properly trained, the dog can make that distinction easily. The **Whoa** command takes precedence over all others and must be obeyed immediately.

Voice

Finished trained hunting dogs that will find birds for the gun and retrieve after the shot must know about 10 voice commands. The words used for these commands are strictly personal preference. Most of the commands referenced in this book are those commonly used and include the typical voice commands: **Whoa, Come, Heel, Fetch, Out** (fetch release), **Hie-on** (hunt), **Back, Over, Leave It** (negative).

Any word other than okay tells the dog that the lesson or work is over and that he is on his own. The word **Whoa** is used for the stop command because it can be projected to a greater distance than **Hup** or other words sometimes used.

You perhaps wonder why sit and stay are not included among the voice commands. If you have a flushing dog, the **Whoa** command means stop and sit. If you have a pointing dog, **Whoa** means stop and stay there. Most dogs, with experience, will sit if they have been given the **Whoa** command and there is nothing to hold their attention. There is no need for the **Stay** command since **Whoa** means stop and don't move. When the pointing dog sits or the flushing dog lies down following the **Whoa** command, this is a key indicator during the **Whoa** training for duration. You know that the dog intends to stay there.

A dog has excellent hearing, therefore, there is no need to use a loud voice. If greater range is needed, use your whistle. It is difficult to keep an angry tone out of your voice when you are trying to project it over a long distance. When you scream at a dog, you have lost control and he knows it.

During all phases of training on lead, a voice command or caution precedes lead action and the intensity of the lead matches the intensity of the voice command.

Voice commands and corresponding lead actions are defined as follows:

Voice	Lead
Caution -- soft, soothing, slightly drawn out	Tap -- gentle, move dog's head, **finger** and **wrist** action only
Firm Command -- firm, normal tone of voice, crisp	Snap -- crisp, unweight front end, **wrist** and **forearm** action
Stern Command -- urgent, lowered tone, short	Pop -- stop dog's forward motion; get his attention, **forearm**, **upper arm**, and **shoulder** action
Sharp Command -- harsh tone, demanding	Crack -- explosive, stop all motion; put him on his hocks, **body action** set and locked.

Hand

The most commonly used hand signals are: **Whoa** -- hand held up and palm facing dog; **Over** -- hand and body move vigorously to the left or the right; **Back** -- hand and body move toward the dog. You may vary these hand signals, but be sure that they are clearly obvious to the dog.

Whistle

The whistle commands you use, with the exception of **Whoa**, are matters of preference. All dogs should know at least two whistle commands: **Whoa** and **Come**. All dogs should know these two commands since the whistle will carry much farther than the voice and will do so without sounding angry as the voice often does when projected a great distance. Other whistle commands such as **Turn**, **Back**, **Over**, etc., may be used to suit your preferences.

The **Whoa** command should, in all cases, be only one toot. The **Whoa** command is the only command that can keep the dog out of trouble. For this reason, the command must be as short and as clear as possible. The number of toots or trills for other commands will be determined by the number of whistle commands that you intend to use.

Alternate Command

As you work with dogs, you will find that more than one sound or sign for a given command is very useful. This will not cause the dog any problems as long as you teach the alternate command properly. In fact, having alternatives allows you to add nuances to your commands. Refer to the section on **Whoa** and note that there are four different handler initiated ways to command the dog to stop: voice, hand, whistle and shotgun. In addition, the dog will be taught that a thrown dummy or a flushing bird is an alternate **Whoa** command. Later on, when it is time to teach backing and honoring, another dog on point will serve as an alternate **Whoa** command. During the discussion that follows, we will refer to the voice command as the primary command since it should be the first command taught.

The prerequisite to teaching the dog an alternate command is that the primary command be thoroughly learned and accepted by the dog. It will be the control that prevents the dog from disobeying the alternate command. In some instances, the alternate whistle command actually becomes stronger than the primary voice command.

To train the dog to the alternate command, give the alternate command followed immediately by the primary command, i.e., whistle then voice. Praise the dog as soon as he obeys. Repeat the combination about 10 times then check to see if the dog is attempting to obey the alternate command before the primary command is given. Now give the alternate command, delay the primary command, and allow the dog time to obey. If he obeys the alternate command promptly, praise him profusely. If the primary command is needed give it harshly. Repeat the combination until the dog responds promptly to the alternate command. If the lead is needed to enforce the alternate and primary commands, the dog does not know the primary command. Remember that the command being taught is always given first followed by the control or enforcement command.

RELEASE WORD

When the work or training is over, a dog must know that he is free to do as he pleases. If you do not teach him a word that releases him, then you force him to disobey the last command given. The dog must be taught a release word which he understands to mean that he is free to do as he wishes, therefore, the release command should not be the same as the **Hunt** command.

Whatever word you decide to use is up to you. The dog will learn its significance very quickly. Every training session must end with a release command followed by some play time. When the training work is over, stand by the dog, take off the lead, give the release word in a happy upbeat voice, move a step or two away and brace yourself, If you are working with a puppy, kneel or sit beside him. It will not take many training sessions for him to learn the release word.

Note: The **Hunt** command as taught in Chapter 18 should not be the release word. The **Hunt** command means get out in front of me and hunt -- it does not mean do as you please.

DISTANCE OF CONTROL

For every command that you teach a dog, you must know the distance at which he will obey the command and never use the command beyond that distance. Remember that there is a tremendous difference in the distance over which you can control a dog in water as compared to on land. This is especially true with the **Whoa** command as you progress from the table to over the hill and out of sight. Every time he disobeys a command when you give it beyond your control range, the job of training is made more difficult.

Many think that as long as there is a lead or check cord on a dog that he is in control. That's why you see so many dogs running around the fields hunting with check cords trailing behind. Any dog with a check cord or shock collar on him in the field is out of control.

The only way to gain control of a dog at greatly extended distances is to begin by gaining complete control with the dog beside you. You must be in a position to insure flawless correct repetitions. If there is any minor flaw in the dog's response when he is beside you in calm conditions, there will be no control when he is excited, particularly when he is some distance from you. As you study this book, you will notice that each time a new command is introduced, the training sequence is initiated with the dog right beside you on the short lead or off lead at short range while maintaining eye contact. This approach facilitates the utilization of all forms of control.

The primary control that any animal has over another, including humans, is the force of physical presence. It is this aura that you must extend during training so that the dog believes he must obey at any distance. It has much to do with attitude and body language since dogs understand body language very well. This physical presence or sphere of influence at times seems to have an energy of its own that radiates outward and demands obedience from the dog. The voice command complements the sphere of physical presence and all commands must be given with a tone, not volume, which demands action. It is assertive and you are telling the dog to do it -- not asking him.

The first tool that you will use to extend and enforce vocal control is the short lead followed by the use of the long lead. In order for a lead to be effective when a dog is moving, you must be holding it at all times. If the dog is stationary, the lead is a form of control that can be used in various ways such as holding it, laying it on the ground while it remains attached to the dog, laying it across the dog's body, or laying it on the ground near him. The lead will be used in all of these ways during training, but not in the presence of game. The object of the training is to get the lead off the dog as soon as possible and to rely on voice or whistle commands and hand signals.

As long as the dog is on a lead, he knows that you have control of him if you use the lead properly. The problems start when the lead is removed. All too often the lead is removed and the dog is given a command at 50 yards or more which he promptly ignores. He probably would have ignored it at 20 yards. Therefore, all commands that will eventually be used at considerable distances must be taught beginning at very short distances and worked outward. Such commands should start at about 5 to 10 yards, depending on the command, and not increased 'until the dog is performing flawlessly. If you only have mediocre performance at 10 yards, you will have no useful control at 50 yards. You must obtain flawless work at each increment out to the maximum range that you intend to use it. The commands **Whoa** and **Come** must also be taught with the dog at a distance, and also when he cannot see you. In most cases, when a dog will obey at 100 yards he will obey at any distance at which he can hear or see the command.

Once the dog is performing the basic **Heel, Whoa** and **Fetch** commands on lead, you are then ready to teach these commands off lead. By starting the dog very close to you so that you can use your physical presence and eye contact, it is relatively easy to establish control of the dog off lead. Now that the dog believes that you can control him off lead as well as on lead, it is easy to extend the range providing you do so in small increments. This prevents the dog from ever learning that there is a limit to your control.

You must be aware of the problems inherent in making the transition from teaching commands on land to teaching those same commands while the dog is in water. Take the time to determine the distance at which the dog will obey a given command while in water. You may be surprised. However, as on land, you must start in close and work outward.

TAP ON THE HEAD

The major problem most people have is getting a dog to be steady, that is, to not move until told to do so. The dog will use any motion or sound as an excuse to move. A technique that you will find very helpful is to teach a young dog that a tap on the head means go. This method should not be taught separately but instead should be used during any activity that sends the dog out and away from you. This is particularly true in the case of the **Hunt**, **Fetch** and **Release** commands. The young dog learns unconsciously to go only when tapped on the head.

Every time you get ready to send the dog to hunt, give him a light tap on the head the instant before you give the **Hunt** command. At the end of each lesson when it is time for his roughhouse session, tap his head just before the **Release** word.

Retrieving is the activity that allows the greatest opportunity for repetition. Once the dog has learned the elements of the command **Whoa,** the retrieve can be set up and you can start to use the tap on the head. Every time he is sent to retrieve, give him a tap simultaneously with the **Fetch** command. If the *tap-fetch* is well taught, it will overcome many temptations to break before the **Fetch** command is given.

Conscientious use of the tap on the head when training young dogs will so ingrain the action that they will wait for the tap even after the command has been given, especially if the dog is not sure that the command was intended for him, or if he was disciplined on the previous repetition. Repeating the command sends him on his way. After the dog is well trained on steadiness, it is very easy to back off on this routine.

EYE CONTACT

Eye contact, cooperation and the desire to please are closely related. The dog that will look you in the eye will try to do what you ask of him. You have his attention and he is receptive to your commands. Whether he completes what you ask of him depends on his ability and preparation, not his lack of cooperation or desire to please. In contrast, the dog that will not look you in the eye or deliberately turns his head to avoid looking at you, does not want to cooperate or do the job and he will ignore you.

Eye contact has three major elements that you must consider in training a dog: (1) it gives you added control in enforcing any command, (2) it indicates the dog's acceptance of a command and his willingness to obey the next one, and (3) it is an indication of cooperativeness as opposed to the obedience of the dog. Most dogs find it very difficult to disobey a command if they are looking at you.

When you give a command while the dog is facing another direction and he turns to look at you, there is no doubt that the command has registered and he has accepted it. If he continues to look at you, he is waiting for the next command. If he looks away, he is not likely to obey the next command and you must get his attention again before giving another command.

During basic and intermediate training, It is pointless to give a dog a command if you do not have his attention. When the dog is on lead, you can get his attention quickly by snapping the lead. The dog may not be able to make eye contact but he can become alert to you. Whenever he is away from you, the dog can look at you and make eye contact. **Caution:** Do not make or expect the dog to hold eye contact for long periods. That action constitutes staring which is a form of aggression and dominance. You must be prepared to give the command the moment you and the dog make eye contact. You have his full attention at that moment. Use it.

Even during advanced training, you should utilize eye contact whenever possible to introduce a tough new phase of work since it will make the job easier for you and the dog. During much advanced work, training and hunting, eye contact is not possible, nor can you always have the dog's attention at the time a command is given. You must be aware of the difference that eye contact makes to the dog and take advantage of it when possible. The dog that looks to you on his own, i.e., with no stimulus from you, is either checking with you to be sure that he is doing what you want him to do or is asking you for guidance. That is cooperation. It takes very little to send such a dog to do whatever you wish.

CONCENTRATION

If we consider what eye contact can tell us about a dog's attitude, it is obvious that we must concentrate on the dog at all times when training him. This is particularly true when a trained dog has a very difficult task ahead of him. You cannot learn to "read" a dog if you do not concentrate on him during training. This is where you must learn his body language as well as he has learned yours. You cannot make good progress in training or working a dog if you have not learned how to understand what he is communicating to you. Anyone can learn to read a dog if he concentrates on the dog at all times during training.

REINFORCEMENT

A reinforcement is any stimulus, which when presented following a response, increases the frequency of the response. There are two types of reinforcement, positive and negative. *Positive reinforcement* is (or may be) praise, food, etc., applied after a response; *negative reinforcement* involves an unpleasant or noxious event removed contingent upon a response, like the ear pinch.

The only command that can be reinforced is one that has been learned by the dog. You cannot reinforce a command that has not been well taught. If you try reinforcement too soon, you will only succeed in teaching the dog some minimum performance that should not be accepted. Once learned, a command can be reinforced by (1) tempting the dog to make a mistake, or (2) forcing him to make a mistake.

In tempting a dog to make a mistake on a given command, you actually set up a situation in order to prevent it. This technique is very effective in teaching a command since it allows you to repetitively prevent an improper behavior under controlled conditions. You must have sufficient control over the situation to allow the dog to start to break the command, yet you must be able to stop him from doing so. Depending on the command, this will be done with voice, whistle, hand signals or a combination of these. Praise the dog generously when he corrects himself and does not err.

When the dog handles temptation well, only then is it appropriate to force a mistake. The dog should know the command well enough so that when the mistake is forced, he shows discomfort. Therefore, the only discipline needed is a good scolding and some shaking. No check cords or pain of any kind is required. *Do not under any circumstance give the dog any other command or repeat the broken command.* Keep quiet and go to him. If you give any command after the break and he obeys it, all is lost; and all that you can do is praise him for obeying that command. Be sure that he succeeds on the next command and praise him profusely when he does.

PUNISHMENT

Is there a place for punishment in training a dog? Yes, under very limited circumstances. There are only two situations in which punishment is appropriate: (1) willful disobedience of a thoroughly learned command and (2) unwarranted aggression toward people or other dogs.

All definitions of punishment define it as inflicting pain for making a mistake. The primary purpose is retaliation or retribution, and only incidentally for prevention. Compare this with negative reinforcement.

THE LESSON

If the dog learns to do his work correctly in the beginning, he will do it correctly for the rest of his life. If he learns it incorrectly, you will be troubled by it for the rest of his life. Therefore, it is far better to train the dog correctly and prevent mistakes than it is to correct them after they become bad habits. Like any teacher, you must have a lesson objective and a plan for reaching that objective.

The first step in preparing for a lesson is to decide exactly what you plan to accomplish on each command. You will probably work on more than one command during most lessons. Be realistic in the progress expected during each lesson and remember that the object of every lesson should be just one small improvement for each command. If you plan for giant leaps, you will surely miss some detail that will come back and bite you down the line.

The second step to consider is whether or not the dog has learned the basics needed for the work and whether or not you have taught the controls needed to prevent mistakes. Be honest with the dog and be honest with yourself. Is the incremental increase controllable?

The third step is to be sure that you know the sequence thoroughly for what you must do and what is expected of the dog. Make sure that you know where your hands should be at all times. The more precise you are in directing the dog, the quicker he will learn. Review the questions and learn them well so that you will know what to anticipate and what to avoid.

The fourth step is to get into the proper mood for the lesson. If you are angry or upset about something, the dog will sense it and react adversely to it, and as a result, no effective work can be accomplished. Delay or cancel the lesson if you are not in the appropriate frame of mind for training. You must come to the lesson in a pleasant frame of mind. Sweet-talk the dog as you prepare him for the lesson. Select some simple basic command he knows well, give the command and praise him as he obeys. Now you are both happy and ready to work.

The fifth step to consider is the length of the lesson. There are two considerations. Most important is the dog's attention span, for without his attention on the job at hand, no real work can be accomplished. When you have lost the dog's attention and cannot get it back, it is time to stop the lesson. You must be very conscious of this with puppies. Have the objectives of the planned lesson been accomplished? If so, stop! When the desired work has been accomplished for one command, ease off on it and concentrate more on the other one or two until you have covered them all as planned for the lesson. Both you and the dog are happy. All lessons must end on a pleasant note. If it has been tough for the dog, go back to something simple and praise him when he does it right so that you both finish on a positive note. The length of a lesson should not be measured in minutes, but rather by attention and accomplishment.

The lesson is not over. The sixth step, and a very important one, is the release word followed by roughhouse play with the dog for a few minutes. You should do whatever he wants to do after the lesson and remember, no commands. His actions will tell you how well he took the lesson. Watch him closely and note how long it takes him to fully relax and regain his happy disposition if he lost it during training.

Questions

You will notice that there are questions listed at the end of each section in which there are detailed sequences for teaching a command. This is done to get you to stop and think about exactly what you and the dog did. In addition, if someone is watching you and the dog, he or she will know what items are critical and can tell you how they were performed. Answer each question and it will force you to analyze the work, eliminate your mistakes and insure that the dog is doing correct repetitions each time. Remember that the dog learns from the repetitions. Correct repetitions mean correct training, and incorrect repetitions mean problems. When you review the sequence prior to training also review the questions to alert yourself to key items.

The answers to the questions can be varied. Some can be answered *yes* or *no* whereas others will require detailed answers. *Yes is* not always the correct or desired answer, nor is *no* necessarily the incorrect response. The introduction to the lesson will give you the desired answer.

HUNTING THE PARTIALLY TRAINED DOG

Can a young or partially trained dog be used for and profit from hunting? If you have the required self-discipline, the answer is an emphatic *yes.* If you do not, the answer is a more emphatic *no.* This applies to you and your hunting partners. You have to decide whether a bird today is more important than a finish trained dog next year. There is only one way for a dog to gain hunting experience and that is to hunt wild game. He learns quickly that when he makes a mistake he does not get the game, but when he does his job properly he does. The wild game will do its part. You must do yours. It is very difficult while hunting to control events well enough to train by correct repetitions. Decide which is more important to you on that day and do that only. The only thing that truly causes problems in future training is when the dog learns that he does not have to obey your commands. Therefore, there are a few things that you should keep in mind.

Do not try to use any command that the dog does not know thoroughly. The two most often disobeyed commands are **Whoa** and **Come.** Every time you order **Whoa** or **Come** and the dog does not obey, his training takes another step backwards. Keep quiet, go to him and get him. One of the major causes of the **Whoa-Come** problem is that hunters work dogs in an area where danger is so close that the dog is hacked constantly to try and keep him safe. He soon learns to ignore you.

Do not expect or command the dog to do something that he has not been trained to do. A dog that has not been trained to steadiness cannot be expected to remain steady. There is no instinct for steadiness. If your **Whoa** is not strong enough to stop and hold him, let him go. There is no point in letting him disobey. If he is a pointer wish him well; he can't catch a wild bird. If the dog is a retriever, tie him to the blind or boat.

Use the dog's instincts to get the work done for which he has not been trained. If that fails, do not hack the dog or get angry with him. If a dog has not been force-trained to retrieve, he is working on instinct and desire. If he has not been taught hand signals and blind retrieving you cannot help him. Remain calm and go and pick up the game yourself. The biggest problem you will have is passing up the easy shot when the dog has made a mistake.

TRAINING EQUIPMENT

There are all types of products on the market for training dogs and most of them are not needed to train a hunting dog. The items required for training a hunting dog are few and quite simple: leads (short and long), collar (hunting and plain chain), dummies (necked down buck and standard), whistle (your choice), shotgun, decoys, a training table, and at the proper time, birds. (See Figure 1.) Shock collars, bark collars, spike collars, check cords, etc., are used to break dogs because the training has not or will not be done properly. Dummy launchers and bird launchers and other gadgets may be used when you do not have a training partner, but they are not as effective.

Training Table

The training table is used for basic training in **Whoa**, **Heel**, **Fetch** and calmness on game. In other words, for all work that requires you to have your hands on the dog or to have the dog very close to you. The primary contributions of the table to training are: (1) concentrates the dog's attention on you, (2) makes you less intimidating to the dog, (3) helps you see, feel and read the dog better, (4) makes your job a lot more comfortable, and (5) it makes the dog feel less secure, therefore, more tractable.

Introduction of the Dog to the Table

Make as long an approach as possible so that you and the dog get lined up with the table. Approach the table with the dog at tight heel on a slack shortened lead so that he cannot go left or right to avoid the ramp. If he balks, reach down and drive him up the ramp. Remember, your hand is right behind and above his head. Slide your hand down the lead to the snap, grip it and drive the dog up the ramp. Use as much pressure as is needed to keep him in the heel position. If he balks on the table, continue to drive him across it. Do not get in front and pull him since that loses the heel position and you cannot snap the lead properly for the **Whoa** command. Many dogs will cross the table the first few times on their toenails. Don't worry, they will relax and drop onto their pads after a few trips.

With a very young puppy, sit on the table, pick him up and let him walk around on and explore the table. Do this several times before you **Heel** him up the ramp.

Collars

There are two types of collars used to train and work hunting dogs: a training collar and a hunting collar.

Training collars: A training collar (a plain chain collar with a ring on each end) is all that is needed to train a hunting dog of normal sound temperament. Many people erroneously refer to them as "choke chains." They are never used in training in the sliding or "choke" condition. That would defeat the purpose of the chain collar which is to concentrate the applied pressure and insure instantaneous transfer of the pressure from your hand to the dog. The lead is attached to the ring that prevents sliding or by catching both rings. Therefore, the collar should be just large enough to slide snugly over the dog's head. The only time the lead is attached to the ring that allows the collar to tighten on the dog's neck is when the dog would be in danger if he slipped his collar off.

Figure 1   The Training Table

Hunting collars: Hunting collars come in all sizes and materials. The most common are leather or nylon webbing. Wide fluorescent collars are becoming popular for dogs working in heavy cover. Take your choice. However, the chain collar that can tighten is *not* a choice. Shock collars, pinch collars, spike collars, bark collars are neither hunting nor training collars. They are "breaking" collars and are specifically designed to hurt a dog.

Leads

There are four basic styles of leads: standard, long, special and short. The most useful leads for training are flat leather and nylon webbing although they are made from a variety of different materials. All of the work described in this book can be done with two leads.

Standard lead: A standard lead is normally about 4 to 6 feet long, made of flat leather or nylon webbing, and is all that is needed for table work and most basic ground work.

Long lead: A long lead is 20 feet or longer. While it can be made of flat leather, it is very expensive; therefore, it is usually made of nylon webbing. One end should be clean and smooth with no loop, snaps or knots. While it is used in a variety of training activities, the actual time of use is very short in each activity. The long lead will be used for teaching **Fetch**, the basic **Come** command, early trailing work and for introducing puppies to birds. If **Whoa** has been trained properly, there is no need for a lead when working birds in the field.

Special leads: Although there are many, the most useful is the Jaeger or over the shoulder type made of flat leather or nylon webbing with various snaps and rings to adjust length. Its primary use is to leave the hands free while restraining the dog.

Short lead: The short leash is about 16 inches long with a snap on one end and loop on the other, and is usually made of leather or nylon. The short lead is very easy for a hunter to carry in the field for use when needed, especially when hunting or working near roads.

Whistles

There are many styles of whistles made of many different materials. Pick the one that suits you since it makes no difference to the dog. Make sure that it has the power to project sound over a long distance.

Any command that you train a dog to obey can be given with a whistle. It is a simple matter to teach the dog that a certain whistle sound means the same as the voice or hand command. As a matter of safety, all dogs should be trained to stop instantly on one blast of the whistle. The real advantage a whistle has is that the sound can be projected a long way without an angry tone which is very difficult to do with your voice.

Decide what whistle commands you plan to train the dog to obey before you train him to obey any, otherwise, you may have problems selecting the right combinations of whistle toots. The number of toots should be in the order of urgency of response, i.e., one toot means stop. Make sure the dog has been trained well to a given command before you transfer that command to the whistle.

Dummies

There are two types of dummies needed to force train a dog to retrieve: (1) necked down in the middle and (2) full-bodied floaters. The necked down dummies are used for basic training and the full bodied floaters for advanced work. There are two styles of necked down dummies: (1) light weight and (2) heavy weight.

Light weights are made with a wooden dowel wrapped with about 3/16" diameter rope. The ends are constructed so that at least 1" remains between the bottom of the dowel and the surface on which it rests. The space between the insides of the ends should be just wide enough to be comfortable for the dog when gripping it. The diameter of the dowel plus wrapping should be so that your thumb can hook over it and lock it down on the dog's premolars when your hand is under the dog's jaw. The large diameter pads should be about 3" long making the total dummy length about 10 inches.

Weight lifters' hand weights are the easiest to find and use as *heavy weight* dummies. Many sporting goods stores stock them. The weight of the dummy can be easily adjusted as the dog progresses. A mature 50-pound dog can handle a 20-pound weight with no trouble. Make sure that the space between the weights is well wrapped with rope of at least 1/4" in diameter. The metal bar must be well padded with the rope to protect the dog's teeth. In contrast to the light dummy, the distance between the insides of the weights should be about 7" so that the dog learns to be conscious of weight distribution and balance.

These are the dummies you will use in the basic training of **Fetch.** The light dummy is used for training all steps of hold, reach and pick up. The heavy dummy (with increasing weight) is used only after the dog will pick up and carry properly. The heavy dummy should never be put into the dog's mouth since you cannot guarantee proper balance. Therefore, it must be picked up by the dog.

The full-bodied dummy is used to train the dog to **Fetch** under widely varying conditions on land and water. It is used to teach **Fetch** for marked, blind, combinations and multiples under a variety of conditions. Full-bodied dummies are also used to teach hand and voice directional signals.

Shotgun

A hunting dog should have all shooting done for him in training with a shotgun. No other gun sounds like a shotgun and a shotgun is the gun that will be used on all game that the dog will be asked to hunt. If you must use blank rounds use shotgun blanks, not a starter pistol or other blank pistol loads. The first objection voiced about using shotguns is the cost of the ammunition. Any dog properly trained to **Whoa** can be finished trained steady in both upland and waterfowl work with less than 5 boxes of shells.

The advantages of using a shotgun during training are: (1) it is one of four commands for **Whoa** (voice, whistle, hand, gunfire), (2) if the dog can see the gun come up, he directs and concentrates his attention in the area where action should take place and (3) it gives the dog experience in learning to take the direction of the mark when neither the gun nor the game can be seen.

There is one phase of training, however, that will require more shells and it can only be done with a shotgun -- marking the fall of game by the sound of the gun. Seasoned hunting dogs learn this in time if enough game is shot for them. You can help the dog learn it by the proper safe use of a shotgun during training. Proper and safe use is to aim right at any object being "shot" for the dog to retrieve if you are using blanks. If you are using live rounds, shoot as close to dummies and birds, that are not to be killed, as practical. If the dog can see you, he will look in the direction you point the gun. Over water he can see the wad hit. (How many times have you seen a young dog go to the wad?) If the dog cannot see you or another gunner shoot, he can hear the shot and determines the direction in which it is fired. He can do none of these things if you fire a blank or starters pistol in the air.

Bird Harness, Pole and Line

The bird harness, pole and line has very limited and specialized use in dog training. A loop tied around a bird's wings will usually eliminate the need for a harness.

There are actually only two uses for these pieces of equipment: (1) to introduce a young pointing dog to birds to see if he has any pointing instinct and (2) to train a dog to be calm in the presence of game on the table. This should not be tried until the dog is thoroughly trained in **Whoa** and it is always better to use a strong bird released properly.

Forget about the bird wing on a pole with a puppy. It neither proves nor demonstrates anything useful about the puppy. Dogs should retrieve dead game, not point it. A sight point on a wing is no proof that the dog will scent point live game, Let any puppy get tired enough and he will quit chasing and sight point the wing.

SUMMARY

The easiest and only sure way to train a dog to hunt at an intermediate level is to first train him to the finished dog level and then back off to an intermediate stage. No intermediate stage performance ever gets complete control over a dog. Since complete control has never been established, backing off from an intermediate level means that you have no control.

How many times have you heard, "I want my dog to break to shot so that he can get to the bird quicker"? That is wrong for two reasons: (1) the steady dog marks better and retrieves quicker and (2) why should a dog break and chase a missed bird? The average hunter shoots less than 50 percent on game farm birds and worse on wild birds. Therefore, the dog spends over half his time chasing missed birds. For the opening statement to have any possible validity it should have been, "I want my dog to break on hit (shot) birds." To achieve that, a dog must first be steady to wing, shot and fall and only fetch when told to do so. Then there is safety as well as other considerations.

Train the dog to **Heel** flawlessly both on and off lead. Then let experience determine how much leeway a dog can effectively utilize without interfering with the hunting.

Before a dog is allowed to move with game that has been pointed and pushed out, he should be trained to complete steadiness. There is much to be said for a dog with the self-discipline and experience to handle a running bird or covey strictly on his own. If you try to teach this before the dog is a dependable pointer you will wind up with many prematurely flushed birds for many years to come.

These are but a few examples of the problems hunters cause themselves because they will not take the time to train the dog properly. Trying to correct problems is always more difficult than training the dog properly and is a chore for the entire hunting life of the dog. All dogs, and men, backslide in their discipline at times. It is easy to get a dog that has been finish trained back under control. This is not the case for the partially trained or untrained older dog.

The preceding pages define our philosophy of training and introduce you to the methods used in this book. Go back and read them several times. Understand them before you start to train your dog. Your dog will profit greatly from the time you spend doing so.

<table>
<tr><td>2</td><td></td></tr>
</table>

2 | The Lead

The lead in all its forms is, if used properly, the most important piece of equipment you have. It is the tool that allows you to control the dog. It is used to teach and to enforce all basic commands. It allows you to get, keep, and concentrate a dog's attention. Yet, to be effective, it is slack 99.9 percent of the time. It has only two conditions: slack or snapping. It should never be pulled or tugged if you are on one end and the dog is on the other. There are few things a dog loves more than a good tug-of-war where he can lead you around. Do not play the game. Because the lead is slack virtually all of the time, is the reason that the dog pays attention and reacts to it's tap, snap, pop or crack.

The snap of a lead can be defined as a quick forceful application of pressure followed immediately by the complete release of pressure. It should not be thought of as having duration. If there is measurable duration it is not a snap. Think of the snap of a whip. Four degrees of pressure will be used to describe the use of the lead:

1. **Tap** -- very light if used. Pressure is applied with the fingers and wrist. The tap is used with puppies and as gentle reminder or caution for older dogs.
2. **Snap** -- implies medium pressure. Pressure is applied with a secure grip, a locked wrist and a quick movement of the hand upward. The hinge or breakpoint is the elbow. This pressure will unweight the dog's front feet but not lift them. It will not stop all forward motion.
3. **Pop** -- implies hard pressure. Pressure is applied with a tight grip, locked wrist and elbow, and a quick movement of the arm. The

hinge or break point is the shoulder. This will lift the dog off his front feet and stop all forward movement.

4. **Crack** -- pressure is applied with a very tight grip, locked wrist, elbow and shoulder. This movement is an explosive backward movement of the entire body. The pressure generated picks the dog off the ground and either flips him over or jams his rump to the ground, depending on his balance at the moment of the action. If there is a need to crack the leash there has been a mistake made during training.

Remember that the object is to focus the dog's concentration on you and the task at hand. The amount of pressure that you apply depends on the dog and is primarily a function of age, temperament and stage of training.

Caution: A lead that is taut cannot be snapped -- it can only be pulled. Whenever the dog is pulling on the lead you must take a quick step or two toward him to get slack in the lead. Plant your lead foot and pop that lead. The dog must learn that he must not pull on the lead.

In order to use the lead, you must learn how to hold and control it. If you heel and work a dog on your left, the lead is held as follows while the manner of holding is obviously reversed if you work your dog on your right:

1. The controlling hand is your left hand while your right hand handles the excess lead.
2. Hold your left hand waist high with the thumb up and the palm facing forward. Open your thumb forming a "V" with your fingers. Move your right hand to place the lead in the "V" with the lead coming from a chair or any other convenient object (dog) up past your little finger, over the palm and over the top of your thumb, and across in front of your body to your right hand. (See Figure 2.)
3. The excess lead is controlled in the right hand. If you are working with the long lead it will be coiled. (See Figure 3.)
4. To pop the lead, close your fingers around the lead and apply downward pressure on your thumb by moving your right hand to the right and down. To crack the lead, bring the right hand over and grip the lead with both hands.

Figure 2   Note the lead across palm, between the thumb and index finger.

Figure 3   Note the lead lightly gripped by left thumb, excess lead lightly coiled, not wrapped around right hand.

Figure 4   Open left hand stays still in the position. Right hand moves over and grips the lead near left hand.

Figure 5   Right hand moves to the right, shortening the lead from the hand to the dog. The left hand does not move.

5. To shorten lead (distance from left hand to dog), bring your right hand over to the left, grip the lead, relax grip of your left hand on the lead, but do not move your left hand, and pull the excess lead through left hand and regrip it. (See Figures 4 and 5.)

6. To lengthen the lead, relax grip (both hands) and let the dog take the slack lead as needed, regrip the lead with left hand.

7. Practice griping, lengthening and shortening the lead while you have it tied to a convenient object. If the object is anchored, practice some taps, snaps and pops. Note the pressure on your hand when the object is anchored.

To control the dog, the lead must be held in the proper positions to work with the dog. With the dog on the ground at your left, grip the lead in your left hand at about waist height. The section of lead from your left hand to the dog should be slack, but only slightly so. If there is too much slack, you cannot control the dog when necessary. When the dog is on the training table, the left hand should be above the dog's head and just behind the ears. The distance your left hand is held above the dog's head will be determined by your height, the dog's height and the height of the table. In general, the shorter the distance the better. (See Figures 6-10.)

Figure 6 Note lead snap and collar ring --- slack lead.

Figure 7 Position of hands to shorten lead.

Figure 8 Position of hands after lead is shortened.

Figure 9 Front view hand position crossing table.

Figure 10   Position of hands crossing table.

Whatever the distance, the lead must be slack. The one exception to this will be during Step 1 of the **Whoa** lesson for flushing dogs. As the left hand must be free to push the dog's rear end down, the lead must be controlled by the right hand. You normally reach over with the right hand to take up slack as the dog comes up the ramp and onto the table. As soon as you have taken up the slack, reach back over with the right hand and grasp the lead just above your left hand. Maintain the grip with your right hand and position your left hand over the dog's rump. Do this whether you plan to **Whoa** the dog or not to eliminate the dog's anticipation of the **Whoa** command. (See Figures 11 and 12.)

Figure 11   Position of hands and body approaching table.

Figure 12   Position of hands crossing the table.

3 | Heeling

Heeling means that the dog must walk beside you when and wherever you walk, stop when you stop, and stand when you stand with the lead remaining slack at all times. To do that his attention must be primarily on you. The proper use of the lead when heeling sets the stage for its use in all other activities. Whenever, a dog is on a lead that you are holding, he should be at heel unless told otherwise. Therefore, training starts the moment the lead is attached -- regardless of age. If you are not ready to train him do not put him on one end of a lead while you hold the other. This means that you must leave him in the kennel or let him run free. Otherwise he will do the training and you will be heeling. Remember, any time the dog makes the lead go taut tap, snap, pop or crack it, whatever it takes to make him slacken it.

There is little doubt that the best heel position is the one that lets the dog *read* you most easily, and that is when his head is even with and close to your leg. Some may prefer to give the dog more leeway than that; however, you should train the dog to the optimum level and then ease off. You will have full and immediate control when it is needed as a result. It will also be much easier to teach heeling off lead if the dog has been taught the best heel position while on lead.

When working with puppies up to 16 weeks of age, you must be very gentle. To start the heeling lesson, physically hold the dog beside you and calm him. Then give the **Heel** command clearly and step out. If the dog hesitates, tap the lead to encourage him forward. Any time that you start with the dog standing, use this procedure. **Caution:** Do not move your hands, feet or lean forward before the **Heel** command is clearly given. Make the lesson very short and do not expose the pup to long sessions on lead. Pick him up, put him in his crate or stake him out. He him out. He must learn to be calm when he is at heel with you.

When working with puppies 4 to 10 months of age, tap or snap the lead hard enough to get the dog's attention on you, not the surroundings. The lead will never be taut enough for him to tug or pull if his attention is on you. Every time the dog tugs at the lead it gets snapped with increasing force until he pays attention. He will come to heel when he pays attention. Never pull him to heel.

If you begin teaching a dog to heel at 12 months or older, you will have many bad habits to overcome. In most cases this will require hard pops on the lead. However, you must only pop the lead hard enough to get the dogs attention. You will know that you have his attention when he comes to heel and looks up at you. It will take many repetitions of hard pops or even cracks over several sessions. Remember that he has been in the habit of leading. If it is necessary to crack the lead, take one quick step toward the dog to slacken the lead, plant your left foot (for dog heeling on your left) firmly, crack the lead, and immediately relax it. One of two things will happen. His forward motion will be stopped and his front end unweighted or he will be flipped onto his back depending on how hard you crack the lead. In either case, you have his attention. Praise the dog when he comes to heel and looks up at you.

STEP 1

Do whatever it takes to make the dog stand beside you with the lead slack. That means hold the young puppy; tap, snap, pop or crack the lead as needed when training an older dog. You have to be mentally ready to give the **Heel** command the moment he stops and relaxes. Do not give him time to get interested in something else. With the dog standing still and the lead slack:

1. Give the **Heel** command. (It cannot be repeated or emphasized too strongly that you must not make any body movements of any kind before you give the **Heel** command.)
2. Step forward.
3. Tap the lead with forward motion to encourage the dog if he hesitates.

4. Take 5 or 6 steps in a straight line and at a steady pace. The object is to try and stop before the dog has made a mistake so that he can be praised.
5. Praise the dog.

Repeat the sequence and each time he responds correctly, praise him. If he does not walk beside you with a slack lead, give the **Heel** command and snap the lead with enough force to get his attention and bring him to heel. Remember to give the **Heel** command before you snap the lead. Praise him when he comes to heel. Pick up the sequence at item 4 and repeat the sequence at this short distance until the dog is flawless for an entire session, i.e., until only the initial **Heel** command is needed and the lead remains slack at all times.

STEP 2

Increase the straight line distance in increments of 4 or 5 steps. The total distance will depend on the length of the area in which you are working, but there is no need to go over 30 yards. Use the same sequence as in Step 1. When the dog performs flawlessly for an entire session, it is time to vary the speed.

STEP 3

Vary the speed. This is the first step in teaching the dog that he must pay attention to what you are doing and adjust his actions accordingly. Do not underrate the importance of this. When you stop, the dog must come to a complete stop and stand beside you with a slack lead. Dogs that have learned this well can be brought to heel quickly, if they start to stray or edge ahead, even when off lead, if you stop and stand a moment -- there is no need to give any command. With the dog standing beside you:

1. Give the **Heel** command (remember-no body movement prior to command)
2. Step off at a normal pace
3. Cut speed-not abruptly-give dog a moment to adjust
4. Tap the lead if needed
5. Praise the dog when he has adjusted speed properly
6. Resume normal pace

7. Praise the dog when he is in the proper heel position
8. Stop with no command and praise the dog lavishly

Repeat the sequence using both acceleration and deceleration -- running to a very slow walk.

If the dog does not adjust his pace to yours, you must get his attention on you and your movements. Apply only as much force as is needed. Start with a tap of the lead and work up as needed. The sequence will be:

1. Give the **Heel** command
2. Change pace
3. Give the **Heel** command
4. Immediate lead tap, snap or pop as needed to get the dog's attention on you (do not pull him to you -- he must come on his own)
5. Dog comes to heel
6. Praise the dog as you maintain your pace a short distance
7. Stop and praise the dog

Repeat the sequence reducing the force as the dog adjusts quickly to your pace changes.

STEP 4

When the dog will handle pace changes flawlessly, it is time to start changing directions. Do not make these too abrupt or too quick at first. Start with gradual turns since there is no way the dog can handle an abrupt turn correctly if it is his first turn with you. He has no reason to expect or anticipate such a move. Therefore, you will have forced him into a mistake with the consequential reactions. Start with turns of 30 degrees, then 45, 60 and finally 90 degrees. Be sure that he will handle 90 degree turns well before you move on through steps to 180 degree turns. You want to put special emphasis on turns into the dog as opposed to turns away from him due to the lack of reaction time before he is in trouble. There is also no movement of the lead to help him. When the dog has learned to handle all changes of pace and direction, he will know that he must pay attention to your movements and the movements of the lead.

Turn away from the dog.

1. Dog walking beside you at heel
2. Give the **Heel** command
3. Tap lead in direction of turn
4. You turn 30 degrees (items 2, 3 and 4 are done in rapid sequence)
5. Dog turns and comes to heel position
6. Praise the dog as you walk
7. Stop and praise the dog

When the dog handles this well, eliminate item 3 (tap of lead). When he handles that well, eliminate item 2 (**Heel** command). In the event the dog does not turn with you or come to the heel position, you must apply enough force to get his attention on you -- snap, pop or crack the lead as needed. If physical force is needed, work back through the sequence until no command of any kind is needed.

Turn into the dog.

You must be careful not to step on the dog's feet. His *leading leg* will determine how quickly he can turn. When you turn away, the dog has the slack in the lead with which to work. On the other hand, when you turn into the dog, contact can be immediate. The sequence will be the same as in *turn away.* The only change is the direction of the *tap* in item 3. Make sure the tap is in the direction of the turn. If he has been taught to heel with his head at your knee or slightly behind, he will learn to *read* your knee very quickly. Make certain that the early turns into the dog are no more than 30 degrees. Work through all angles until he performs flawlessly on sharp, abrupt directional changes through 180 degree turns.

Review the questions.

STEP 5

The final step on lead will be to stop and remain at heel and then resume heeling when you walk on without any command at the stop or start. This will have many more uses than you may think.

1. Dog walking beside you at heel
2. Give the **Heel** command

3. Tap on lead
4. Stop (items 2, 3 and 4 are done rapidly)
5. Dog stops
6. Short praise (good dog)
7. Resume walking
8. Dog heels
9. Praise the dog as you walk

Review the questions and repeat the sequence several times until you and the dog are at ease. On the next sequence, delay the tap on the lead to see if it is needed. Repeat the sequence without the tap until the dog performs flawlessly. Next, stop without the **Heel** command. Pick up the sequence at item 5. Repeat the sequence until the dog heels, walks, stops, and resumes walking at heel flawlessly.

Before you can effectively start teaching a dog to heel off lead, you must be certain that he understands that he can never take the slack out of the lead. Therefore, he can never pull or tug on the lead. How do you recognize when the dog has learned this? When the lead is slack, the weight of the snap hangs from the collar. As the dog moves away from you and starts to take the slack out of the lead, the snap is lifted. The dog knows the instant it happens and reacts immediately by moving quickly toward you. You can check this by taking the slack out of the lead and watching the dog's reaction.

Drill the dog hard on turns into or across in front of him.

Anytime the lead goes taut, give the lead slack and pop it. He must learn to correct himself before the lead goes taut.

When you have to pop the lead be sure and give the **Heel** command just before the pop. Remember that you are trying to teach the dog to heel to voice alone.

Questions

1. When starting, did you give the **Heel** command clearly before making any movement with your hands, shoulders or feet?
2. Did you pop the lead hard enough to command attention when the dog strayed?

3. Did you give the **Heel** command before popping the lead?
4. Did you give slack immediately or tug on the lead?
5. Did you pull the dog to heel?
6. Did the dog come to heel and look up at you?

OFF LEAD

Heeling off lead is only used when there is no danger. Whenever there is potential danger the dog must be on lead. When the dog is heeling flawlessly on lead it is time to start heeling off lead, go to Step 6.

STEP 6

Acclimate the dog to a crop, old broom handle, or dowel rod by carrying it with you for a lesson or two of heeling without using it. Give the **Heel** command and walk him at heel on lead. Stop and remove the lead. Give the **Heel** command and walk forward. Hold crop diagonally in front of the dog's chest at the start. If he is heeling properly, move the crop in front of your leg, not too far away at first. Any time that the dog moves ahead, give him a **Heel** command and gently rap his chest with the crop. If he persists in trying to move ahead, tap him on the top of his muzzle. This is done to annoy, not to hurt. Every time his muzzle goes ahead of your leg, tap it. This will become very annoying to the dog and he will get the message. If he strays to the left, shift the crop to your left hand; give the **Heel** command and rap his left forearm hard enough to get an immediate and proper reaction back to heel. Progress through all the steps as listed above on lead -- varying speed, stop and start, turns, etc. Whenever a correction must be made, give the **Heel** command followed by a tap. Repeat each step until he performs it flawlessly using only a single initial command. (See Figure 13.)

Questions

1. Were you motionless when the first **Heel** command was given?
2. Did you rap hard enough to get the correct response immediately?
3. Did you praise him when he was heeling properly?
4. Did the dog come to heel quickly and look at you?

Figure 13   Use of rod to position dog heeling off lead.

5. Did the dog stay at heel?

4 | Whoa

Whoa *is the most important command a dog will learn.*

Properly taught, the **Whoa** command greatly reduces the time required to teach all other commands and activities. **Whoa** and **Heel** are virtually complementary in teaching, as one naturally leads to the other or becomes a logical counter command. **Come** should not be taught until **Whoa** is thoroughly learned since it can easily lead to anticipation or to the dog attempting to come to you instead of staying on **Whoa**. Never call a dog to you or give him a command while you are away from him until he has learned **Whoa** thoroughly. Always walk to him, take the heel position, praise him and give him the next command.

Until **Whoa** is thoroughly learned through Step 16, Chapter 5, Duration and Temptation, the **Whoa** command should be given only when you are at the dog's side. Always praise him before giving another command. This approach prevents anticipation and promotes happiness while on **Whoa**.

Teaching the **Whoa** command will be done in 3 phases: *basic, intermediate* and *advanced.*

The *basic* phase of **Whoa** will be taught on lead to voice, whistle, and hand signals.

Intermediate training in the **Whoa** command will be taught off lead in a confined area by voice, by whistle, and by hand signals when the dog is looking at you from short range.

Advanced training in the **Whoa** command will be used while the dog is at a distance from the handler, and while running or swimming. Voice, whistle and shotgun signals will be used. Hand signals will be used when the dog is looking at you or in the presence of game.

The dog well trained to **Whoa** will always stop, look to the handler eagerly, as if to say "What do you want?" He is not cowed, on the contrary, he is alert.

STEP 1

Whoa to a pointing dog means stop, plant four feet, and look to the command. Let's take a moment to explain what snapping the lead does. It unweights the front end -- it does not lift a foot or feet off the ground. (See Figure 14.)

The skier knows this well. To get the feel of it stand up, crouch as if to jump off the floor, spring the body up but keep your feet on the floor. Better yet, if you have a spring scale, step on it, crouch, spring your body

Figure 14   Note feet on the table, lack of weight on the front feet, height of neck and withers.

up but keep your feet on the scale. Your weight seems to increase at the spring then goes down to nearly zero when your legs are fully extended. Unweighting the dog's front end changes some of the forward (horizontal) motion to upward motion, puts some of the weight on the rear end and lets the dog maintain good balance. If the dog's front feet are lifted off the ground he will be pawing the air and trying to move forward for balance when he comes down. The snap of the lead is not a sustained tug or hold that lifts the dog, instead it is a quick application of force released instantly. The snap of the lead must be straight up perpendicular to the dog's movement and sharp enough to unweight the dog's fore end. If the line of force generated by the lead is to the left or right of the dog's midline, he will be thrown off balance which requires foot movement to regain his balance. (See Figure 15.) If the snap is backward it will tend to push the rear end down causing many dogs to sit. You do not want to encourage this if it is a pointing dog.

The beginning of **Whoa** for puppies up to about 4 months of age is the acceptance of restraint. When the **Whoa** command is given, the puppy is

Figure 15   Note weight on the feet, height of neck and withers, slack lead, and position of hands.

Figure 16 Dog held firmly but gently, your head tilts down looking at dog as **Heel** command is given.

held until he stops struggling. If the puppy is heeling on your left, the sequence will be:

1. **Whoa**
2. Reach down and hold the puppy's rear end with your left hand and his front end with your right hand
3. Repeat **Whoa** soothingly until the puppy stops struggling
4. Give short praise ("Good dog") followed immediately by **Heel**. Keep both hands in place on the dog and look straight at the top of his withers until you give the **Heel** command. (See Figure 16.)

Continue this for several weeks or until the puppy stops and does not struggle during two complete 5-minute sessions.

A pointing dog should not be taught to sit until after he is steady to wing and shot. **Sit** is a superfluous command for a dog that knows **Whoa**. It does not take a dog very long to sit or lay down if he has been given the **Whoa** command and ignored.

As a prerequisite to teaching the **Whoa** command to both pointing and flushing dogs, walk the dog over the training table several times or until he relaxes (refer to the section on training table for proper control).

Hook the chain collar so that it will not slide and be sure that you have your hands in the proper position. The control hand should be about 6 inches above the dog's head and just behind his ears. Check your hand position every time the dog crosses the table and don't get lazy. You are now ready for the first step in the **Whoa** training, which is to get the dog to stop.

For pointing dogs the sequence is as follows:

1. Give the voice command **Whoa**
2. Snap the lead immediately after **Whoa**
3. You stop
4. Dog stops
5. Voice praise, "Good dog" (nothing else -- quick and short)
6. Give the **Heel** command
7. Step out

Do not allow the dog to make a mistake. Do not take time for patting or stroking, use voice only. How do you know if the dog has responded correctly? The key is what he does with the unweighted foot at the time of the Whoa. If the unweighted foot is put down even with or behind the weighted foot he has stopped on the command. If he puts it down ahead of the weighted foot he has taken a step after the command. He is praised if he stops on command. If he takes a step after the command, snap the lead harder the next time.

Questions

1. Was your hand in the correct position (above and behind the ears) before **Whoa** command to avoid anticipation?
2. Was the sequence correct?
3. Was the snap done with a straight up hand movement? Remember that a backward snap will promote sitting.
4. Did the snap lift the dog's feet off the table?
5. Did you give body signals before **Whoa?**

6. What happened with the unweighted foot?
7. Was the duration of the stop and praise short enough to prevent a mistake? Remember you are only trying to teach the dog to stop in this lesson.
8. Are you sure that you said **Heel** before you moved a hand or foot or leaned forward?

Answer each of these questions for yourself before you give the next **Whoa** command. It will concentrate your attention on the job at hand and reduce your mistakes. When you and the dog are performing flawlessly on this sequence for two complete lessons, go to Step 2.

The only difference between teaching a flushing dog to **Whoa** and teaching a pointer to **Whoa** is Step 1. **Whoa** to the flushing dog means stop, sit and look to the command. The stop and sit must be quick and continuous with no hesitation or break in the sitting motion. A break or hesitation in the sitting motion by the flushing dog is the same as the pointing dog taking another step or putting the unweighted foot ahead of the weighted foot. Reread the section on Lead, Chapter 2, that pertains to lead control and hand positions. You must practice this to avoid anticipation of the command. When the dog is moving across the table well and you have your hands in the right position it is time for **Whoa.** The snap of the lead must be in the line of movement and not at an angle to it. A dog snapped off balance will not sit; he will try to regain his balance. The snap should be hard enough to unweight, not lift the front end. Therefore, the snap must be up and since you want to load the rear end, it must also have a backward slant of about 45 degrees. At the same time you snap the lead, you will drive the rear end down to the table with your left hand to fully seat the rear end. This sequence must be accomplished in one forceful, quick, continuous motion. (See Figure 17.)

Caution: You will need to overcome the following:

1. To hold the rear end down -- don't. Release the pressure as soon as his rump hits the table.
2. To "hang" the dog on the lead -- don't. Remember that it is a snap of the lead. (See Figure 18.)
3. To move your hands before you say **Heel** -- don't. Keep your left hand an inch or two above the dog's rump and the lead slack

Figure 17   Note position of hands, snap of lead, pressure on the rump.

Figure 18   Note position of hands and slack lead.

Figure 19   Note position of hands, slack lead, head could be tilted more.

in your right hand. It will also help to prevent anticipation if you keep your head tilted down and look straight at the top of the dog's withers while you say "Good dog" and **Heel**. (See Figure 19.)

Note: The **Whoa** command will be given while you are still moving to prevent anticipation of the command followed almost simultaneously by snapping the lead, pushing the dog's rear down and stopping. Snapping the lead and rocking your body backwards to push the dog's rump down will, in effect, stop you.

The flushing dog sequence for **Whoa** will be taught in two parts, A and B. The primary difference between sequences A and B is that the dog's rump is not pushed down in sequence B. The dog must sit to voice **Whoa** and a snap of the lead only.

FLUSHING DOG SEQUENCE A

With the dog moving across the table well on the lead:

1. Give the **Whoa** (voice) command
2. Snap the lead; push the rear down (simultaneously and with one smooth motion)
3. You stop
4. Dog sits
5. Praise the dog, "Good dog." (Nothing else, quick and short.)
6. Give the **Heel** command
7. Move on

Make the stop very short and do not give the dog time enough to make a mistake. Make sure that the **Heel** command is given clearly before you move your hand, foot or lean forward. This sequence must be repeated until the dog sits in one smooth, quick continuous motion. That hitch or hesitation must be eliminated completely. Do not try for duration of sit at this stage.

Repeat the sequence until it is flawless. The dog is not sitting on command if he hesitates; he is resisting and sitting sometime *after* the command. He must be flat on his haunches.

Questions

1. Were your hands in the correct position for a quick reaction and to avoid anticipation?
2. Was the sequence correct?
3. Did you give body signals before the **Whoa** and **Heel** commands?
4. Was there a distinct time lapse between **Heel** and any movement on your part?
5. Was the snap of the lead and push with your hand done simultaneously?
6. Did the dog sit down in one quick, smooth motion?
7. Was an increase in pressure needed to finish the sit?
8. Was the lead slack when the dog's rump hit the table?
9. Did you release the pressure on his rump as soon as it hit the table?
10. Was the praise short enough to prevent a mistake?

Answer each of these questions for yourself before you give the next **Whoa** command. Answering the questions will concentrate your attention on the job at hand and reduce your mistakes. Are you sure you clearly said **Heel** before you moved a hand or foot or leaned forward? When you and the dog are flawless on Flushing Dog Sequence A, it is time to go to Flushing Dog Sequence B -- not before.

Walk the dog over the table a few times to relax him. Is he properly at heel and are your hands properly positioned to use lead if needed?

FLUSHING DOG SEQUENCE B

The sequence is as follows:

1. Give the **Whoa** voice command
2. Snap lead
3. You stop
4. Dog sits
5. Voice praise, "Good dog"
6. **Heel,** move out

Did the dog sit in one quick, continuous motion? If so, praise him and repeat the sequence. If he did not, go back to Flushing Dog Sequence A and use a sharp pop and forceful push on the rump. If that is done correctly try Flushing Dog Sequence B again. This time make the voice command sterner and pop the lead sharply. If he stops and sits properly praise him, give the **Heel** command and step out. Each time he fails to stop and sit properly go back a step. If Flushing Dog Sequence A was taught properly, it will not take long to get Flushing Dog Sequence B done properly.

Flushing dogs and pointing dogs are now on equal footing or rump. They both know that **Whoa** means stop now to the **Whoa** command and snap of the lead; the flushing dog sitting and the pointing dog standing. It is now time to train them to stop to the **Whoa** command by voice only.

STEP 2

Stop on lead and voice command.

The sequence is as follows:

1. Voice command, **Whoa**
2. You stop
3. Dog stops
4. Voice praise, "Good dog"
5. **Heel**
6. Move out

The flushing dog now knows that **Whoa** means stop and sit -- not just stop. Throughout the remainder of the text, whenever a reference is made that the dog must stop that means the flushing dog must sit.

With the dog at heel walk him across the table a time or two. Is your hand in position to use the lead if it is needed? Give the **Whoa** command and stop. Look down to see how smooth and quick the dog sits or what happens to the unweighted foot if he is a pointing dog. If he is correct, praise him, give the **Heel** command and move out. If he tries to keep moving, stand or take another step, pop the lead immediately. Heel him around on to the table and this time repeat Step 1 with a pop. If this performance is flawless, try Step 2 again. Each time the dog fails to stop immediately on the **Whoa** command, pop the lead and repeat Step 1. It will not take as long as you may think if Step 1 was learned well. Repeat the sequence until the dog's performance is flawless for a full lesson to voice only, and then go to Step 3.

Review questions for Step 1 paying special attention to question 5, unweighted foot for pointer, and also to Flushing Dog Sequence A, question 6, smooth sit for flusher.

STEP 3

Stop on lead and hand command.

You must now teach the hand command for **Whoa** as it will be needed to avoid mistakes by the dog as he is taught that **Whoa** means stop and stay. The hand command for **Whoa** will also be used to stop the dog when handler does not stop.

*Hand command for **Whoa**.* Since the hand command for **Whoa** may serve as an alternate command, reread section on Alternate Command, Chapter 1. For this sequence you must control the lead with your right hand if the dog is on your left. The hand command is the open palm in the dog's face. If the dog is on your left, you must use the left hand for the command. If you try to use the right hand, the dog will be able to anticipate the command as you turn your body to bring the hand over. Later when the dog is away from you, use your hands alternately.

1. Walk the dog onto the table and transfer the lead completely to your right hand by bringing your right hand to your left hand
2. Release the lead with your left hand and
3. Move it quickly in front of and towards the dog's face
4. Give voice **Whoa** command immediately
5. You stop
6. Praise, "Good dog"
7. **Heel**
8. Move out

Review the questions. Do not work on duration of **Whoa** yet. Repeat the sequence about 20 times or until the dog indicates that he has made the association between the hand and **Whoa.** Now you must eliminate the voice command from the sequence. Repeat the above sequence, but delay the voice command (item 4) to see if the dog stops. If he does, praise him generously. If he does not, give a stern voice command and pop the lead. Repeat the sequence again with a delay of the voice command. Any time the dog does not stop use a stern voice command and pop of the lead. Repeat the sequence until he stops on hand command only. When the dog's performance is flawless on the hand command only, it is time for Step 4.

Questions

1. Did you get your open palm in the dog's face before you gave the **Whoa** command?
2. Refer to the questions in Step 1.

STEP 4

*On lead **Whoa** means stop and stay.*

We now have two commands that can stop the dog without resorting to the use of the lead, voice or hand commands. It is now time to start extending the time on **Whoa**. From here out we will be including duration on **Whoa** with the other **Whoa** work as needed. We start the extension of **Whoa** by first extending the duration of praise. Walk the dog across the table and give the **Whoa** command. (Use voice and a lead-snap the first few times to make sure that you really have the dog stopped.) If he has stopped correctly, extend the praise time by speaking softly and give him a pat or two. Give the **Heel** command and move out. During this first lesson, fill all of the delay time with praise. This not only starts the duration part of **Whoa** training happily, it also teaches the dog that praise is not a release word. The dog must learn that praise is not a release word for later work. Gradually work on the duration with praise until the dog is stopping and staying on **Whoa** to voice alone and to the hand command alone with you at his side. You will move through these steps quickly. When the dog will stay on **Whoa** for a minute or two with you beside him giving praise, it is time for you to move away from him.

Whenever you are going to start something new or make a major extension of a command, you should use the strongest command that you have. Recall that until now you have always stood beside the dog while he was on **Whoa.** This will be the first time that you leave the dog. At this stage your strongest command for **Whoa** will be your voice command and a pop on the lead. Therefore, the first time you plan to step away from the dog the sequence will be:

1. Voice **Whoa**
2. Pop the lead
3. You stop
4. Dog stops
5. Short praise
6. Voice **Whoa**
7. Take one step at a 45 degree angle forward, turn and face the dog bringing up your free hand for the **Whoa** command (remember that you want to prevent any mistakes)
8. Praise the dog -- make it short
9. Step back to the dog so that he is at heel
10. Praise lavishly (See Figure 20.)

If the dog moves at any time, correct him. Replace the foot or rump and give a stern **Whoa.** Repeat the sequence until his performance is flawless. Now you want to eliminate all commands but the initial **Whoa.** The first item to drop is the **Whoa** in item 7. When that is no longer needed, drop the voice **Whoa** in item 6, not item 1. When the voice **Whoa** is no longer needed, drop the snap of the lead in item 2. Repeat the sequence until the dog will stop and remain on **Whoa** to voice alone while you take a step away from him. Repeat the sequence until the dog will stop and remain on either a voice or hand command. When the dog stops and remains flawlessly it is time to extend the duration. The distance is determined by the length of the lead at this stage, since you must hold it at all times. Work the full semicircle in front of the dog and include some stops and starts. You must watch the dog closely and anticipate any attempt to move and prevent it with a voice or hand command. Use both voice and hand command if you feel more comfortable. If the dog moves, correct him and repeat the **Whoa** command. This must be done every time he moves. If the dog walks off, pick him up roughly, put him back into the correct position forcefully and repeat the **Whoa** command sternly. Do this every time that he moves. Make sure that the dog is performing flawlessly in the forward semicircle before you start the rearward semicircle.

Figure 20   Note: Pointer will be standing. Check position of hands and control of slack lead.

Most dogs that are flawless while you are in front of them will want to move when you go behind them. The dog wants to keep you in sight.

1. **Whoa** the dog on the table
2. Praise
3. Voice **Whoa**
4. Snap the lead
5. Step back obliquely
6. As the dog turns his head, reinforce the **Whoa** with a hand command
7. As you stop, give a calming **Whoa**
8. Praise the dog (See Figure 21.)

If you anticipate movement (other than the turn of his head), give a firm commanding **Whoa**. That does not mean loud. Use a firm, forceful or stern tone. Work back through the commands as outlined above until the dog will stop and remain on the initial **Whoa** command while you take one step back. When the dog accepts this sequence flawlessly, extend the distance, change directions, and move in a semicircle behind him. The first time you start to move completely behind the dog, give a firm voice command to prevent the anticipated movement. You may have to do this for several repetitions. Continue to work on this until the dog will remain still (except for his head) while you move anywhere in the circle while holding the lead.

Questions

1. Did the flushing dog sit quickly and smoothly?
2. How did the pointing dog handle the unweighted foot?
3. Did the pointing dog move a foot to follow you or come to you?
4. Did the flushing dog stand up to follow you or come to you?
5. Did he move anything other than his head and neck? Tail wagging is permissible.

Figure 21   Maintain control of lead as you step behind the dog. Do not tug it --- very light pressure.

STEP 5

*Off lead **Whoa** means stay.*

You must teach the dog that **Whoa** means do not move although you are not holding the lead.

1. Give the dog a **Whoa** command on the table; praise him
2. Snap the lead
3. Drop the lead
4. Give voice **Whoa**
5. Step obliquely forward
6. Give hand **Whoa** command as you turn facing the dog
7. Short praise
8. Step back to the dog quickly
9. Praise generously if he has stood correctly

Review the questions for Step 4. If he has not stood correctly, pop the lead on the next step and use a sterner **Whoa** command. Repeat the sequence that you went through while holding the lead. When the dog is performing flawlessly with the lead dropped, go through the sequence again with the lead off. Each time you bring the dog onto the table and **Whoa** him take the lead with you. Remember to put him back on lead each time before you heel him off. When the dog's performance is flawless he is ready for Step 6.

Note: You may now want to refer to Chapter 5, Duration and Temptation. Temptation will greatly reinforce **Whoa.** Do not get carried away with temptation, however. It is an aid to training, not an end in itself.

STEP 6

On lead, dog stops, while you keep moving.

We now know that the dog will stop on three different commands for **Whoa** and once stopped will stand for a reasonable time with the lead on or off, while you move around him at reasonable distances. He must now learn to **Whoa** on command while you keep moving. When you start this training, you should go to your strongest **Whoa** command the first few times, using the command or combination that has the best chance of preventing a mistake.

With the dog crossing the table:
1. Stern **Whoa** command
2. Snap lead
3. Drop lead
4. Keep moving 2 or 3 steps
5. Stop
6. Short praise
7. Return to dog
8. Lavish praise if done correctly
9. **Heel**

Review the questions for Step 4. If not done correctly, use a sterner voice and a sharper pop on the lead. If you do not have the dog heeling properly and your control of the lead is not proper, this exercise will be most difficult. This is the point at which problems with the unweighted foot become very clear. It also highlights how quick and smooth the sit has been for the flushing dog, as well as the commitment to stop. Continue this sequence at a walk until the dog stops flawlessly. The unweighted foot at the time of the command must not come down ahead of the weighted foot. When the dog is flawless with the snap and voice command, it is time to use a voice command only.

1. Voice command **Whoa**
2. Drop the lead
3. Walk on
4. Turn to face the dog
5. Short praise
6. Return to the dog
7. If done correctly, praise lavishly

Review the questions for Step 4. If the sequence is not done correctly on the next attempt give a voice command sternly and pop the lead. Next time across the table use a stern voice command only. Repeat the sequence until the dog is flawless through the entire lesson as you are walking on. You are now ready to vary speed, that is, walk slowly, normally or rapidly, jog slowly or jog rapidly. If you plan to vary this sequence some

with practice on duration, go back to the dog and praise him. Now move away for duration practice.

STEP 7

*Whistle command for **Whoa**, on table, on lead.*

You will want to use the whistle in later work so now is a good time to teach the alternate command. As **Whoa** is used many times to keep the dog out of trouble and sometimes out of danger, it must be a short quick command that can reach out. Therefore, one short blast on the whistle is the most effective command.

Use the following sequence:

1. **Whistle** command
2. Snap the lead and **Whoa** simultaneously
3. You stop
4. Dog stops
5. Praise

Repeat the sequence 10 to 20 times. Then substitute the **Whoa** command for the snap (item 2) and repeat about 10 times -- until the dog associates the **whistle** with stop. Now it is time to delay the **Whoa** command to see when the dog commits to stop. If the dog commits to stop immediately, stop and praise him. If he hesitates or continues forward, give a stern **Whoa** and pop or crack the lead as needed. Repeat the sequence until the dog commits to stop immediately on the whistle only. When the dog is stopping properly, teach the dog to stop while you move on. Refer back to Step 6 with this sequence:

1. **Whistle** (single short blast)
2. Snap lead
3. Drop lead
4. You keep moving
5. Dog stops
6. Praise the dog as you walk back to him

Review the questions. When the dog is stopping properly to the whistle, give a **Whoa** command in place of the lead snap. When that is done properly the sequence will be:

1. **Whistle**
2. Drop lead
3. Keep moving

When this is done flawlessly at a walk, vary speeds until the dog stops under all conditions.

Questions

1. Did the dog commit to stop to the Whistle? **Whoa**? Lead Snap?
2. Did the dog **Whoa** properly?

STEP 8

Off Lead, voice command, you stop.

If you have taught the dog to **Heel** off lead, it is now time to teach him to **Whoa** off lead. Whatever you used to teach **Heel** off lead (crop, dowel etc.) will be of great help in teaching **Whoa** off lead. It will keep the dog in a good heel position and block his forward movement if needed.

Walk the dog over the table several times while praising him. Then proceed with the following sequence:

1. **Whoa** (normal voice)
2. You stop
3. Dog stops
4. Praise ("Good dog")
5. **Heel** and move out

Review the questions. If the dog performed correctly continue the exercise. If he did not stop properly, use a stronger **Whoa** command (whistle, voice, hand, etc.); block the dog with the crop as you stop. If the dog is successful, praise him profusely. Repeat this sequence several times, then eliminate the use of the crop. If he is very stubborn, instead of blocking him with the crop, rap his front leg hard enough to get his attention. Very few dogs will require the use of the crop in this manner.

Repeat the sequence with lighter raps on his leg until the crop is no longer needed and he stops on voice alone. The time required to do this is basically dependent upon how well you taught **Whoa** on lead. Before you go on, be sure that the flushing dog stops, sits with one quick continuous motion, and that the pointing dog will stop to all **Whoa** commands. Do not try to achieve duration during this step.

STEP 8A

Take the dog through the sequence on the ground around the table until he is flawless.

Questions

1. Did the dog commit to stop instantly on the **Whoa?**
2. Did the dog need to be blocked?
3. Did the dog **Whoa** properly?
4. Did you praise the dog?
5. Did you move before you said **Heel**?

STEP 9

Off Lead, voice command, you keep moving.

Review Step 7 and consider which command was most effective, i.e., which command stopped the dog the quickest. That command will be the one that you use first during this sequence. Walk the dog over the table several times with praise and proceed as follows:

1. Give the **Whoa** command
2. Give the **Hand** command as you move on
3. Dog stops
4. Turn and face the dog
5. Give praise as you walk back to him
6. Use hand **Whoa** if needed
7. Take position so the dog is at heel
8. Praise
9. Give the **Heel** command, move out

Review the questions. If successful, continue repetitions until you are sure that the dog has learned it well. If he has not learned it well the next sequence will be:

1. Give the **Whoa** command
2. Strong **Hand** command
3. Block with crop
4. Move on
5. Turn to face the dog
6. Praise as you walk back if he is correct
7. Assume position with the dog at heel
8. Praise
9. Give the **Heel** command and move out

Review the questions. If the dog still has not learned it, give the **Whoa** command and rap the dog across his front with crop simultaneously with sufficient force to get the desired reaction. If successful, continue exercise back through the sequence until the dog performs flawlessly on all three **Whoa** commands -- voice, whistle and hand.

STEP 9A

Take the dog through each sequence on the ground around the table until he performs flawlessly.

Questions

1. Did the dog commit to stop instantly on **Whoa?**
2. Did the dog **Whoa** properly?
3. Did the dog try to move with or to you?
4. Did you praise him as you moved to the heel position?
5. Did you move before you said **Heel**?
6. Did you need to block the dog?

You must now teach the dog that is running, hunting etc. to stop, look to you and not move until you give another command. A dog that will do this on a single command can be easily trained for other activities, kept out of trouble, and will be a pleasure to handle and hunt with in the field. If additional commands are needed (stay, etc.), the dog may get into trouble and much time will be lost during training and hunting. When the dog looks to you it should be with a happy alert look that seems to say, "What do you want?" With that attitude, there is no question about the dog's willingness to do what you command him to do.

There are two things to be very careful about during this phase of training, one you do not want to do and the other you must do.

1. You *do not* want to change the dog's hunting range or style. If that needs to be done due to variations in cover, it should be done later. Therefore, repetitions must be spaced about five minutes apart, and some thought must be given to the dog's location at the time of command. The **Whoa** command is best given when the dog is coming nearer to you or crossing in front of you, not when he is moving away from you at high speed.

2. Every time you give the **Whoa** command and the dog obeys *walk to him,* praise him and with the dog in the heel position send him on to hunt.

STEP 10

With the dog working in front of you:

1. Wait for the dog to come within 10 to 15 yards approaching and looking at you (This is IMPORTANT.)
2. **Whoa** command (voice or whistle) simultaneously with **Hand** command (you want two strong commands plus eye contact)
3. Dog commits to stop
4. Dog stops
5. Praise dog but keep **Hand** command in force as you walk to him
6. Praise him while at heel
7. Send the dog to hunt from the heel position

Questions

1. Was he within 15 yards? How far?
2. Was the dog looking at you?
3. Were the simultaneous commands sharp and clear?
4. How quickly did he commit to stop?
5. Did he **Whoa** properly as quickly as possible after the commitment?
6. Did he look at you when he stopped?

7. Did he look away when he stopped?
8. What was his attitude? Happy? Alert? Dispirited?
9. Did he stand or sit steady as you walked to him?
10. Did his attitude change as you approached him, and if so, how?

Know the answers to these questions before you give the next **Whoa** command. If your answers to **Questions 1, 2** and **3** are not yes, *you* are making the job difficult. The dog must acknowledge you and must be close enough to feel your presence.

Question 4. The commitment to stop will be clearly seen before the dog stops. A running dog cannot stop instantly, but he can commit to stop instantly-that is the key.

Question 5. If he does not commit to stop instantly, the **Whoa** command must be firmer the next time, the dog closer and his attention on you. If the dog still does not get it, put him on lead at heel for a few minutes and get his attention with a harsh **Whoa** and crack of the lead. If he did not commit to stop instantly, go and get him, but do not praise him. Get there quickly, pick him up, carry him back to the location at which he was when you gave the **Whoa** command, put him down roughly and command **Whoa,** walk to where you gave the command and give the **Whoa** command again. Praise him as you walk back to him.

Question 6. If he looked at you, you have no problem. He will be happy and alert.

Questions 7 and 8. If he looked away, he will usually be dispirited or unsubmitting, therefore, he is reluctantly stopping. Review your entire **Whoa** training program to see if you can find the areas in which the problem occurred. You must praise the dog by every means (voice, attitude, body language, etc.) as you walk to him.

Question 9. If he stood steady, you have no problem. If he tries to move, anticipate it and reinforce the **Whoa** with a stronger voice or whistle, and hand command. If he moves, get stern with him, pick him up and put him back forcefully with a sharp **Whoa** command. Review your duration work. Walk away and praise him while he stands. Then go to his side, and praise him.

Question 10. Did his attitude change for the better as you approached?

If his spirit sank, you need to give much more praise. Now you can see why it was necessary to teach the dog that praise is not a release word. Further, if you are praising the dog as you walk toward him, you cannot appear intimidating and he will welcome your approach. If you want to check this, approach him saying nothing with a scowl on your face and watch the difference.

Repeat the sequence until it is performed flawlessly and the dog is happy and alert, commits to stop instantly, and stands or sits steady. If you allow him to cheat here, it will cause great trouble later. He must commit to stop immediately on command. Review these questions after every command. Do not go to Step 11 until his performance is flawless through Step 10.

STEP 11

Drop the eye contact during this step. You want to keep the distance short (10 to 15 yards). The dog should be crossing in front of you or at most, at a 30-degree angle away from you. Now is a good time to start thinking about the dog's mental concentration. Try to give the **Whoa** command when the dog is between objectives, i.e., when he is not concentrating on something. If he glances at you as he passes, give the **Whoa** command just after he looks away. When you learn to *read* your dog these early commands will be easier to teach. You must concentrate on your dog.

1. The dog is crossing in front of you
2. Give the **Whoa** command
3. Dog commits to stop
4. Dog stops
5. Dog looks at you
6. When he looks to you reinforce the **Whoa** command with the hand
7. Praise him as you walk up
8. Praise him at your side
9. Send him on to hunt

Review the questions for Step 10. Know the answers particularly to questions 2, 8 and 10 before you give the next **Whoa** command.

Take time to be sure that Steps 10 and 11 are learned well. If they are, you and the dog will advance rapidly through the remaining steps. You will have taught him to stop on command when running free. Now you need to extend that control to much greater distances. Reread Chapter 1, Distance of Control. Remember that you started with two aids to stopping the dog-eye contact and force of presence. You overcame the need for eye contact at close range and now you will use it to help eliminate the need for closeness. When that is done you can control the dog at any distance from which he can hear the command, even if he is out of sight.

STEP 12

Remember that any time you make an incremental step in training you will use all of the help that you can to get that first command obeyed. Your plan here is to increase the distance of the **Whoa** command. It may be out of the force of presence range as perceived by the dog. Therefore, you must use everything at your disposal. Be sure to use eye contact on the first few commands with the dog working at about 30 yards (flushing dogs 25 yards or less). Proceed as follows:

1. Establish eye contact with the dog
2. **Whoa** command **(voice** or **whistle** and **hand** simultaneously)
3. Dog commits to stop
4. Dog stops
5. Give praise as you walk to him and maintain the **Hand** command
6. At dog's side praise him
7. Send him on to hunt

Answer the 10 questions in Step 10.

Repeat this sequence until the dog does it flawlessly for several repetitions. If the dog does not commit to stop immediately, go to him, pick him up roughly, take him to the spot where he should have made the commitment, give the **Whoa** command and put him down forcefully. If the dog's stop is very ragged, put him on lead at heel and give a simultaneous **Whoa** command and crack the lead -- he knows better. Anytime the dog fails to commit to stop immediately in subsequent steps 13-16, do the same thing.

STEP 13

Now discontinue the eye contact. With the dog working at 30 yards more or less and crossing in front of you or angling slightly away, the sequence will be:

1. Give the **Whoa** command
2. Dog commits to stop
3. Dog stops and looks to you
4. Immediately reinforce with the **Hand** command
5. Praise dog as you walk to him
6, At his side praise him
7. Send him on to hunt

Answer the 10 questions in Step 10.

Repeat this sequence until the dog's performance is flawless for several consecutive repetitions. Stop him when he is going straight away and take note of how quickly he looks to you. When you see that the dog is going to stay there and wait for you, drop the **Whoa** signal.

STEP 14

Increase the distance to 40 to 50 yards and when several consecutive repetitions have been flawless, go to 60 to 70 yards. As soon as he has several consecutive flawless repetitions, increase the distance and work out to 100 yards and more.

Caution: Do not *repeat* commands too close together -- space them out well. You do not want the dog looking over his shoulder waiting for the command. Four or five commands during a 20-minute run are enough. The dog will learn this faster than you think.

STEP 15

You now come to the acid test. Will the dog stop out of your sight and wait for you to come to him? It is not as difficult as you may think, but you may need help. Someone must be in position to see the dog at the time when the **Whoa** command is given. Make sure that he knows or has a copy of the 10 questions since he will have to answer them.

1. The dog is hunting out of your sight (try to set this up at about 40 to 50 yards since anything less will be difficult to do)
2. Give the **Whoa** command (voice or whistle)
3. Dog commits to stop
4. Dog stops and looks to the sound (the person watching must signal or tell you quickly what happened)
5. Walk quickly into the sight of the dog
6. Praise the dog as you walk to him
7. At his side praise him and send him on to hunt

Get the answer to the pertinent questions in Step 10 from your helper. Do the same things in response to these answers as you would have if you had seen the dog. Dogs with temperament problems will have trouble with this sequence especially when the command is gunfire. When the dog obeys flawlessly through several consecutive repetitions it is time for the next step.

This is an alternate command step, but it is most important to hunting dogs. No hunting dog will ever be at a disadvantage if at the sound of a shotgun he immediately stops and looks to the shot. In many cases he will have a definite advantage (for example, a potentially blind retrieve may be turned into a marked retrieve). This also adds to his safety and to yours. If you are hunting an area where there are other parties, don't worry about the sound of their shot. He knows where you and your partners are and will only respond to your shooting. Remember that in teaching an alternate command, the command being taught is followed by the command that the dog knows.

STEP 16

As the dog works out about 50 yards ahead of you in view, the sequence is as follows:

1. One shot from a shotgun (fire in a safe direction)
2. Follow immediately with the **Whoa** (voice or whistle) command
3. Dog commits to stop
4. Dog stops
5. Praise the dog as you walk to him
6. At his side, praise him and send him on to hunt

Answer the pertinent questions in Step 10. Repeat the sequence a few times. Now change the sequence:

1. Fire one shot in a safe direction
2. Delay the **Whoa** command
3. The dog commits to stop immediately
4. Dog stops
5. Praise him as you walk to him

Review the questions for Step 10. If the dog does not commit to stop, pick him up and take him back to where he was when the gun was fired, put him down sternly and have someone fire the gun, walk to where you were when the gun was fired the first time, praise him as you walk to him. When you are at his side praise him and send him on to hunt. Work on this until the dog is flawless at 100 yards or more and when he is out of sight.

Note: When you can walk over the hill and see the dog on **Whoa** and looking your way consistently, your dog is ready to work birds.

The dog understands that **Whoa** means slam on the brakes *now*, look to the command, stay there and wait for you. He will do this at any distance when he can hear audible commands or see hand commands. He will **Whoa** to any of four commands -- **Voice, Whistle, Gunfire,** or **Hand.** All other training will be made much easier because you can stop the dog from making mistakes, and as a result, have the work at hand done correctly.

You must now teach the dog to respond to **Whoa** in the water. Don't worry, flushing dogs will not sit nor will the pointers sink. **Whoa** to a dog in the water is not meant to have duration. It is meant to direct his attention to you. Anytime a dog is given the **Whoa** command in the water, it will be immediately followed by another command. Therefore, you must have decided what command you will give before you say **Whoa** and give it the instant the dog looks at you.

Virtually all **Whoa** commands given to a dog in the water are given during retrieving work. This is because you are either trying to help him or because he was not steady and you are trying to stop him. This is a situation where having the dog stop, turn and look at you is very important. If the dog does not do that, there is no need to give any other command. He will not obey it.

Whoa, Come, Hand Signals and a **Negative** command are the prerequisites for teaching **Whoa** in the water. You also must be able to get eye contact with the dog and hold it long enough to break his concentration on what he is doing. The first attempts to **Whoa** the dog in the water must be at close range. You want the dog to feel your presence. Be prepared to go and get him if he disobeys, Use a boat, waders, hip boots or swim, but you must get him if need be.

With the dog swimming no more than 15 feet from you:

1. Decide which command (Come for instance) you will give when the dog looks at you
2. Get prepared to give it
3. Give **Whoa** (voice or whistle)
4. Dog looks at you
5. Give **Come** immediately
6. Dog comes toward you
7. Keep eye contact and praise the dog as he comes
8. Meet him at the water
9. Praise and pat the dog while he shakes

Review the questions. If the dog does not look at you when the **Whoa** is given -- go and get him. Handle him roughly back to land, put the lead on him and **Heel** him. Give a very sharp **Whoa** and crack the lead. If the dog went back to what he was doing in disobedience to the **Come** command -- go and get him. Put the long lead on him and put him on **Whoa**. Walk out to the end of the lead leaving some slack so that you can really crack it. Give the **Come** command and immediately crack the lead. He now knows that you can get him in the water as well as on land.

Repeat the sequence in the water until you get the proper response with single **Whoa** and **Come** commands for several consecutive repetitions at 15 feet. When that has been done, start to increase the distance in 10 to 15-foot increments, Make sure that you get proper work at each incremental increase. Continue until you can stop the dog at about 100 yards.

Questions

1. Were you prepared to give the **Come** command?
2. Did the dog turn and look at you the instant **Whoa** was given?
3. Did the dog just look and keep going?
4. Did you give **Come** instantly?
5. Did the dog obey **Come?**
6. Did the dog go back to what he was doing?
7. Did you go get him immediately?
8. Did you praise the dog as he came to you?
9. Did you praise the dog while he shook?

5 Duration And Temptation

Now that the dog off lead will let you walk completely around him, start, stop, and stand behind him without moving anything but his head, it is time to start tempting him to move. Tempting the dog to move and preventing him from doing same or correcting him, reinforces that the **Whoa** command means do not move regardless of the temptation. This must of necessity be done one step behind a strong **Whoa** command. If the **Whoa** command is not strong enough to stop the dog when you see that he is about to move, a mistake will be made. Remember that it is always better to prevent a mistake than to have to correct one. It is always best to introduce a new temptation on the training table whenever possible.

The first temptation should be a tug on the lead. One thing that you will have to watch out for here is how well the dog is balanced when the **Whoa** command is given. It may be necessary, as you pull harder, for the dog to take one short step to brace himself to resist the pull. Do not fault him for that. It only takes one step to brace for the pull.

1. Dog on the table on **Whoa**
2. Training lead on
3. You step about 3 or 4 feet in front of the dog and turn facing him
4. Give the **Whoa** command
5. As you pull lightly on the lead, give the **Whoa** hand command -- held about 2 feet in front of his nose
6. Praise him as you walk back to him
7. When at his side, praise him
8. **Heel** him away (See Figure 22.)

Figure 22   Note strong hand **Whoa**. Very light pressure on lead. Flusher will be sitting.

If he moves, pick him up and put him back where he was with a stern **Whoa** command. Gradually increase the force of the pull. Repeat the sequence with light pulls until the dog is flawless through several consecutive repetitions. Gradually reduce the use of the **Hand** command to stop the dog. If needed, replace the **Hand** command with a soft or cautioning **Whoa** command. This lets the dog know that he is right in resisting and you will want to use it during later training. Decrease the use of the hand command as the dog progresses, but you must be ready to use it or the **Whoa** command if the dog is about to make a mistake. If the table is smooth and not sticky to his pads, you should be able to slide the dog across the table as he resists all the way. Remember to praise each good performance lavishly. Now put him on the ground and repeat each step as you did on the table. He will not slide, but make sure that he digs in. (See Figure 23.)

The second temptation is rapid movement away from the dog in all directions. With the dog on lead, **Whoa** him on the table -- remember the praise.

Figure 23   Note strong pressure on lead met by strong resistance of dog.

1. **Whoa**, drop lead
2. Move forward quickly
3. Give quick hand **Whoa** command
4. Turn and praise as you walk back to the dog

If the dog is steady, repeat several sequences forward. Then move to the side and back as long as the dog is steady. If he is not steady, the sequence will be:

1. Stern **Whoa**
2. Snap or pop the lead
3. Drop the lead
4. Move forward quickly
5. Quick **Hand** command
6. Turn and praise dog as you walk back to him

If the dog is steady, eliminate the snap of the lead on the next repetition and continue the sequence above. When he is steady to all movements, take off the lead.

1. **Whoa**
2. **Hand** command
3. Move out quickly
4. Turn and praise the dog as you walk back

If he is not steady, put the lead back on and start the sequence with a stern **Whoa** and a sharp snap on the lead. Now work the dog through the same sequences on the ground, starting with the lead on. When he is consistently steady off lead, it is time for the next step.

It is during the third temptation sequence when he learns that every time you return to him or near him he will not necessarily be released from **Whoa.** With the dog on **Whoa** on the table off lead as you walk back to him:

1. **Whoa**
2. You keep on going
3. Turn and praise as you walk back to the dog

If he is steady, vary the direction and speed at which you move away. If the dog is not steady, on the next approach give him a stern **Whoa** combined with a firm **Hand** command, turn and praise him as you walk back to him. As he improves, drop the **Hand** command and eliminate the sternness. When he is under control with the normal **Whoa,** vary your speed and direction as you move away. When this performance is flawless, go through the above sequence on the ground until he is consistent.

The fourth temptation will take you out of sight of the dog with distracting sounds. With the dog on lead, **Whoa** him on the table and the sequence will be:

1. **Whoa** command
2. Drop the lead
3. Walk out of sight and do not look back
4. Stand a moment or two
5. Praise the dog the moment you can see him right up to his side
6. Praise him profusely when you are standing by him

If the dog is steady, continue the sequence and extend the time out of sight in gradual steps until you can stay out of his sight for several minutes. Take the lead off. While out of sight, talk so that he can hear you, he must remain steady. When he is steady through the talking distraction, it is time to fire a shot. Take the shotgun with you for several repetitions before you fire the first shot. The first time you fire, fire only once. If he is steady for several repetitions, increase the number of shots to two with a 10 to 15 second delay between them. You may fire more shots but not much will be gained by firing more than 3 or 4. When the dog is steady on the table through all of this, go through the sequence on the ground until he is steady to gunfire. Remember to praise him lavishly when he does well.

A fifth temptation can be someone trying to call the dog. With the dog on lead, on the table on **Whoa:**

1. Step a short distance away
2. Give light tap on lead
3. Give the **Whoa** command
4. Have someone call the dog
5. Praise the dog as you walk back to him

You will have to watch the dog closely during this sequence so that you can see the commitment to move, stop it with a stern **Whoa** command and snap on the lead. The better the dog knows the person calling, the greater the temptation. If the dog breaks with no hesitation, give the lead a hard pop. Go to him, pick him up and put him back where he was on **Whoa**. Continue the sequence until he will resist the call while you are out of sight. Remove the lead and repeat the steps.

The last temptation is birds. Here we have to separate the flushing dog and the pointing dog. The flushing dog must be bold and forceful in the presence of all birds on the ground or on the water. The pointing dog, on the other hand, must learn to differentiate between birds that are to be pointed and those to be retrieved. However, both must be steady to flushed and flying birds.

Let's take the pointing dog first. You will need a partner to control a har-nessed bird (a quail is the easiest to handle) on a short line attached to a pole. Do not pull any feathers -- pulling feathers gives the bird a *crippled* scent. While you walk the dog at heel off lead, the bird is placed near the far end of the table. If outdoors, put the bird at the windward end so that the dog can get the bird's scent and point it. If he points, praise him and staunch him up. Use **Whoa** softly in a cautioning manner. When you are satisfied with the dog's performance, give a quiet firm (as opposed to cautioning) **Whoa** command. Your partner should immediately move the bird on the table a foot or two. Watch the dog carefully. If he starts to move, give a harsh **Whoa** command. Have your partner pick up the bird and take it out of the dog's sight. Release the dog to sniff out the table and **Heel** the dog away while your partner sets up the bird for the next try. Repeat the sequence until he is flawless on one firm **Whoa** command.

The next step is to repeat this with the dog working down wind to the bird. It may be necessary to give a sharp **Whoa** command. Use whatever **Whoa** command it takes to stop him quickly. Praise him, use the cautionary **Whoa,** and when he is calm give a firm **Whoa** command and have your partner move the bird on the table. Anticipate any movement by the dog and prevent it. Repeat the sequence until the dog is performing flawlessly.

With the flushing dog, we almost have a contradiction in purposes since you want him to move in quickly, flush the bird boldly and then stop immediately. The problem for the dog is understanding that flushing boldly and stopping is great -- flushing boldly and chasing is not. The problem for you is to teach the dog to stop without affecting the boldness of the flush. Therefore, no command, caution or restraint can be used before the dog flushes the bird. You must show complete pleasure in the bold flush. In the early stages there must be a delay between the flush and the **Whoa** command that is perceptible to the dog. However, it must not be so long that the dog has time to get up a full head of steam chasing. For the pointing dog, scent was used to stop him which made the job easier. To help yourself with the flushing dog, do not use scent in early work. By the time the dog rides up the scent path of the bird, he will have built up a full head of steam and will be difficult to stop. In order to get ready for birds, you must leave birds and start with dummies, i.e., first teach the dog to stop to unscented flying objects. Refer to Chapter 25, Steadiness, Phase 1.

When it is time to teach the dog that you will leave him on whoa, go out of sight, shoot or do something else, and then call him to you to retrieve. But be careful. Do not do too many repetitions at one time or the dog will begin to anticipate the call and move toward you, whine or fidget. Mix things up between calling him to you and your going to him and heeling him to the next task.

A point on the North Dakota prairie.

A covey of sharptail grouse on the rise. The shooter takes a double.

6 | Retrieving

In the "good old days" when game was plentiful, retrieving (except for the market hunters) did not hold the place it does today. If the retrieve could be made easily, that was done; if not, it was not considered a great loss. With present day scarcity of game, all dogs afield or afloat should be dependable retrievers under all conditions. If the hunter intends to be a game conservationist, all game shot must be retrieved and that requires a well-trained retrieving dog. Therefore, the hunting dog must be capable of retrieving all game shot, dead or crippled. The dog must retrieve under all conditions: land, marsh, water; single and multiple falls (marked and blind) and above all, find and retrieve all cripples. Crippled game or dead game found by anti-hunters is their most effective weapon. Any hunting dog worthy of the name must be able to retrieve. Otherwise, he cannot be said to conserve game.

With this in mind, what is the best way to produce an effective retriever? The discussion of "force" versus "natural" trained retrievers gets rather heated at times -- and will remain so as long as the terms are so ill-defined and the denotations and connotations of each are so misunderstood. The popular perception of force training is continual punishment and physical abuse as opposed to natural training, which is all fun and games. Neither is correct. There is some force applied in training the finished natural retriever, and there is fun involved in developing the force-trained retriever.

Force training when done properly establishes the will of the trainer over the will of the dog. The mechanism is 99% correct repetitions with praise, positive reinforcement and 1% negative reinforcement, the ear pinch. Force training to retrieve is accomplished by dividing the total job into small segments so that you can control and ensure correct performance virtually every time. That approach never allows the dog to believe that he can do anything other than what you command. No matter what he tries to do or to avoid doing, he ends up doing what he is told. The dog learns that when the **Fetch** command is given he must go and get the object and deliver it cleanly to hand every time. There is no punishment involved. There are 24 steps to reach simple marked retrieves. The ear pinch is used in only one, the thirteenth, to accomplish a very narrowly defined goal. The ear pinch is eliminated in the fourteenth step. The dog that is force trained properly is an eager, happy and above all, *a very dependable retriever.*

Natural retrieving relies only on the dog's retrieving instinct, his desire to retrieve at any time, reinforced by exposure and encouragement. If it is truly natural, there can be no right or wrong. Whatever the natural retriever does or does not do must be accepted graciously, since he has not been taught differently. Thus, such a dog will fail to make some retrieves that could and should be made. The dog will rarely retrieve all game for which he is sent cleanly to hand. That is wasteful and disrespectful of the game hunted.

There is little doubt that the dog that is properly force trained is a more dependable and efficient retriever than the natural retriever. The question is how do you produce a happy enthusiastic force trained retriever with an acceptable level of pain? There are two things that must be faced and accepted: (1) once you start, you must complete the process, and (2) you must take the time to teach each step flawlessly before going to the next step. Failure to do these things, coupled with the misapplication of pain, are what has given the concept of force training its bad reputation. If you do not complete the training properly you will have a confused, reluctant retriever,

There are two cautions that must be heeded:

1.   Do not start this program of retrieving until all the dog's permanent teeth are in and well seated.
2.   The command **Fetch** cannot be used at any other time, other than during training, until the program is completed. Everyone involved with the dog must accept and follow this rule. This does not mean that you cannot do play or fun retrieving with the dog.

However, you *cannot* use the word **Fetch** or whatever word you plan to use to send the dog to retrieve.

To the dog, the single command **Fetch** is going to mean:

1.   Hold the object put in his mouth until told to release it
2.   Reach, grasp and hold the object until told to release it
3.   Go anywhere, pick up anything, and deliver it to hand

There is no need for any other commands such as **Come** or **Whistle** blowing when the dog gets to and picks up the object. Praise as he is returning -- Yes! There is only one other command needed -- the release command at the time of delivery. When the dog needs help locating the object, directional commands should be used.

There are 3 basic steps in teaching a dog to retrieve properly: (1) hold the object, (2) reach and grasp, and (3) pick up the object off the ground and in that precise order. Any dog worth hunting over will fight you at one or more of these three steps. A good donnybrook at Step 1 is what you hope to see because that is the easiest step to control and in no way hurts the dog.

HOLD THE OBJECT

You must divide the "object" training into small enough increments to en-sure that you can achieve correct repetitions. The first step requires that you hold the dummy in the dog's mouth and grip the dummy with your thumb. You will open the dog's mouth, say **Fetch,** put the dummy in his mouth, and hold it there. **Caution:** Do not start this step unless you are relaxed and calm. Under no circumstances should you show anger when the dog fights to get the dummy out of his mouth -- that is a normal reac-tion on his part. Make sure you have plenty of time -- it may take up to 30 minutes or even more to achieve the first hold and you must win this battle. Remember, when you say **Fetch,** the dog must hold the dummy before you stop; otherwise, his will has won over yours and you are in trouble. How do you do it?

STEP 1

1.   Open the dog's mouth

2. Give the **Fetch** command
3. Put the dummy in
4. Hold it there
5. The dog grips
6. Praise
7. **Out** (Dog opens mouth. *Gently* take dummy.)
8. Lavish praise

Review the questions. The sequence is simple; its execution is not. Yet, it must be done properly.

1. The dummy must be necked down, that is, larger on the ends than in the middle. If the center is a wooden dowel, it should be wrapped with heavy twine or light rope to soften it against the dog's lower teeth. The center section must be small enough so that when held in the right hand you can close your thumb over it and touch your middle finger. If it is larger, you will not be able to place your right hand under the dog's jaw and hold the dummy down against the lower teeth behind the canines with your thumb.
2. Walk the dog over the table several times and do a few simple **Heels** and **Whoas** so that you can praise the dog. Set a good mood.
3. Stop the dog but *do not* use the **Whoa** command. He will only disobey when he starts to resist the dummy. Pointing dogs should definitely stand and we believe flushing dogs should also, as it makes it easier for them when it comes time to reach for the dummy.
4. With the lead in your left hand behind the dog's head, let out just enough lead so that you can bring your left hand over the dog's head and down on the muzzle. With your thumb on the near side and fingers on the far side of the muzzle, reach down and clear his lips so your thumb and fingertips are on his teeth. Open the dog's mouth. If you have trouble opening the dog's mouth, press the upper lip against the side of the teeth. With some determined dogs, it may be necessary to use the index finger and press the lip against the upper left canine. Practice opening the dog's mouth until you can do it smoothly before you use the dummy. Make sure to get the left hand working well so that you do not lose control. Don't worry, the dog will not bite you. If he intended to bite you, he

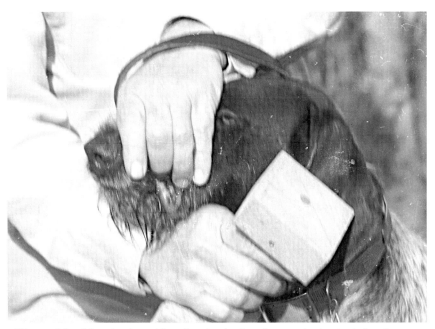

Figure 24   Note lead position, hand gripping dummy locks dog's head, short movement to put dummy in dog's mouth.

would have bitten you long before this. (See Figure 24 for control of the dog prior to opening his mouth.)

5. Prior to opening the dog's mouth you have been holding the dummy in your right hand with the palm up and the dummy held by your thumb. Open the dog's mouth, say **Fetch** and quickly bring your right hand to the dog's mouth with your fingers and palm going under his jaw. Slide the dummy over his canines and grip with your thumb. Press the dummy down on the lower teeth and against the backside of the canines. (See Figures 25 & 26.)

6. Hang on! For how long? Until he stops struggling and puts light pressure on your thumb with the roof of his mouth or incisors. That is your signal that he has accepted the dummy in his mouth and is holding -- gripping it. Hang on! He may buck like a mule, stand on his hind legs, paw at the dummy, attempt to lay down, jump off the table, twist his head away -- anything. Just hang on! If he gets the dummy out, open his mouth, say **Fetch** and put it back in again. If he spits it out a hundred times, put it back in

Figure 25 Note position of right thumb, lips clear of teeth, left hand ready to release lips and grip lead.

Figure 26 Note middle finger between jaw bones can feel tongue move if the dog starts to spit out the dummy.

again. You must win this first battle. Do not get angry -- laugh -- this is what you want. Have the big test of wills now.

7. What has the left hand been doing all this time? After opening the dog's mouth, the left hand has regripped the lead up short behind the dog's head. This keeps him in close to you and lends support for the right hand to work against. Each time you say **Fetch,** you must immediately snap the lead. As long as the dummy is in the dog's mouth, you will be repeating **Fetch** and snapping the lead.

8. The dog has yielded and closed his mouth with light pressure on your thumb. Do not wait, say "Good dog!" quickly followed by **Out** or whatever command you will use for the dog to release game. Praise him generously. If the dog has stopped struggling and gripped the dummy for one second that is plenty long enough. Remember -- do not allow time for a mistake to be made. Walk the dog off the table at heel and do a few stops and starts. Praise the dog when he is right. Take a few minutes before the next repetition. Review the questions.

Repeat the sequence:

1. Open the dog's mouth
2. Give the **Fetch** command
3. Put the dummy in
4. Hold it in and wait for the dog to stop struggling and grip the dummy
5. Quick praise
6. **Out**
7. Dog opens mouth. *Gently* take the dummy.
8. Generous praise

Three or four repetitions is all that is needed for the first session. The dog that fights you will not be a problem. The difficult dog will be the one that does nothing -- just stands there limp and slack-jawed. He will truly try your patience. Do not get angry. To overcome the slack-jaw, you will have to press up with your right hand and close his mouth until the roof presses on your thumb. Hold that pressure for a couple of seconds while you repeat **Fetch** and tap the lead. Hold the pressure, praise the dog, give the **Out** command and take the dummy. Do not try to hold the dog's mouth shut on the dummy by squeezing down on the top of the dog's muzzle. It won't work and you will stop his normal breathing. If he rises up with the upward pressure of your right hand, hold the lead with your thumb and press your left palm down on the top of his head, not his muzzle. If your left hand is in the proper position, all you need to do is roll it over and down. (See Figure 27.)

When the fighting dog no longer fights and the slack-jawed dog is no longer slack-jawed, but accepts the dummy and grips it along with your thumb firmly for a complete lesson throughout 10 repetitions, it is time for Step 2.

Questions

1. Was the lead held correctly?
2. How did the dog resist the mouth opening? Violently? Hard? Locked jaws? Mildly? Not at all?
3. Did you command **Fetch** before putting the dummy in the dog's mouth?
4. Did you place the dummy properly (on the premolars and press against the back of the canines)?

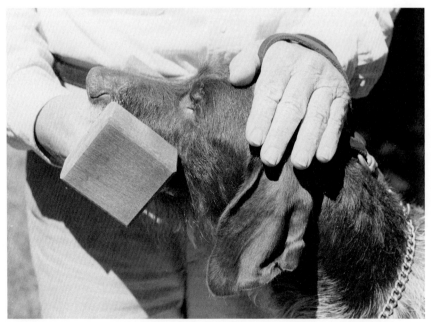

Figure 27   Note left hand blocking head to prevent backward movement.

5. Did your thumb hook over the dummy in the dog's mouth?
6. How did the dog resist the hold? Violently? Every which way? Hard? Mildly? Not at all? Slack-jawed? Laid down, etc.?
7. How long did the resistance last?
8. When the dog gripped the dummy, did you give quick praise and an immediate **Out** command?
9. Did you delay the **Out** command and thereby allow (no-force) the dog to make a mistake by relaxing his grip?
10. Did you control your temper and keep a normal tone to your **Fetch** command'?
11. Did you praise the dog lavishly after the **Out** command?

STEP 2

Walk the dog across the table, stop him and do 1 or 2 repetitions of Step 1. Praise the dog for each correct repetition. The new sequence will be:

1. Open the dog's mouth
2. Give the **Fetch** command
3. Put the dummy in the dog's mouth as you did before
4. Snap lead
5. Do not hook thumb over dummy; press upward with your right hand on the dog's jaw to keep his mouth closed
6. Feel the dog grip the dummy. (Keep contact with the underside of the jaw with your index and middle finger and grip the dummy with your thumb and little finger.)
7. Short praise. If too long, he may relax his grip before you take the dummy
8. **Out** command, dog opens mouth, *gently* take the dummy
9. Praise the dog

Review the questions. The dog's grip is felt with your right hand that keeps contact with the underside of the jaw and through your index finger and thumb. It is important to establish a firm grip at this point. The word is grip, not contain. The dog can contain the dummy without gripping it. Do not be misled. Make sure that he is gripping. Many later problems are caused by failure to teach the grip as opposed to containment. Do not make the duration of the grip too long, 3 or 4 seconds is long enough. As long as he grips, praise him. If you feel he is about to relax, say **Fetch,** and tap the lead and feel the grip firm up. Continue the sequence until the dog completes a lesson flawlessly. **Caution:** Never give the **Out** command unless the dog has a good grip on the dummy. (See Figure 28.)

STEP 3

This will be the step at which the dog must hold without your right hand as support. What will be your control? The voice command and tap of the lead. Anytime you anticipate a problem, give a **Fetch** command and tap the lead. Anytime you start to do something with your right hand, you first say **Fetch** and tap the lead. Walk the dog across the table a time or two and *stop* him.

1. Open the dog's mouth
2. Voice command **Fetch**
3. Put dummy in dog's mouth (fingers touching the underside of the jaw)
4. Dog grips the dummy

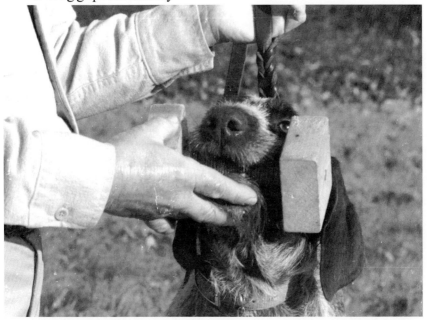

Figure 28   Note middle finger under jaw for control, thumb and little finger on dummy to feel grip, lead hand in proper position.

5. **Fetch,** tap lead
6. Lower right hand about 1 inch below the jaw
7. Short praise
8. **Fetch,** tap lead
9. Put finger on underside of jaw
10. **Fetch,** tap lead
11. You grip dummy (index finger and thumb)
12. Check dog's grip
13. Give the **Out** command
14. Dog opens mouth, *gently* take the dummy
15. Generous praise

Review the questions. The key to this sequence is the **Fetch**/tap lead sequence used three times before you take your hand away, before you put it back and before you grip the dummy This firms up the grip each time and eliminates anticipation. Anytime the dog relaxes his grip, give a firm **Fetch** and snap (not tap) the lead. Do not make the dog's grip time too long yet -- 5 or 6 seconds is plenty. Remember that you are still trying to teach the dog to grip. Prolonged hold comes only after the grip is thoroughly learned to voice alone. Repeat the sequence until the dog performs flawlessly for an entire lesson. (See Figure 29.)

Note: Start to be conscious of when the dog is no longer resisting having his mouth opened; when he allows it to be opened, when he starts to open on the **Fetch** command and when his mouth figuratively floats open as you touch the sides of his muzzle. You will need this response before you start the Reach/Grasp.

STEP 4

During this step you will drop the tap of the lead but still use the **Fetch** before any movement with the right hand. Do not try to drop the tap of the lead on all three right hand movements in one sequence the first time, pick one. Make it a different one each time, then two out of three and then all three. It may well be that you have more trouble with one than others. Don't worry, just work it out. If you have trouble, back up a step, that is, to the **Fetch** and snap lead sequence. It shouldn't take more than one or two times to get the message across.

Figure 29   Always hold dummy and check the dog's grip before giving the **Out** command.

1. Open the dog's mouth
2. Give the **Fetch** command
3. Put dummy in the dog's mouth (fingers touching the underside of the jaw)
4. Dog grips the dummy
5. Give the **Fetch** command
6. Lower right hand about an inch
7. Short praise
8. Give the **Fetch** command
9. Put fingers on underside of jaw
10. Give the Fetch command
11. You grip dummy
12. Check the dog's grip
13. Give the **Out** command
14. Dog opens mouth, *gently* take the dummy
15. Praise the dog

Review the questions. Repeat the exercise until the dog is flawless through all three right hand movements. (See Figure 30.)

STEP 5

During this step you will change your grip on the dummy. Instead of holding it in the middle and riding it over the canines from straight on, grip it at one end and after you open the dog's mouth, put the dummy into his mouth so that he grips it in the middle. You will want to keep the right hand near and below his muzzle after he grips it, in case a light tap on the underside of the jaw is needed as a reminder. Walk the dog across the table, stop him and take him through a repetition or two of Steps 1-4. Praise him for good work and set a good tone for the lesson.

1. Open the dog's mouth
2. Give the **Fetch** command
3. Put dummy in dog's mouth
4. Dog grips dummy

Figure 30   Keep hand under jaw to quickly prevent a mistake, lead held to quickly tap as a reminder to grip the dummy.

5. You release dummy
6. Keep right hand near his muzzle
7. Short praise
8. You grip dummy
9. Check dog's grip
10. Give the **Out** command
11. Dog opens mouth, *gently* take the dummy
12. Lavish praise

Review the questions. If the dog starts to relax his grip, tap the underside of his jaw with your fingertips or give a light tap on the lead, whichever is appropriate. Continue the sequence until the dog is flawless for a complete lesson to voice command only.

You now have a dog that knows he is supposed to hold the dummy when it is put in his mouth. It is time to start extending the time of the hold and tempting him to make a mistake. It is also time to have him hold objects other than the dummy. You can alternate between extended holds and temptation with different objects to break up the routine and avoid boredom. When varying objects use a variety of textures, hard, soft, fragile, you name it. Use any objects around the house: aluminum cans, bottles, sticks, a wood rasp, a very soft box (he should not crush it), hairbrush, or anything and everything. However, do not introduce a lot of new things during the first lesson. While we are at it, do not use heavy (2 lbs. and up) dummies until the dog will pick up light dummies from the table and the ground. You may not hold the dummy so that the dog gets a grip that balances it and when you let go -- disaster.

STEP 6

Let's start with the extension of the duration of the grip. Extend the time gradually -- 10 seconds, then 15, 20, 30, etc. Remember to keep the lead in the proper position so you can stop relaxation of the grip by a light tap on the lead. You must watch the dog carefully and use voice and lead to keep the grip firm. The sequence will be:

1. Open the dog's mouth
2. Give the **Fetch** command
3. Put the dummy in his mouth

4. Release the dummy
5. Mix praise with cautionary **Fetch**
6. You grip the dummy
7. Be sure dog has firm grip
8. Give the **Out** command
9. Dog opens mouth, *gently* take the dummy
10. Give praise

Gradually extend the time. When he will hold for 30 or more seconds, it is time to step a short distance away. Keep hold of the lead and move in front of the dog when you first start. Vary this until you can walk around the dog. You will find that a light flip of the lead when you are in front of the dog will get the same reaction as the tap. Use the cautionary **Fetch** frequently to keep the grip firm.

STEP 7

In tempting the dog to make a mistake (relax the grip) start with a light tap on the dummy -- just hard enough so that you can feel if there is any relaxation of the grip. There is no need to hit it hard enough to jolt the dog. As you work up, use a push rather than a tap. Grip the dummy and push or pull it, push it up or down to tilt the dog's head. Start softly and work up gradually. Grip the dummy as you would if you were going to take it and use the take out movement. The first few times you do this, use the **Fetch** command or a tap on the lead immediately before the take out movement. Remember the purpose of all this is to ensure that the dog will keep a grip firm enough to control the dummy. **Caution:** Do not rotate or try to spin the dummy in the dog's mouth. For some reason dogs will not maintain a grip while you rotate the dummy. Also, the taking of the dummy should not be a rotating movement. You would not want to rotate game in the dog's mouth while taking it from him. Any time there is a mistake made, set the dog up again and use the **Fetch**/tap lead sequence before repeating it. Praise him generously when he does it right. (See Figure 31.)

STEP 8

As you start to introduce different objects, be sure that you start the lesson with something familiar so that the dog does it right and earns praise,

Figure 31   Notice how the dog's
head is tipped upward.

the lesson will then be off to a happy start. Be gentle and always remember to put all new objects in the dog's mouth and do not let go of them until you are sure that he has the grip needed to hold them and that he is holding. If you feel a reluctance on the dog's part, keep the right hand close by so that you can tap the underside of the jaw or tap the lead to firm up the grip. Make sure that the dog will hold a variety of shapes (for balance), textures (for feel in his mouth), hard items (will he grip metal or glass?), soft items (does he grip softly as needed or does he crush or puncture?). Aluminum cans are a great test of the uniformness of grip since any variation makes the can snap and pop. A tightly rolled magazine is also useful since each time he relaxes his grip the magazine will open a little more.

The next step is to have the dog walk at heel with the dummy. There is more to this than just the dog walking with the dummy. This will be the point at which you teach the dog to hold the dummy and yet obey other commands. It reinforces the hold until the **Out** command is given. In later work, he will be asked to do other things while holding the dummy. You introduce the concept here, and it is a major step. This step must be well learned before the dog reaches for the dummy.

Remember, when you introduce a new concept or make a major step forward, you want to be sure that the first attempt has every possibility of success. How do you reinforce **Fetch** and still give the **Heel** command? Many dogs will refuse to move, some will drop the dummy and others will do both. If you have used the lead properly, a light tap will mean both **Fetch** and **Heel** -- remember that you have used it to reinforce both commands. You will also need the free hand held lightly under the jaw so that you can tap it for reinforcement.

STEP 9

With the dog on the table standing near the up ramp:
1. Open the dog's mouth
2. Give the **Fetch** command
3. Put the dummy in the dog's mouth
4. Praise him for holding
5. Position your free hand
6. Reinforce the **Fetch** command with voice and lead tap
7. Give the **Heel** command
8. Step forward
9. Praise the dog
10. Stop short of the down ramp
11. Praise the dog
12. Grip the dummy
13. Check the dog's grip
14. Give the **Out** command
15. Dog opens mouth, *gently* take the dummy
16. Praise the dog lavishly
17. Give the **Heel** command and walk the dog down the ramp and away

Review the questions and if all has gone well, repeat the sequence until it can be done flawlessly with no reinforcement of the **Fetch** command and only the voice command for **Heel** is needed.

Now, what do you do if the dog refuses to move, tries to drop the dummy, or both? As you may recall, it was suggested at the start that you not give a **Whoa** command when you stopped the dog to start the **Fetch** sequence -- this is one reason. If the dog does not start to move with you, repeat the **Heel** command and tap the lead with a forward motion as you did during early heel training. Keep a sharp eye on the dog to be sure that he is maintaining a good grip. If he still refuses to move, stop and go back to the standing heel position. Encourage the dog while he holds the dummy. Remember that he is confused. Reinforce the **Fetch** softly, give the **Heel** command, step forward and snap the lead with a forward motion. Remember to keep the right hand ready to tap the jaw if the grip loosens. It may take several repetitions to get the dog to move while holding the dummy. Be patient and prepared to prevent the dog from dropping the dummy. Work through the sequence until the dog will move willingly on the voice command only.

STEP 10

The dog is now ready to be taught to go down the ramp to the floor or ground. With the dog on the table near the up ramp:

1. Open the dog's mouth
2. Give the **Fetch** command
3. Put the dummy in the dog's mouth
4. Praise the dog
5. Give the **Heel** command
6. As you approach the down ramp, softly reinforce the **Fetch** command
7. Be alert with the right hand as the dog starts down the ramp, as there will be a strong temptation for him to drop the dummy
8. Give the **Fetch** command; tap lead and tap the lower jaw if needed to firm up the grip
9. Walk the dog around and back up on the table
10. Grip the dummy
11. Check his grip
12. **Out**, dog opens mouth, *gently* take the dummy
13. Praise him generously

Repeat the sequence until he is flawless up and down the ramp with only the initial **Fetch** and **Heel** commands.

STEP 11

Now that the dog is holding the dummy, while walking flawlessly at heel, it is time to tempt the dog to make a mistake and correct him in order to reinforce the hold. Lightly bump the dummy with your leg. The first bump or two must be preceded by the **Fetch** command. If the dog's grip is secure, gradually increase the force of the bump. Each time you bump the dummy check to see if the dog has a grip or if he is merely containing the dummy. Reinforce the grip if needed with a voice command **Fetch** or a tap on lead. When the dog handles this lesson flawlessly, he is ready to hold another object -- your hand. (See Figure 32.)

Figure 32   Note extreme tip of dog's head, showing firm grip on dummy.

STEP 12

Now comes the real test for the grip and hold. Open the dog's mouth, give the **Fetch** command, put your open hand into his mouth. Most dogs will be quite reluctant to grip your hand. It may take a light tap on the lead to firm up the grip. It also may take quite a few repetitions before the dog grips without reluctance. When he is gripping your hand well, tempt him to relax his grip by pulling and pushing your hand in all directions. If you have real trouble getting the dog to grip your hand, you may have to start with a glove on your hand. When the dog grips your gloved hand well, take the glove off. This is where you truly get a feel for how he grips and how well he maintains the pressure. When he will hold your hand standing still, have him hold your hand while you walk. Be gentle, he is confused. (See Figure 33.)

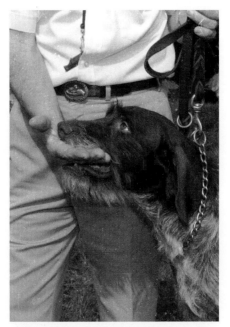

Figure 33   Note firm grip on hand.
Most dogs do not like to grip hand.

A further check on the dog's acceptance of the hold/grip is the way he opens his mouth. Do you have to apply pressure and physically open his mouth? If so, he is still resisting. On the other hand, if his mouth starts to open as soon as your hand drops over his muzzle or when your fingers touch the sides of his muzzle, he has accepted it and is no longer resisting. If he still resists opening his mouth when the **Fetch** command is given, keep working on it. Do **not** go on to the Reach/Grasp sequence until the dog opens his mouth without resistance and accepts the dummy.

Questions

1. Was the lead held correctly and in the proper position?
2. Did the dog resist opening its mouth?
3. Was the **Fetch** command given before putting the dummy in the dog's mouth?
4. Was the dummy placed properly?
5. Was the right hand used properly as detailed for each step?
6. Was the lead held and used properly for each step?
7. Was the lead tapped or snapped immediately after each **Fetch** command?
8. Did you check to be sure the dog was gripping before and as you gave the **Out** command'?
9. Did the dog maintain his grip on or merely contain the dummy as you extended the duration and as the dog walked with the dummy?
10. Did the dog maintain his grip when you tempted him to release or pressured him to release the dummy?
11. Did you vary the time between the dog's gripping the dummy and your giving the **Out** command to prevent anticipation and premature relaxation of the grip?

REACH FOR AND GRASP THE OBJECT

You have done all of the previous work to get the dog to grip the dummy in order to minimize the amount of force or pressure needed to induce the dog to reach and grasp the dummy. It does no good for the dog to reach out and grab the dummy if he drops it when the pressure is removed. Therefore, you had to make sure that he would hold on once he grasped the dummy. The reach and grasp will be divided into 3 phases:

1. Dummy held 6 inches away from the dog's nose at eye level.

2. Dummy held at varying distances and gradually lowered to the table with your hand still in contact with it.
3. Dummy resting free on the table.

Your biggest problem during the first phase will be your natural empathy with the dog, which results in your putting the dummy into the dog's mouth rather than forcing him to reach out and take the dummy from you. We all have this problem. To prevent it, you must mentally, and often physically block the hand holding the dummy so you cannot move it toward the dog. It may be helpful to hold your elbow tightly against your side. Since you will not put the dummy in the dog's mouth, he must be free to move to the dummy. This means that your hand on the lead and/ or collar must move forward on the command **Fetch.** This is why the dog should not be on **Whoa** or sitting while teaching **Hold**, **Reach**, and **Pick up** on the table. He must feel no restraint. When the **Fetch** command is given the dog must be compelled to move forward quickly, grasp the dummy and keep moving. In fact he should forcefully take the dummy out of your hand as he goes by. He must grasp the dummy eagerly.

If the dog nibbles at the dummy, apply more pressure and get a sharper yelp since hesitation at any point is not acceptable. When the **Fetch** command is given, the dog must move quickly to the dummy, grasp it and move on in one smooth continuous motion, He does not need to stop to grasp or pick up the dummy. You must not go to the next phase until the dog is performing flawlessly at each phase. When hunting there will be many times when you cannot see the dog and when the dog cannot see you, therefore, one **Fetch** command must get the job done. If he does not move, quickly, grasp the dummy and move on each stage of retrieving, the problem will come back and bite you later.

With the dog on the table, grasp the lead with your left hand in the normal manner. Now reach down and take the leather part of the dog's right ear between your left thumb and index finger so that the fingernails are the primary contacts. Pinch the finger and thumb together hard and quickly so that the dog yelps. Your fingernails will be required to make most dogs yelp. Many dogs will reach around and mouth your hand and some will grip it but not bite. If the dog had wanted to bite you, he would have. Do not flinch and do not allow it to continue. Pop the lead and show the dog that you do not approve of this behavior. A whine will not do; it must be a yelp. Release the pressure as soon as he yelps. If you cannot make him yelp with your fingers alone, you may need a hard object (metal) placed on one side of the ear to press against. There is no point in trying to get the dog to reach for the dummy if you cannot make him yelp. The yelp is his way of saying "OK you win." Release the pressure as soon as he yelps. You must be sure that you can make him yelp before you hold a dummy in front of him, otherwise, you are teaching him that he doesn't have to obey the **Fetch** command.

The dog will try to avoid or anticipate the command after only a very few repetitions during this phase of training. You must prevent it by keeping all of your movements to a minimum and the time interval between the grasp of the ear and the **Fetch** command as short as possible. You must also control the dog's movements. The dog can be held in place by the lead or with your fingers hooked in the collar. The problem will be to get the dummy into the proper position quickly and smoothly with a minimum of delay after you have grasped, but not pinched, the dog's ear. With the dummy held by one end pass it under the dog's neck and put your wrist against the junction of the dog's head and neck. This places the dummy out of the dog's sight and yet you have to move the dummy only about a foot to have it in the proper position for the **Fetch** command. It also allows you to use your wrist to help control the dog when necessary.

PHASE 1   Reach and Grasp at Eye Level

STEP 1

Now that you have everything set, lead the dog onto the table and do a few simple exercises with lots of praise for success.

1. Hold the dog's lead (and/or collar)
2. Take his ear between your left thumb and index finger
3. Hold the dummy about 6 inches in front of and level with the dog's nose (block your hand)
4. Give the **Fetch** command
5. Pinch his ear until he yelps, reaches out and grasps the dummy; do not push or pull his head toward the dummy and do not restrict

his forward motion; let your hand flow with his head; the dog must reach for the dummy

6. Release the pressure as soon as he grasps the dummy -- not before
7. Praise him profusely
8. **Heel** the dog around and back onto the table, praising him as you go
9. You grip the dummy and check his grip
10. Give the **Out** command
11. Dog opens mouth, *gently* take the dummy
12. Praise him lavishly

Review the questions. If all goes well, repeat the sequence about five or six times. That is enough for one session. In the event that the dog will not reach and grasp the dummy, do not get angry and do not put the dummy in the dog's mouth. Get a secure grip on his collar and ear, pinch the ear sharply and when he yelps, drive him toward the dummy -- do not move the dummy toward him. If he does not grasp and hold the dummy, back up and review the hold sequences in detail. You have missed something. When the dog reaches for and grasps the dummy eagerly and flawlessly 5 or 6 times consecutively with only a mild pinch, go to Step 2. Remember that he must not stop and grasp the dummy. The dog must grasp it as he drives through and continues his forward motion. (See Figures 34, 35 and 36.)

Questions on Step 1

1. Had you made a few dry runs to coordinate your left hand actions and made sure that you could make the dog yelp'?
2. Was the dummy held in the right position?
3. Did you give the **Fetch** command before the ear pinch?
4. Did the dog yelp when you pinched his ear and did you maintain pressure until he grasped the dummy?
5. Did the dog reach for the dummy quickly, hesitantly, or not at all?
6. Did the dog reach for your hand?
7. Did you restrain the dog's forward movement?
8. Did you hold your right hand still, move it toward the dog, put the

Figure 34   Note ear gripped with thumbnail ready for use, dummy is at muzzle level about 3 inches away.

Figure 35   Note speed of dog going for the dummy.

Figure 36   Note dummy being pulled from handler's hand, handler slow on the release.

dummy in the dog's mouth?
9. Did the dog grasp the dummy quickly, hesitantly, or not at all'?
10. Did the dog move through the dummy and pull it out of your hand?
11. Did you release the pressure as soon as the dog grasped the dummy?
12. Did the dog drop the dummy after you released the pressure?
13. Did you praise him profusely?

STEP 2

Next you will eliminate the need for and use of the ear pinch.

1. Hold the lead
2. Take the dog's ear
3. Hold the dummy about 6 inches in front of the dog's nose (do not let him reach before the **Fetch** command)
4. Give the **Fetch** command
5. Do not pinch his ear immediately -- give him a moment to reach and grasp the dummy
6. If he hesitates, pinch the ear sharply until he grasps the dummy
7. Release the pressure as soon as he grasps the dummy
8. Praise him well when he grasps the dummy
9. Continue the praise as you **Heel** him off and back onto the table
10. Grip the dummy
11. Check the dog's grip
12. Give the **Out** command
13. Dog opens mouth, *gently* take the dummy
14. Praise the dog well

Review the questions. Anytime that the dog does not grasp the dummy quickly, pinch his ear immediately after the **Fetch** command on the next sequence. Repeat the sequence until he reaches for and grasps the dummy quickly 5 or 6 times consecutively without an ear pinch.

Questions on Steps 2 and 3

1. All the questions for Step 1 (except the ear pinch and yelp) apply to Steps 2 and 3. Did you review them?

2. Did the dog try to reach before the **Fetch** command?
3. Did you restrain him?
4. Did the dog reach quickly, hesitantly, or not at all on voice command?
5. Was the car pinch needed?
6. Did you handle deliveries correctly -- grip the dummy, check the dog's grip, and vary time from when you gripped the dummy until the **Out** command was given?
7. Did you praise him profusely?

STEP 3

Now you will eliminate the grasp of the dog's ear.

1. Hold the lead
2. Hold the dummy about 6 inches in front of the dog's nose (do not let him reach before the **Fetch** command)
3. Give the **Fetch** command
4. The dog should move forward and quickly grasp the dummy
5. If he hesitates, grasp and sharply pinch his ear
6. Praise the dog as you **Heel** him off and back onto the table
7. Grip the dummy
8. Check the dog's grip
9. Give the **Out** command
10. Dog opens mouth, *gently* take the dummy
11. Praise the dog

Review the questions. Repeat the sequence until you have flawless work for 5 or 6 consecutive repetitions. The dog's work is flawless when he moves forward immediately on the **Fetch** command, eagerly grasps the dummy quickly and keeps on moving. Be sure to give him enough slack lead at the time you say **Fetch** to allow him to do so.

PHASE 2   Reach and Grasp Object at Various Levels

The sequence for this phase is the same as in Step 3, Phase 1, except for the location of the dummy. Make sure that you have several consecutive perfect repetitions at each location. The first step will be to increase the distance from 6 inches at the dog's eye level out to as far as you can reach while still maintaining control of the dog with the lead. Do this in about 6-inch increments. The second step will be to lower the dummy below the dog's eye level starting about 6 inches out and 6 inches below his eye level. As you work the dummy down, move it out so that the dog can move smoothly as he moves forward, grasps the dummy and moves on **Heel**. Work the dummy down until it rests on the table while you grip it with your hand. Finally, you will only touch the dummy with one finger. **Caution:** The first time the dummy is placed on the table, you should grasp the dog's ear. This is the first time that you have not held the **Fetch** object. It is a major step and you must be prepared to prevent any hesitation. Review the questions after Steps 1 and 2. When you have 5 or 6 consecutive flawless repetitions (on **Fetch** command dog moves quickly forward and grasps the dummy eagerly and moves on), you are ready for the last phase. (See Figures 37 and 38.)

Figure 37   Lower the dummy to the table in stages, get driving grasp by the dog.

Figure 38   Dummy on table, hand on dummy, ear grip.

PHASE 3 Reach and Grasp a Free Lying Dummy

Place the dummy on the table so that the dog can step to it smoothly (about 2 feet out) when the **Fetch** command is given. Be sure you have several consecutive flawless repetitions at each location. Review the questions listed for Steps 1 and 2. When the dog is picking the dummy up quickly and cleanly at this comfortable range, it is time to increase the distance. On the next repetition, stop him as close to the up-ramp as possible and place the dummy at about the middle of the table. Step back to the dog and give the **Fetch** command. The dog should move forward quickly, pick up the dummy eagerly and move on. If he does not, quickly grasp his ear and give a hard sharp pinch; it will drive him forward. Gradually work the distance out until the dummy is at the edge of the down-ramp. **Caution:** Be sure to give the dog enough slack lead as he moves forward so that he feels no restraint. Make sure that you stand still until the dog picks up the dummy; then walk briskly to the heel position with the dog. You must make sure that this step is well learned, which means that the dog handles this flawlessly and eagerly through a full lesson. There must be no hesitation when moving to the dummy and no hesitation at the pick up. The dog should not stop; he should scoop up the dummy on the move. (See Figures 39, 40, and 41.)

Figure 39   Note loose lead above and below dog's neck, giving plenty of slack for the dog to drive through the dummy with no restraint.

The dog now knows that **Fetch** means go to an object, pick it up, bring it back and hold it until told to release it. The basics have been learned and he knows how to retrieve. Now the dog must be trained to retrieve under any and all conditions. The dog must be given the experience and confidence that will enable him to handle the unexpected. You must teach him that he can depend on you and trust you. You and the dog must come to believe that there is nothing that the two of you working together cannot retrieve.

GO, PICK UP, AND DELIVER

Now the dog comes off the table and works on the ground with both the short and the long lead. Two new items will be introduced at this stage: (1) The heavy dummy and (2) The dog's delivery position at the time you

Figure 40   Dog close to dummy, slack lead.

Figure 41   Off lead, dummy on table.

take the object. You must decide how you want him to present game standing or sitting; at heel position or facing you. Neither is right or wrong, it is your preference. However, one part is important -- the dog should present the game to you. That is, take the position you want him to, tip his muzzle up and look at you with an attitude that says, "Here it is boss." Do not chase after the dummy if the dog lowers his head or turns his head away. He must present it to you. That truly adds the final touch.

STEP 1

With the dog at the **Heel** position on a short lead:

1. Give the **Whoa** command
2. You take one step forward
3. Give the **Mark** command and drop the dummy on the ground (See Chapter 7 for a description of the "mark" command.)
4. Step back to the dog
5. Praise the dog
6. Give the **Fetch** command
7. Give the dog enough slack lead to move through the dummy as he picks it up
8. Dog picks up dummy eagerly (if he does not, step to him and give his ear a sharp pinch)
9. Praise the dog at the pick up
10. Dog starts back to you on his own (if he does not, give the **Fetch** command and snap the lead)
11. Praise the dog as you guide him to the position you want for delivery (standing or sitting facing you or at heel); for hunting, standing facing you is more efficient
12. Give the **Whoa** command
13. Put one hand under the dog's chin and tip his head back, get eye contact and smile
14. Grasp the dummy with your free hand
15. Check the dog's grip
16. Give the **Out** command
17. Dog opens mouth, *gently* take the dummy
18. Praise the dog

Review the questions and repeat the sequence until you have several consecutive flawless performances to voice alone. (See Figures 42, 43, and 44.)

Figure 42   First retrieve on the ground is done on lead and very short.

Figure 43   Lead the dog to the position you want for delivery.

Figure 44   Tip dog's head back and hold for a moment, grip dummy and hold for a moment.

STEP 2

With the dog at **Heel** on the short lead:

1. Give the **Whoa** command
2. Drop the lead
3. Take two steps forward
4. Give the **Mark** command and drop the dummy
5. Step back to the dog and pick up the lead
6. Praise the dog
7. Give the **Fetch** command
8. Feed out lead as he moves forward
9. The dog should pick up dummy eagerly
10. Praise the dog
11. Gently turn him and lead him back to the delivery position
12. Give the **Whoa** command

13. Put one hand under the dog's chin and tip his head back so that you make eye contact
14. Grasp the dummy (occasionally hold it for a few moments)
15. Give the **Out** command
16. Dog opens mouth, *gently* take the dummy
17. Praise the dog

Review the questions and repeat the sequence until you have several consecutive flawless performances. This is the step at which you can effec-

Figure 45   Note attitude of dog with heavy dummy.

tively introduce the heavy dummy. For large dogs start with 5 or 6 pounds, for small dogs 2 or 3 pounds. Gradually increase the weight until the large dogs are carrying 15 to 20 pounds and the small dogs can carry 10 to 12 pounds. Three or four retrieves with the heavy dummy per session is enough. Mix heavy dummies in with light dummies. If the dog has been somewhat subdued carrying the heavy weights, mixing in light dummies during this step usually puts more sparkle back into his performance. (See

Figure 46   Note handler's foot under heavy dummy at delivery.

Figures 45 and 46.)

STEP 3

Now put the dog on the long (20 to 50 feet) lead, gradually increase the distance using the sequence in Step 2 until the dog is flawless at the extended length of the lead. If the dog hesitates to pick up the dummy when he reaches it, give a stern **Fetch** and pop the lead. That is usually all the reminder he needs. **Caution:** Do not get lazy -- walk the dummy out and drop it. Do not throw it out. Make sure that the dog is driving through normal dummies at each distance before going to the next one. When the weights get heavy, most dogs will stop and pick up.

STEP 4

By this time you may have had enough repetitions of the head tip and eye contact during the presentation so that you can gradually eliminate the head tipping movement with your hand. However, the dog may still need some encouragement to make eye contact. When you grasp the dummy, press upward lightly until you have eye contact with the dog before giving

Figure 47   Note eye contact
between dog and handler. Dog
may stand or sit at heel.

the **Out** command. If more than light pressure is needed, continue using
the hand under the chin and try again later. When only very light upward
pressure is needed, if you speak gently, he will usually look up and make
eye contact. What you say is not as important as how you say it. Make it
sound like praise. When you have eye contact, grasp the dummy, check
the dog's grip and give the **Out** command. Remember to vary the time
between the grasp and the **Out** command. (See Figure 47.)

Questions on Ground Steps 1-4

1. Did the dog move after the **Whoa** command?
2. Did you walk the dummy out and drop it?
3. Did you praise the dog when you got back to him?
4. Did you allow enough slack lead for the dog to get to the dummy
   unhindered?
5. How did the dog go to the dummy -- rapidly, slowly, or wander-
   ing?

6. Did the dog pick up the dummy eagerly and quickly or halfheartedly? Did the dog need another **Fetch** command, snap of the lead, or pinch of his ear?
7. Did the dog turn to you and make eye contact on his own or did you need to turn him with the lead?
8. Did the dog return to you on his own, or was the lead needed?
9. Did the dog return to you eagerly, happily, sedately, or reluctantly?
10. Did the dog come to the delivery position on his own, or did he need to be guided?
11. Did you handle the delivery correctly?
12. Did the dog present the dummy correctly, or did he need assistance?
13. Did you praise the dog profusely?

STEP 5

It is now time to work the dog off lead. With the dog at **Heel,** remove the lead.

1. Give the **Whoa** command
2. You take one step forward, **Mark** command and drop the dummy
3. Return to the dog at the heel position
4. Praise the dog
5. Give the **Fetch** command
6. Dog should move forward quickly and pick up the dummy eagerly
7. Dog should return to you, stop and present the dummy
8. Grasp dummy
9. Check the dog's grip. (Vary the time you hold.)
10. Give the **Out** command, dog opens mouth, *gently* take dummy.
11. Praise the dog

Review the questions. Gradually increase the distance in increments of a step or two until he works cleanly out to about 50 feet. Remember you are still walking the dummy out and dropping it. If the dog has not learned the proper presentation, refer to Step 4. If he does not come directly to you, put him back on the long lead and after he turns to you, give a stern

Fetch command and pop the lead, take up the slack quickly and draw him to the delivery position. On the next repetition (off lead) give him a stern **Fetch** command to send him and as soon as he picks up the dummy, give another stern **Fetch** command. If that does not get the job done, put him back on the long lead and this time give a harsh **Fetch** command to send him. After the dog has picked up the dummy and turned toward you, give a harsh **Fetch** and crack the lead. Draw him in to the delivery position roughly. Repeat this several times and then take the lead off for the next sequence. Use a harsh **Fetch** command the first time or two and then a stern **Fetch** or two before resuming a normal tone. If he is really stubborn, on the next repetition give a harsh **Fetch** command and a very sharp ear pinch. Continue repetitions until the dog's performance is flawless through a complete session.

Questions on Step 5

1. Did the dog move after the **Whoa** command?
2. Did you walk the dummy out and drop it?
3. Did you praise the dog when you got back?
4. Did the dog go to the dummy rapidly, slowly, or did he wander?
5. Did the dog pick up the dummy eagerly and quickly, or halfheartedly?
6. Was another **Fetch** command and/or ear pinch needed?
7. Did he turn and look at you immediately or hesitantly? Was a command needed?
8. Did the dog return to you quickly, slowly, or did he require a command?
9. Did the dog return eagerly, happily, sedately, or reluctantly?
10. Did the dog come to the delivery position on his own, or was a command needed?
11. Did the dog present the dummy correctly?
12. Was it necessary to give a voice reminder or tip the dog's head back?
13. Did you handle the deliver correctly?
14. Did you praise the dog profusely?

STEP 6

The final step on the long lead is done at the water. It is best to have a
partner help you with this so that you do not have to throw the dummy. If
you must place the dummy, try to find a gradual sloping area and get a pair
of waders or hip boots. Of course, if it's summer, there is no problem.
With the dog on the long lead at **Heel**:

1. Give the **Whoa** command
2. Step forward a step or two in shallow (wading depth for the dog)
   water
3. Give the **Mark** command and drop the dummy
4. Return to **Heel** position
5. Praise the dog
6. Give the **Fetch** command
7. Dog goes out quickly, picks up dummy eagerly
8. Lead him back to delivery position
9. Praise him
10. Grasp presented dummy
11. Check the dog's grip
12. Give the **Out** command
13. Dog opens mouth, *gently* take the dummy
14. Praise the dog lavishly

Review the questions and repeat the sequence several times in shallow
water. Remember to vary the time between the grasp and the **Out** command. If you want a dog to return eagerly to you and deliver quickly, be
prepared to praise and pet him after the delivery while he shakes. Wear
clothing that will allow you to do this comfortably. Do not jump away or
scold him when he shakes on you -- he then thinks that he's done something wrong on the retrieve. (See Figures 48 and 49.)

STEP 7

Work the dog out in increments of 3 or 4 feet into swimming depth water.
Now is the time when you need someone to throw the dummy. Try and
find an area where the thrower can stand on the opposite shore and throw
the dummy the distance from the near shore that is needed. If that is not

Figure 48   At water, dog on lead by handler, moving to water. Note proper attire for work, slack lead, dog going for dummy.

Figure 49   Handler praising dog while he shakes. Man that water is cold! Praise while he shakes --- every time.

possible, put the thrower in a boat. If that isn't possible, position him at a right angle to you about 20 yards down the shore. The thrower should throw the dummy straight in front of the dog at the distance needed for the lesson. You must tell the thrower how far to throw the dummy each time.

1. The dog is at **Heel** on long lead
2. Give the **Whoa** command
3. Give the thrower the distance
4. Give the **Mark** command
5. Dummy is thrown immediately on **Mark** command
6. Give the **Whoa** command (restrain dog if he tries to break and wait until he relaxes)
7. Give the **Fetch** command
8. Dog should enter water boldly (leaping is not necessary and is sometimes dangerous)
9. Swims to dummy and grasps it
10. Turns to start back
11. Lead him back to delivery position
12. Dog presents dummy
13. Grasp dummy and check dog's grip
14. Give the **Out** command, dog opens mouth, *gently* take dummy.
15. Praise dog

Review the questions and repeat the sequence until the dog works cleanly at the full length of the long lead. (See Figures 50 and 51.)

If the dog does not turn back to you immediately after grasping the dummy, enforce the command with a stern **Fetch** and pop the lead. Take up the slack in the lead and guide him to you. If the pop does not turn him, give a harsh **Fetch** and crack the lead. Take up the slack and haul him in roughly. Bring him to the delivery position and praise him. Take the dummy and praise him while he shakes. Work back through the steps of harsh and stern **Fetch** commands until a normal **Fetch** command sends the dog out and back to the delivery position with the dummy. Work on the single command until a complete lesson is done properly.

Figure 50 Dog nearing dummy on long lead. Note lead in the water near the dog and out of the water near the shore.

Figure 51 Dog with dummy, turning, on long lead. Note lead out of the water as light pressure is on the lead.

STEP 8

It is now time to work the dog in the water off lead. With the dog at **Heel**:

1. Give the **Whoa** command
2. Give the **Mark** command
3. Thrower throws dummy into wading depth water 3 or 4 feet from the dog
4. Give the **Fetch** command
5. Dog wades out and retrieves dummy to delivery position
6. Praise the dog
7. Dog presents dummy
8. Grasp the dummy and check dog's grip
9. Give the **Out** command
10. Dog opens mouth, *gently* take the dummy
11. Praise the dog while he shakes

Review the questions. Repeat sequence until dog handles it cleanly for a half dozen repetitions.

STEP 9

You will now start to work in water of swimming depth. With the dog at **Heel**:

1. Give the **Whoa** command
2. Give the **Mark** command
3. Thrower throws dummy into water at the shortest distance that requires the dog to swim
4. Give the **Fetch** command
5. Dog enters boldly and swims to dummy
6. Dog grasps the dummy and retrieves to delivery position
7. Short praise
8. Dog presents dummy
9. Grasp dummy (remember to vary duration of grasp) and check dog's grip
10. Give the **Out** command
11. Dog opens mouth, *gently* take the dummy

12. Praise the dog

Review the questions. Repeat the sequence at shortest swimming distance until the dog does about 6 consecutive clean repetitions. Increase swimming distance in increments of about 5 to 10 feet out to about 50 to 60 feet. Be sure that you get several consecutive clean repetitions at each distance before making the next increase.

Questions on Steps 6-9

1. Did the dog move after the **Whoa** command?
2. a. Did you walk the dummy out and drop it?
   b. Did your partner throw it the correct distance?
3. Did you praise the dog for steadiness?
4. Did you allow enough slack when needed?
5. Did the dog go to dummy eagerly, calmly, or hesitantly?
6. Did the dog approach the dummy eagerly and forcefully, or hesitantly?
7. Did the dog grasp the dummy quickly and eagerly, or hesitantly?
8. Was a **Fetch** command needed?
9. Did the dog turn to you immediately or hesitantly and was a command needed?
10. Did the dog make eye contact?
11. Did the dog return to you eagerly, calmly, or hesitantly?
12. Did the dog approach you eagerly, happily, sedately, or reluctantly?
13. Did the dog come to the delivery position on his own, or did he need commands?
14. Did the dog present the dummy correctly?
15. Was it necessary for you to give a reminder, tap or hold the dog's head back?
16. Did you handle the delivery correctly?
17. Did you praise the dog profusely?

Now that the dog has learned to retrieve, it is time to tempt him to make a mistake -- break for the object before the **Fetch** command is given. You must be ready to prevent the mistake. Put him on lead even though it will not likely be needed. You will tempt the dog with both words and movements. If you have been using **Fetch,** use any word that starts with a similar sound, i.e. fletch, fiddle, finch, etc. As soon as a standing dog leans forward or a sitting dog raises his rump a fraction of an inch, give a stern **Whoa.** If he does not rock back immediately, pop the lead. If anything more than one **Whoa** is needed, do not let him make the retrieve. After a few repetitions with the **Whoa** command, do not let him retrieve if a **Whoa** is needed. Do not over do this in any one session -- mix it in with some **Fetches**. When he is flawless to voice temptation, add hand and body movements as added temptation. The dog must learn not to move until a clear and distinct **Fetch** command is given. It will be a great help later during steadiness work.

When the dog is performing flawlessly, he knows that **Fetch** means: go pick up the object, bring it back, present and hold it until told to release it. He will handle the retrieve properly from both land and water. The fundamentals, that is, simple single marked retrieves, have been learned.

It is not reasonable to assume that all retrieves will be simple marked retrieves while hunting. Therefore, we must prepare the dog to handle complex retrieves under any and all circumstances and conditions that he will encounter while hunting. Game conservation demands this of us. This training and preparation will have two very important effects on the dog: (1) it will develop his self-confidence in strange circumstances and (2) it will increase his confidence and trust in you. Both are vitally needed to accomplish truly difficult work.

Before you can guarantee correct repetitions off lead at distances over 20 yards both on land and in water, there are other controls and concepts that both you and the dog need. Take the time to acquire and train them. They are not all needed immediately but they will all be needed if you want a finished trained retriever that you can expect to get anything for which you send him. The sooner these concepts are learned, the sooner you will have a trained dog. Some of these concepts will be taught in conjunction with retrieving work, while others must be learned separately. Of course, the dog's response to **Whoa** must be flawless regardless of whether it is voice, hand, whistle and/or shotgun. Other concepts and controls must be achieved if you wish to develop a finished trained retriever. These include

Come, steady at your side, **Mark**, hand signals, concept of the far shore, trailing, stop to flush, and steady to wing, shot and fall.

A youngster with his father, German wirehaired
pointer, and wild pheasant in South Dakota.

7 | Mark

The word "mark" is usually used in conjunction with retrieving and generally refers to where the fallen object is that has to be retrieved. While all dogs can mark a fall, some naturally do it better than others. There are many uses for the term when training a dog to retrieve that will prepare him to mark better when hunting.

A dog can mark an object or game by sight, sound, scent, or a combination of these. The use of sight is self-explanatory as is scent at close range, particularly in cover that hides the object. Marking by sound is often overlooked by most trainers and handlers. Most obvious is the sound of the object hitting the ground or water. Dogs can also hear certain game moving over ground or in the air and know the direction it is traveling when the shot is fired. Most properly trained and experienced hunting dogs get a sense of direction from seeing the direction a gun is pointed when shot. The properly trained and experienced dog can take direction from the sound of the shot even when he cannot see the gun. This is easy to demonstrate with a shotgun, a dummy and an experienced dog. It may well be that the dog can hear the shot moving through the air. With this in mind, any shooting used in training a hunting retriever should be done with shotguns as they would be handled while hunting and not blank pistols. There is no comparison between the sound and effect of a shotgun and a blank pistol. Clearly, it is much more difficult to indicate direction with a blank pistol that is virtually always pointed straight up. Whenever a shotgun is fired, it should be pointed (by *the handler)* as near as possible at the object to be retrieved. If you stand and watch a seasoned dog work, you will see how the movement and firing of a shotgun increases his alertness and concentration.

During training all shooting must be done by you or someone near the dog such as in a blind, in front of a pointing dog or behind a dog that has flushed. No noise, shot or otherwise, should be made by anyone throwing objects for the dog to mark and retrieve. Likewise, the object to be marked and retrieved should not come from the handler or near the dog. If the object comes from you or near the dog during training, you have taught him that all retrieve objects come from you. His attention, therefore, will be on you, not out there where the game is.

During training the command **Mark** may be used to alert the dog to potential retrieving action, get his attention focused in the right direction, prepare him for the next command, and signal the thrower to throw the object to be retrieved. As soon as you start having dummies thrown for the dog, they should *not* be thrown by you, but rather someone else out away from you and the dog. When hunting, you will never throw the game and shoot it. Therefore, you do not want the dog to concentrate on you at shooting time. You want his attention out there where the action is so that he can see the object and mark it. When things are set up, the use of the command **Mark** will be used to alert the dog and signal the thrower to throw the dummy. This will be especially important when you start multiple retrieves. It will concentrate the dog's attention and get each bird marked. You will not consciously have to teach it. The dog will catch on quickly.

During blind retrieve training, the command **Mark** will alert the dog to the fact that directions will be forthcoming -- namely the line of your hand and arm. He will know what is expected before the **Fetch** command is given.

The primary use of the **Mark** command is to concentrate the dog's attention on the job at hand, which is most important during early training.

8 | Concept Of The Far Shore

The biggest problem in water retrieving is to get a dog to go far enough out or to keep going until something or somebody stops him. Many things limit his range over water. Perceived distance over water is greatly magnified when compared with the same distance over land. A hunting dog can cover 40 yards in about 5 seconds on land, whereas, it takes him about 50 seconds to swim 40 yards. Yet, the distance over water appears to be less. Therefore, you need a visual objective to help the dog keep going -- the far shore. The dog learns to keep going until he hits the far shore unless stopped by you.

You can start teaching the concept of the far shore as soon as the dog knows Step 9 of the Reach and Grasp sequence. That means that he can handle marked retrieves off lead at over 20 yards of water. Rather than continue to throw the dummy into open water as distances increase, find an area where there are varying distances to the far shore, such as an island, across a river or any other configuration. This approach will have the added advantage of the dog being unable to see the thrower.

Every time you work the dog on water retrieves, no matter what the distance, have some retrieves made from the far shore. Start with a short distance, 15 to 20 yards, and work out. Start with the dummy in the water and work it up onto the far shore as you increase the distance. As the dog's skill improves, work the dummy farther inland and into heavier cover. Make sure that you have the controls needed to ensure that the dog can make the retrieve. You will soon begin to notice a change in the dog's attitude and a shift in his point of concentration when he cannot see the dummy in the water -- he will stop looking for it in the water and head for the far shore.

Gradually increase the distance over open water to about 100 yards. The dog that will go 100 yards in training will usually keep going much farther when hunting. However, if the opportunity arises or can be set up, send him farther.

9 | Decoys

Do not introduce a dog to decoys on his first waterfowl hunt. It happens all too often. The proper place and time to introduce a dog to decoys is in the yard during training. If you hunt both ducks and geese, use both types of decoys during training. A spread of 100 or so goose decoys can be overwhelming if a dog has never seen even one. When the dog is handling marked single water retrieves well, it is time to start exposing him to decoys.

Take 8 to 10 decoys and set them on the ground in your normal home training area. Put the dog on lead and **Heel** him through the decoys. If he tries to sniff or bother the decoys, give a **Negative** command and a snap on the lead. Do this until he ignores the decoys. Now step back about 10 to 15 yards and toss a dummy so that it lands well short of the decoys. Send the dog to retrieve. If he tries to go past the dummy, stop him, give a **Negative** command, point at the dummy and give the **Fetch** command. Repeat this until he ignores the decoys and retrieves cleanly. Now work the dummy closer to the decoys. Keep working until he will ignore the decoys and cleanly retrieve the dummy when thrown among and beyond the decoys. (See Figures 52, 53, and 54.)

Take the dog to the water and set the decoys in water that is wading depth for the dog. Start by tossing the dummy just short of the decoys and work outward until he will handle retrieves properly among and beyond the decoys. This lets the dog get his first feel of decoy lines. Now move the decoys to swimming depth water and repeat the process by tossing the dummy short of, then among and beyond the decoys. (See Figures 55 and 56.) Anytime the dog bothers a decoy, give a **Negative** command,

Figure 52   Note slack lead, dog ignores decoys.

Figure 53   Dog ignores decoys.

Figure 54   Note the lie of the lead, dog took straight line to dummy.

point to the dummy and give the **Fetch** command. If the dog persists, put him on the long lead. As he approaches a decoy, give a very harsh **Negative** command and crack that lead. Remember, do not pull the lead -- crack it. Make the decoy lines long enough so that the dog can get the feel of them while swimming. Pull a decoy so that it bumps him and give him the opportunity to pull a decoy as he makes the retrieve. That will eliminate any future surprises with decoys.

When the dog's performance is flawless on lead, take the lead off and repeat the work while the dog is free.

Figure 55   Note dog's concentration on dummy, not decoys.

Figure 56   Note dog's concentration on handler, not decoys. Dog has eye contact with handler.

10 | Hand Signals

The term "hand signal" is a misnomer -- it actually should be "hand-arm-body-voice signals." Rarely is the hand alone used. If you try to train with hand movement alone, you have a nearly impossible job. You must put your whole being into the signal to train effectively especially at long distances. There are four prerequisites for teaching hand signals:

1. The basic **Fetch** command has been well learned
2. The dog is steady to flight and fall
3. **Whoa** has been thoroughly learned to voice, whistle and hand signals
4. The dog should know **Come**

With these four basics well learned it is easy to achieve correct repetitions -- that is, the dog takes the signal and retrieves the correct object. Some "starts" and "stops" may be required but in the end he will be successful. Knowledge of the **Mark** command will also be helpful.

Caution: If you are going to be effective at hand signals, you must *decide* what you are going to do *before you start* to do anything.

1. Which way is the *wind* blowing? You want to send the dog downwind of the mark.
2. Where do you want the dog to *stop?* Remember that **Whoa** means stop and look at me.
3. Can you stop him *there? How* long does it take him to stop when running or swimming at various speeds?
4. You must get into the *correct position. You* must place the correct hand in the correct position and be prepared to give the sig-

Figure 57   Note dog's concentration on handler, alertness; he is ready.

nal the instant the dog stops and looks at you. To command attention the signaling hand must be high over your head, palm toward
the dog, fingers tense and partly spread. (A limp hand and half-
raised arm does not command attention). This gives the dog a
fixed reference that tells him a directional signal is coming and
allows the maximum clearly visible movement of the hand. (See
Figure 57.)

There are three basic hand signals to teach: (1) **Back**, (2) **Over** (right or
left) and (3) **Line**. **Back** seems to cause most dogs more trouble than
Over, so we will start with that. **Caution:** Do not rush to use the "baseball diamond set up." Teach each of the commands separately before you
do advanced work on the "ball field." Remember our earlier discussion
about the distance at which a dog will obey a given command, Therefore,
you will start close to the dog with short marked retrieves. The surface
should be such that the dog can see the dummy at all times.

STEP 1

Begin with the dog off lead:

1. Give the **Whoa** command
2. Step out about 10 feet, turn and face the dog
3. Give the **Mark** command
4. Throw the dummy over the dog so that it lands about 10 feet behind him
5. Raise your hand (alternate between right and left) to the **Whoa** position (arm straight up with the palm facing the dog)
6. Be sure the dog is looking at you (if he is not, he is avoiding the job and will not take the command -- get his attention). Gain eye contact at the moment the **Back** command is given. Whatever it takes. Remember that **Whoa** means stop and look at me.
7. Give the **Back** command and simultaneously take one vigorous, enthusiastic step forward pushing the hand forward and up
8. The dog should turn immediately and head for the dummy
9. Option -- You may want to say **Fetch** as well as **Back** the first few times; very likely you will not need to do so
10. Dog picks up dummy eagerly and turns to you
11. Praise him
12. Dog comes to delivery position
13. Dog presents dummy
14. You grasp the dummy and check dog's grip
15. Give the **Out** command
16. Dog opens mouth, *gently* take the dummy
17. Praise the dog

Review the questions and repeat the sequence until the dog is turning abruptly and going quickly to the dummy. If the dog tries to go left or right, **Whoa** him immediately. **Heel** him back to the proper position and start the sequence again. The dog must learn that he goes **Back** or he goes nowhere. This will be a test of wills with some dogs. Keep at it until he goes back to the dummy. When he has done six or so consecutive correct repetitions quickly, go to Step 2. You should start to notice which way the dog turns, it will come in handy later. (See Figure 58.)

Figure 58   Handler has made vigorous move toward dog; dog is turning to go back. Be sure to note which way your dog turns.

At this point, you may want to skip to Step 4 and teach the **Over** command. Otherwise the dog may think that **Back** is the only command there is. When **Over** at 20 feet away has been learned, you can work both **Back** and **Over** during the same lesson. *Do not,* however, throw 2 dummies out. Throw only one dummy at a time until Steps 1-4 have been learned well. "The baseball diamond" is used for temptation and reinforcement.

STEP 2

You are now ready to move farther away from the dog. The sequence will be the same as above except that you will stand about 20 feet from the dog. Throw the dummy the same distance (about 10 feet) behind the dog. At this stage, the distance from you to the dog (not the distance from the dog to the dummy) is more important. When the dog completes about 6-10 quick clean repetitions, it is time to increase the distance. Make incremental increases of about 5 yards out to about 50 yards. **Caution:** As the distance from you to the dog increases, make sure that the dog stays on **Whoa** when the dummy is thrown. He may turn his head to mark the fall, but the dog should not move his feet or turn to the dummy. If he does, make him turn and face you before the hand signal is given. Be sure that he continues to work quickly and cleanly before the next increment. At longer ranges, it may be necessary to throw the dummy from a shorter distance and then walk on out to the selected distance.

STEP 3

It is now time to increase the distance from the dog to the dummy.

1. Give the **Whoa** to the dog
2. Step out about 10 feet, turn and face the dog
3. Give the **Mark** command
4. Throw the dummy over the dog's head so that it lands about 20 feet behind him
5. Raise your hand to the **Whoa** position and get the dog's attention
6. Make sure that the dog is looking at you (eye contact)
7. Give the **Back** command and simultaneously step toward the dog pushing your hand forward and up
8. Dog should turn immediately and go to the dummy, pick it up, and return to the delivery position
9. Praise the dog as he comes in
10. Dog presents the dummy
11. Grasp the dummy (remember to vary the time of the grasp) and check dog's grip
12. Give the **Out** command
13. Dog opens mouth, *gently* take the dummy
14. Praise the dog

Review the questions and repeat the sequence until you have several consecutive quick clean performances. You are now ready to increase the distance from the dog to the dummy. Do so in about 5-yard increments out to as far as you can throw. Be sure that you have good performance at each stage before you increase the distance again. Even if the dog needs help, it can be a good performance if he obeys the commands given to help him. Work the dog out until he can be sent back 40 or 50 yards.

It is now time to start increasing the distance from you to the dog and from the dog to the dummy simultaneously. This should be done until you can send him 50 yards back while you are 50 yards away when the command is given.

The steps in the **Over** training sequence will be the same as those in the **Back** sequence except for the position of the dummy, the command and the body movement.

STEP 4

With the dog at **Heel**:

1. Give the **Whoa** command
2. Step 10 feet out, turn and face the dog
3. Give the **Mark** command
4. Throw dummy 10 feet to your right of the dog
5. Raise right hand to **Whoa** command position
6. Be sure the dog is looking at you (eye contact)
7. Give the **Over** command and simultaneously look to the right; swing the right hand and arm to the right while taking a vigorous leap to the right
8. The dog should immediately go to the dummy
9. Dog picks up dummy and starts back
10. Praise him on the way to the delivery position
11. Dog presents dummy
12. Grasp the dummy and check the dog's grip
13. Give **Out** command
14. Dog opens mouth, *gently* take the dummy
15. Praise the dog

Irregularly vary the side to which you throw the dummy and give the **Over** direction. Make sure that your signal is given happily and vigorously each time. If the dog tries to go the wrong way, stop him immediately and start the sequence again. Be sure to get about 10 quick clean repetitions before you increase the distance between you and the dog. (See Figure 59.) Work out until you can send the dog right or left from approximately 50 yards for about 10 quick clean retrieves. Take time to be sure that the dog

Figure 59   Note dog's concentration on signal, quick movement in right direction, handler's hand has only moved about a foot, handler's head has turned.

can be sent **Over** about 50 yards. You must work the dog out to that distance gradually.

You are now ready to use the baseball diamond to integrate the **Back** and **Over** commands and send the dog to the dummy that you want retrieved. Do not start with 3 dummies, instead start with only two and when that is well learned, go to 3. The dog is placed on **Whoa** on the pitcher's mound facing you at home plate. Of course, the distances will be considerably shorter as you begin.

Caution: The **Negative** command should be well learned before you start the ball field work. It will often be needed to break the dog's concentration on the wrong dummy. Anytime he starts for the wrong dummy, use a **Negative** command and stop him. Then send him for the right dummy.

STEP 5

With the dog on the pitcher's mound facing you:

1. Give the **Whoa** command
2. Walk out 10 yards, and turn and face the dog
3. Give the **Mark** command
4. Throw one dummy to your right about level with the dog and 15 to 20 feet from him; throw another dummy to your left
5. Mentally select the dummy to be retrieved
6. Raise correct hand to **Whoa** position
7. Be sure the dog is looking at you -- you must break his concentration from the last dummy thrown, talk to him if you must, but get his attention on you (eye contact)
8. Give the **Over** command simultaneous with vigorous hand and body signal
9. Dog goes over and retrieves dummy
10. Praise him as he comes in to delivery position and presents dummy
11. Grasp the dummy and check dog's grip
12. Give the **Out** command
13. Dog opens mouth, *gently* take the dummy
14. Praise the dog
15. **Heel** him to the "mound"
16. Walk back to home plate
17. Send the dog for the second dummy (items 5-14)

Review the questions. Vary the throw from right-left, left-back, back-right, etc. until the dog is handling any and all combinations quickly. Now you are ready to work with 3 dummies. The sequence will be the same except that you throw 3 dummies and the dog makes 3 retrieves. You must be ready with your strongest **Whoa** command (voice or whistle) so that you can stop the dog if he tries to get the wrong dummy. Do not increase distances until you have flawless work at each distance. First increase the distance between you and the dog and then increase the distance between the dog and the dummy.

STEP 6

When the hand signals are learned well on land, it is time to go to the water. Find a place where you can start with the dog standing in shallow water. Use the sequence in Step 3 for **Back** and Step 4 for **Over**, but start at about 5 yards from the dog. The dummy may be in swimming depth water for the **Back** command or in standing depth water for the **Over** command. Repeat these sequences until you can send the dog **Back** or **Over** from about 30 yards. Remember to get several consecutive clean repetitions before making increases and make sure to vary the time between your grasp of the dummy and the **Out** command in order to check the dogs grip. Review the questions after each repetition.

STEP 7

When this work is clean, it is time to work the dog in swimming depth water. However, when you give the **Whoa** command the dog cannot stop completely -- he would sink. The dog can, however, turn toward you and look for the command. Make sure that you have eye contact since it will let you know that he is ready for the next command. Therefore, you must have decided exactly what you are going to do before you give the **Whoa** command and you must do it quickly and smoothly. Make every effort to have someone throw the dummy for the dog and you should have the setup arranged ahead of time. Do the first sequence, if possible, with the dog no more than 10 yards away from you. You want to be sure that the dog is well within your range of control. You may want to practice the **Whoa** with the dog swimming before you start this step. You will be looking for that eye contact. With the dog swimming:

1. Give the **Whoa** command
2. Dummy thrown by thrower on **Whoa** command about 10 feet from the dog (right, left or back as decided beforehand)
3. Hold the dog's attention with your raised arm with palm facing dog (do whatever it takes)
4. Make sure that he is looking at you when you give the command (if he swims toward dummy, stop him and make him look at you)
5. Give appropriate command vigorously
6. Dog retrieves the dummy to delivery position
7. Praise the dog as he comes to delivery position
8. Grasp the dummy and check the dog's grip
9. Give the **Out** command
10. Dog opens mouth, *gently* take the dummy
11. Praise the dog

Repeat the sequence until you get clean work on both **Over** and **Back** at short range, then increase the distance between the handler and the dog and finally between the dog and the dummy. When you have several consecutive clean performances beginning with the dog about 50 yards from you at the start and after you have sent him 50 yards to the dummy, there is no doubt that he knows **Over** and **Back**.

Questions on Steps 1-7

1. Did the dog move on the throw?
2. Did the dog mark the fall?
3. Did you have your hand in the correct location?
4. Was the dog looking at your hand when you gave the signal?
5. Was your signal vigorous and did your whole body move in the correct direction?
6. Was your signal halfhearted or given with the wrong hand?
7. Did the dog start the correct direction?
8. Did the dog go to the dummy?
9. Did the dog need additional commands?
10. Did the dog come to position and present the dummy?
11. Did you handle the delivery properly?
12. Did you praise the dog?

After the dog has learned hand signals, there are some things of which you must be aware and give serious consideration before you stop the dog. Which way does the dog turn on the **Back** signal? Which does the dog do best -- **Back**, **Over** right, **Over** left? Where do you want the dog to stop? Which direction is the wind blowing? You must have the proper hand raised before the **Stop** command is given. You must give the hand signal the instant the dog looks at you -- do not make him wait while you decide what to do.

Now that the dog knows **Over** and **Back,** he needs to learn a signal that will get him started in the right direction when he is standing beside you. There are two philosophies on lining.

The field trialer's philosophy mandates that a dog run a straight line ignoring everything until he hits the mark or is told to stop. The hunter gives the dog a direction and a start toward fallen game that he must find and retrieve. The field trial concept demands rigid obedience, suppression of instincts and loss of initiative; while the hunter starts the dog in the right direction and helps him utilize his hunting skills.

The hunter must be able to send his dog out to make a blind retrieve. Therefore, the dog must go far enough in the direction indicated to get the job done. This does not require strict adherence to a straight line. The primary reason for giving a dog a line is to achieve an efficient retrieve. Never lose sight of that. If a dog will take a line 50 yards on land and your **Back** command can send him another 50 yards, that will certainly serve the hunter's needs. If the mark for a blind retrieve is more than 100 yards, the most efficient retrieve will be for you to walk to within a reasonable distance of the game and then send the dog. Most birds that land more than a hundred yards out are not dead on impact and the dog will have to trail or search to make the retrieve. When hunting over water the story is different. It may be necessary to send the dog more than 100 yards out and that is the reason for the concept of the far shore -- to get the dog way out there. The need to send a dog more than 150 yards out usually means that you have a winged bird. Therefore, more often than not, the hunter will use a boat to help the dog. Do not be unduly influenced by the unrealistic lining distances and situations set up to eliminate dogs in field trials. They have little validity in a hunting situation.

Caution: The biggest mistake most hunters make when giving a dog a line is to send it straight at the mark. That is only valid if the wind is blowing straight down the line. Most dogs will drift off the line to some extent. Therefore, you should give the dog a line that will take him downwind of the mark and that he can drift some on either side of the line and still locate the game. You must realize that a dog's nose is far better than his eyes. Therefore, when sending a dog across a river, give him a line that will take him down river of the game and let it drift to him.

The prerequisites for giving a line are **Whoa**, hand signals (**Back** and **Over**), and **Fetch** on marked retrieves out to about 40 or 50 yards. The experience of the hand signal for **Line** on many marked retrieves will have conditioned the dog that the hand points toward the game.

Lining and blind retrieving are virtually inseparable. You cannot train for one without some use of the other. No hunting dog runs a line on the **Line** command. He is given the hand signal (direction) and told to **Fetch**. **Fetch** is the command that spurs and moves the dog. Refer to the sequences in the section on Blind Retrieves for training the dog to line.

11 | Single Marked Long Retrieves

The next phase in retrieving is to extend the distance that a dog will go for a marked retrieve. A marked retrieve is one that the dog can see in the air and follow downward so that he can judge distance and have an idea where the object hit the ground. The dog does not have to see it on the ground. In fact, rarely will the dog be able to see it on the land, but may often see it on the water. Work on distance retrieving is important before you start blind retrieving because of the time lapse between the **Fetch** command and the dog's seeing or smelling the object when working a blind retrieve. It also gives you time to practice using the hand signal for taking a line.

The previous work has taken the dog out about 20 yards or so, and now it is time to go to 100 yards or more if you can control the dog at greater distances. Make sure that you can control the dog at each incremental distance. Never send a dog farther than the distance at which he will obey the **Whoa** command. If he starts to get into trouble, you will not be able to help him. There are very few dogs that mark well enough at 100 yards or more to get every object they are sent for without some help. **Caution:** As long as the dog is working toward the object, remain quiet and let him work. You should step in only when he asks for help or is getting into trouble.

Remember that the command **Fetch** means go and get the object and bring it back -- that one command is all that is needed. The dog knows at all times exactly where he left you and he does not have to be reminded. Therefore, there is no need for white jackets, trilling whistles, hand waving, hacking and all of the other antics you see when dogs get to the retrieve object and are on their way back. These things are done because the handler does not believe his dog will do the job if left to his own devices. It is purely a lack of confidence in the dog. Do not get into this habit. You should be his reference point, show interest and confidence in his work, and help him when he asks for help. The dog has a right to expect help when he is on a tough retrieve. Step in when you definitely know something that he does not, praise and encourage him, otherwise keep quiet and let him work.

Three prerequisites for this work are: **Whoa,** basic **Fetch,** and the hand signals (**Back** and **Over**). You also need someone to throw the objects to be retrieved. The thrower should not be visible to the dog. If this is not always possible, he should be as immobile and inconspicuous as possible. At no time should the thrower or anyone near him fire a shot or make a noise to draw the dog's attention to the retrieve object. Be sure that you give the thrower careful and precise instructions as to how and where (location and distance) you want each object thrown.

The dog must learn that the object to be retrieved does not come from the handler or from the spot that the shot is fired. It is out there somewhere in the direction that the gun is pointed and/or in the direction that the sound of the shot indicates. Therefore, the dog must look up and outward at all times, not at his handler. All shooting should be done by the handler or someone standing near him. Do not use blank pistols -- no shot at all is better than a blank pistol. Use blank shotgun loads. If blank shotgun loads are not available, live rounds may be used when handled carefully and safely directed. It is during such training that a dog starts to learn to mark by the sound of the shot. In the early stages, make sure all objects are thrown clear of the background so that they are clearly visible against the sky. The thrower has two responsibilities: (1) to throw the dummies properly and (2) to watch the dog's head and eyes to see where his concentration is from the moment of the throw until he is sent to retrieve. In essence, did the dog have a fair chance to mark and did he mark?

With the dog at **Heel**, gun loaded and with safety on:

1. Give thrower location to which the dummy is to be thrown (make the first distance about 30 yards)
2. Give the **Whoa** command

3. Give the **Mark** command (alerts dog and is the signal to thrower to throw the dummy)
4. Dummy thrown
5. You fire at the dummy (but miss it)
6. Dog is steady
7. Set up hand signal for **Line**
8. Give the **Fetch** command and hand signal
9. Dog drives to dummy
10. Dog makes clean quick pick up
11. Dog turns back immediately (makes eye contact)
12. Dog returns to delivery position quickly
13. Dog presents dummy (looks up at you)
14. You grasp the dummy
15. Check the dog's grip
16. Give the **Out** command
17. Dog opens mouth, *gently* take the dummy
18. Praise the dog well

Review the questions and repeat the sequence until the dog handles 5 or 6 consecutive repetitions flawlessly.

When it is clear that the dog broke before the **Fetch** command, get on him -- he has just disobeyed three commands that should have kept him steady: **Heel, Whoa** and **Gunshot.** Do not let him make the retrieve (either you or the thrower must get to the dummy before the dog does). Review your **Whoa** training. The dog's concentration may be on the mark so intently that he ignores your hand signal for the line. If the dog does not drive eagerly to the dummy, you have missed something in the basic **Fetch** training -- probably the reach and grasp at eye level. Lack of eagerness at pickup is indicative of improper work on the pickup from the table. Go back and review it. If the dog will not look at you after the pickup, you have a cooperation problem and you will have to rely on obedience. Reluctance and halfheartedness on the return is a training problem. You may have pushed the dog too fast or praised it too little. Coming to you has not been pleasurable for the dog. When a dog turns his head or lowers his muzzle, he is trying to avoid making another retrieve because retrieving is not fun for him. Go back and identify the problem (review the questions in every step).

Make sure that the dog is handling retrieves over a distance of about 30 yards (no more) with drive, eagerness and happiness during each aspect or step of the sequence. If there is a weakness in any part of the retrieve, the problem will bite you as the distances increase. Time spent here will pay big dividends later.

Questions

1. Did you give the thrower good instructions?
2. Did you give the **Whoa** command?
3. Did the dog become alert to the **Mark** command?
4. Did you shoot close to the dummy?
5. Did the dog break on the throw, shot, or fall?
6. Did the dog acknowledge your hand signal or keep his eyes on the mark?
7. Did the dog go to the dummy eagerly, quickly, halfheartedly, or not at all?
8. Did the dog pick up the dummy eagerly, quickly, halfheartedly, playfully or did be not pick it up at all?
9. Did the dog turn and look at you instantly after the pickup, refuse to look at you, come straight to you, head away from you, or take the long way around?
10. Did the dog return to the delivery position eagerly and quickly, calmly and slowly or halfheartedly and hesitantly?
11. Did the dog present the dummy eagerly with eye contact, refuse to make eye contact, turn his head away, or lower his muzzle?
12. Did you have to tip his muzzle?
13. Did you handle the delivery properly by checking the dog's grip and varying timing?
14. Did you praise the dog generously?
15. Did you check with the thrower to determine where the dog's concentration was?

This same sequence will be used for all single marked retrieves on both

Figure 60   Note dog's concentration is on the mark, not the decoys, nor the man walking on the island toward the right side.

land and water from 30 yards out to as far as you want to work the dog. Work out in increments of about 10 yards (this may vary some depending on conditions). Make sure that the dog is working flawlessly at each distance. **Caution:** Do not send the dog farther on water than you have sent him on land as you work out to 100 yards. (See Figure 60.)

While any new work or extension of old work should be introduced under relatively easy ground or water conditions, the dog must learn to work under all conditions. When the dog is working well at 50 yards on land or in the water, it is time to start giving him experience working under varying conditions. While on land, occasionally throw the dummy into waist-high thick weeds, heavy scrub brush, alder thickets, briars or over a small hill - - anything and everything. For water work, take the dog to a marsh, a river and a beach with breaking surf. Work up to a situation in which the dog gets flipped over and still gets through. The dog must learn how to handle heavy surf. Many of these things are a jolt to a dog that has never encountered them. The dog should be exposed to them during training, not on a hunting trip. When you start these retrieves under varying conditions, start by having the dummy land about 20 yards from you and work out as the dog progresses to long retrieves.

You must be aware that the accuracy of the dog's mark will diminish as the distance increases, therefore, you may have to do more handling to get the dog downwind of the object. **Caution:** Use self-discipline, do not let handling the dog become the primary objective. Handle the dog only as a means to an end -- not as the end.

A good morning hunting Canada geese
on Maryland's eastern shore.

12 | Blind Retrieves

Any hunting dog should be able to make blind retrieves on both land and water, as there is no way to ensure that he will be able to mark all shot game. The longest blind retrieves a dog will make will be over water. It is pointless while hunting to send a dog on a long blind retrieve when it is not necessary. Therefore, most blind land retrieves will be less than 40 yards. It is much easier to walk closer to the fall than to send the dog for a long blind retrieve. Even though you will teach your dog to make a blind retrieve on land out to about 100 yards, this is only done to help the dog prepare for long blind water retrieves. You want to make sure that you can control him well at 100 yards on land before you try to control him at that distance over water.

The prerequisites for teaching blind retrieving are: **Whoa**, hand signals, **Fetch**, the concept of the far shore, and marked retrieves at 50 yards or more. Without these you cannot control the dog sufficiently to prevent complete failure. Failure causes two problems: (1) You lose your temper, with all that entails, and (2) The dog does not achieve a correct or successful performance. Therefore, ground was lost not gained during training. Use the **Whoa** command and hand signals to get the dog to the dummy if needed -- make sure that he gets there. Think before you give a command in order to keep the number of commands and signals to a minimum.

How do you ensure success on blind retrieves to establish a base of correct repetitions? Start with very short retrieves and with the dog working into the wind. You need a place with cover high enough to hide the dummy but not so heavy that the dog has to break through it. You will be able to make more repetitions quicker if you have several dummies to set out at one time and work the dog from one to the next. Do not walk the dummies out -- the dog will follow your trail. Put the dog out of sight. Walk and throw the dummies so that the dog does not cross your scent trail to get to the dummies.

STEP 1

With the dummies set out, walk the dog at **Heel** so that he is about 15 to 20 feet straight downwind from the dummy.

1. Give the **Whoa** command to the dog
2. Give the dog a line and all the time you are giving the line use the **Mark** command
3. Make sure that he is concentrating on the line
4. Give the **Fetch** command and simultaneously give a vigorous forward movement with the hand used to give the line
5. The dog goes out and makes the retrieve (he will not have to move far before he gets the scent)
6. Praise him

Review the questions and continue the sequence until you get good steady performances.

STEP 2

Increase the distance in about 10-foot increments until you can get consistent performances out to about 50 feet. You must get consistent performances at each incremental increase before making the next increase. When the dog is consistent while working into the wind, it is time to start working down wind.

STEP 3

You must start again with the short distance of 15 to 20 feet when you begin the blind retrieves down wind. Using the same basic cover and setup as in Step 1, the sequence will be the same except that you will be on the upwind side of the dummies. Review the questions after each repetition. If the dog has trouble or hesitates, be patient. He will have no scent to work with until he passes the dummy. In fact, he may see it before he scents it. Work the dog on the sequence until you get good consistent performances (straight out to the dummy on the line). If he starts to wander at this short distance, he will be far off course on longer attempts.

STEP 4

Now that he has consistently worked over a short distance, it is time to work the dog out to about 50 yards in small increments (about 5 yards). Review the questions after each repetition. Make sure you get good consistent performances before you make the next increase. If you do not solidly build and establish the dog's trust in you on these intermediate range blind retrieves, you will have very little in the bank with which to work during longer and more difficult retrieves later on. Take the time necessary to do it well.

STEP 5

Now we take advantage of the "concept of the far shore" to make blind retrieving over water easier. Remember that you taught the dog to keep going until he reaches the game or hits the far shore. It is difficult to set up a true blind retrieve if the dummy or game is in calm open water. When you give the dog a line he can, in many cases, see the object in the water that is against the shoreline. Also, you know that he will go far enough to get to the blind retrieve object if he always goes to the far shore. Therefore, it is easier to teach blind retrieving over water if you find an area that gives you a range of distances to a far shore --- starting at about 15 yards and going out to 100, 150, 200 yards or more. When working between 15 yards and 50 yards, increase the distance in 5 to 10-yard increments. Beyond 50 yards you have more flexibility. If you have a training partner, this job is much easier. He can set the next dummy while the dog is finishing off his retrieve. **Caution:** Agree on where the dummies will be set before you start.

With the first dummy set near the far shore at a distance up to 15 yards, the sequence will be the same as in Step 1. Review the questions after each repetition. If the dog does not go out and make the retrieve, put him on the long lead and use a stern **Fetch** command. If he has misbehaved badly, put him on the long lead, give a harsh **Fetch** command and pinch his ear. Try the next repetition with a harsh command but no ear pinch. After you have good repetitions with the harsh command, soften your tone to stern and then to normal commands. Be sure you have good consistent work at the shortest distance before you begin to increase the distance.

STEP 6

Work the dog out in increments of about 5 yards (the distance to the far shore will determine the exact distance), making sure that you get good consistent work at each distance. Review the questions after each repetition. When the dog will work to a distance of about 50 yards, he will know how to make blind retrieves over water. Beyond that depends upon how far you want him to go.

Questions on Steps 1-6

1. Does the dog obey the **Whoa** command?
2. At the **Mark** command does the dog become alert, break and/or ignore you?
3. At the **Line** signal, does the dog pay attention, concentrate on it, look around, deliberately ignore it or try to break?
4. Did you give the **Fetch** command before the dog acknowledged the line?
5. Did you give a vigorous hand, arm and body movement on the **Fetch** command?
6. Did the dog take the line, go off left or right, take off, move uncertainly or stand there?
7. Did the dog go promptly to the dummy, find it efficiently, wander around, or did he need help?
8. Did the dog return to the correct delivery position and present dummy?
9. Did you handle the delivery properly?
10. Did you praise the dog, look happy, and smile?

13 Multiple Marked And Blind Retrieves

The primary reason for training a dog on multiple retrieves is to condition him to the fact that there can be more than one object out there. Also, the dog must learn to retrieve the particular objects that you want in the order that you want them. This is necessary sometimes in order to make the total retrieving job less difficult.

The prerequisites for multiple marked and blind retrieves are: **Whoa**, retrieving through long single marked retrieves, blind retrieves, hand signals, **Mark** and steadiness. If the prerequisites have been well trained, teaching multiple retrieves progresses very rapidly since you can easily prevent mistakes and thereby ensure correct repetitions. The dog will know the required components of multiple retrieves; all he has to do is learn to use them in combinations.

Caution: For all early work and any new combination, set up the retrieves so that the dog will not be downwind of another dummy or game while going out and coming back to you.

As with all new retrieving work, you should start on land that will allow the dog to see the dummy clearly lying on the ground; and start with short retrieves. If you have a partner to throw the objects, it is better for future work if he is hidden from the dog's view. Fire a blank or live shotgun round for each object thrown. Give your partner explicit instructions on how and where to throw for marked retrieves and placement for blind retrieves. Do not leave it to his discretion -- it's your dog and you are the trainer.

The first multiple will be a double marked retrieve on land. With the dog standing at **Heel**:

1. Face the dog squarely toward the first mark
2. Give the **Whoa** command
3. First **Mark** command
4. First dummy thrown to land about 10 yards from the dog
5. Shot fired toward the dummy
6. Turn the dog to squarely face second mark
7. Give the **Whoa** command
8. Give the **Mark** command
9. Second dummy thrown to land 10 yards from the dog and 10 yards from the first dummy
10. Shot fired toward the dummy
11. Give the dog the line to the second dummy
12. Give the **Fetch** command and **Line** signal simultaneously
13. Dog retrieves and presents second dummy properly
14. Check dog's grip and give the **Out** command
15. Dog opens mouth, *gently* take the dummy
16. Praise the dog briefly
17. **Heel** the dog so that he squarely faces the first dummy
18. Give line to first dummy
19. Give the **Fetch** command and **Line** signal simultaneously
20. Dog retrieves and presents the first dummy properly
21. Check the dog's grip and give the **Out** command
22. Dog opens mouth, *gently* take the dummy
23. Praise the dog lavishly

Review the questions and repeat the sequence until you get several eager, happy, flawless repetitions before you increase the length of the retrieves. Increase the distance of the retrieves in increments of 5 yards out to 100 yards. As the distance increases, increase the spread between the dummies -- at least 50 yards at 100 yards. When the dog will handle a double marked retrieve at 100 yards on land, it is time to go to the water. (See Figures 61 and 62.)

Figure 61   Note how close the dummies are to the dog.

Figure 62   Look at dog's face. He is looking right at the dummy indicated by the hand signal.

Anytime the dog tries to go to the wrong dummy, give a harsh **Negative** command, voice or whistle, **Whoa** command, and the proper hand signal to get him to the correct dummy. You must not allow him to retrieve the wrong dummy.

MARKED DOUBLE RETRIEVES ON WATER

The first few double marked retrieves at the water should be about 10 yards long. You must keep the dummies well separated. It is more difficult to prevent the dog from going to the wrong dummy in the water than on land. Eliminate as much temptation as possible during the early sequences. The sequence at the water will be the same as on land. Be sure to get eager, happy, flawless performance at each distance before increasing the distance.

Now that the dog will handle double marked retrieves on land and water, take the time to give him some mixed (land and water) double marked retrieves. Start with short distances again and work out. The dog may be a little confused the first time or two and not want to switch from land to water or vice versa. You must be firm but patient. Encourage him but make sure that he is successful. Repeat the mixed doubles until he makes the switch readily.

Now the dog must learn to do his own marking from your movements and the direction the gun is pointed and fired. Allow your partner considerable flexibility as to where and when he throws the dummies now. The new requirement here is that the dog must shift his concentration from one mark to the next as indicated by the dummy in the air or by the shooting. The sequence is the same as above except that you leave out items 3, 6, 7 and 8. Use the full range of the dog's vision and test his alertness.

Questions

1. Did you give the **Whoa** and **Mark** command both times?
2. Was the dog steady for the throws?
3. Did you fire a shot at each dummy?
4. Did you reset the dog before the second dummy was thrown?
5. Did you give the dog the line, **Line** signal, and **Fetch** command on the first retrieve?

6. Did the dog retrieve eagerly, quickly, calmly, moderately, half-heartedly, or slowly?
7. Did you position the dog so that he faced the dummy squarely?
8. Did the dog present the dummies properly?
9. Did you handle the deliveries properly?
10. Did you praise the dog briefly after the first retrieve?
11. Did you praise the dog generously after the second retrieve?

BLIND DOUBLE RETRIEVES ON LAND

Be sure that you know exactly where the blind objects are before you send the dog; if you do not -- do not send him. Again you will start with short distances -- about 10 yards with the dummies well separated. Use an area with cover high enough to hide the dummy but not so high that the dog has to push his way through it. Check the direction of the wind to be sure that the dog *cannot* "wind" the other dummy on his way out and back, so that you can give him a proper line. Do not pound the dog into the ground with blind retrieves; mix in some marked retrieves frequently. Four or five repetitions of the sequence are enough at one time.

With the dog not able to see, place the two dummies. **Heel** the dog to the starting point.

1. Face the dog squarely toward one dummy
2. Give the **Whoa** command
3. Give the **Mark** command
4. Give the dog the line
5. Give the **Fetch** command and the **Line** signal
6. Dog retrieves and presents the dummy properly
7. Check dog's grip and give the **Out** command
8. Dog opens mouth, *gently* take the dummy
9. Praise the dog briefly
10. Repeat 1-8 for the second dummy.
11. Praise the dog generously

Review the questions and repeat the sequence until the dog is working flawlessly at 10 yards for several consecutive repetitions. Now work out in 5-yard increments and be sure to get eager flawless work each time. When the dog can handle blind doubles properly at 100 yards, it is time to take him to the water.

If the dog breaks off the line at short distances, stop him, bring him back and start the sequence again. Do not let him retrieve the wrong dummy. If he persists in leaving the line, go back and teach single blind retrieves and taking a line. If he starts to drift off the line at longer distances, stop him and give the proper hand signals to get him back on the line.

BLIND DOUBLE IN WATER

The difficulty with blind retrieves on open water is just that -- making them truly blind. For short-distance work use dummies that lie low in the water. The dog will probably see them but he will not have seen them fly through the air. Once a dog is in the water, his range of discriminating vision is greatly reduced and the dog cannot identify the object until he is fairly close. Do not run too many sequences during one session as you do not want the dog to become dependent on you to lead him to the object to be retrieved. Mix in some marked retrieves.

Again, you will start with short (10 yards) retrieves and work your way out to about 100 yards. The sequence for blind retrieves on water is the same as for land. Remember that controlling a dog in water is more difficult than on land, therefore, you must get eager flawless work at each distance.

Questions for Blind Doubles

1. Did you know exactly where the dummies were?
2. Did you give **Whoa** and **Mark** commands?
3. Did you give the dog a good line and **Line** signal?
4. Did the dog go to the dummy eagerly, calmly, halfheartedly, or did he need help?
5. Did the dog return to the delivery position eagerly, calmly, halfheartedly; or did he need commands?
6. Did the dog present the dummy properly, turn or lower his head; or did he refuse requiring commands?

7.   Did you handle the delivery properly?

8.   Did you praise the dog?

Now that you have all of the elements of multiple retrieves in hand, you can use them in any and all combinations. Give the dog experience on all combinations until he has developed confidence in himself and in you. In the event something unique develops, the two of you will be able to handle it. Be sure to mix in some combination of marked retrieves on land and blind retrieves in the water and vice versa.

You are a very slow learner. Don't you
understand the **Heel** command? Come on!

14 | Retrieve By Trailing

Trailing crippled game is essential for any hunting dog that is expected to retrieve, and all hunting dogs should retrieve. While the instinct to trail is stronger in some dogs than others, all dogs can scent trail. This is called trailing as opposed to tracking -- as tracking carries the connotation of head-down, nose-in-the-footprint, slow, plodding progress. This training does not attempt that. Very few sporting dogs will truly track; however, they will work a total scent trail left by crippled game. The dog is told to **Fetch** and he is trained to use the trail to retrieve. Trailing is a logical and necessary extension of **Fetch** on both land and water. A dog can follow scent over still water as well as over water with reasonable wave action.

When hunting in a marsh or on land with cover heavy enough to hide a moving bird, the most efficient and often the only way that game can be recovered is by trailing. If neither you nor the dog can see the game move from the spot where it fell, there is no efficient way that it can be recovered if the dog cannot locate the trail, work it out and catch the game. You cannot help him.

Many people fear that training a dog to trail will make him hunt with his head carried low looking for ground scent. That is not so. When a dog is sent to hunt, he is given a **Hunt** command. When a dog needs to trail, he is given a **Fetch** command and he knows the difference.

The manner in which the dog works a trail is of little importance. He may carry his head high at near full speed or low at a much slower speed. The dog may work downwind of the trail, quarter it variably or slow his gait to a walk and stay glued to the trail. The important thing is that he uses the scent on the ground, on the grass, in bushes, on the water or emergent growth or wherever it may be to retrieve the game.

The end result of trailing is retrieving; therefore, the prerequisites are **Fetch** and **Whoa** thoroughly trained on both land and water. The keys to trailing are calmness and concentration. Therefore, you must calm the dog and ensure that he is concentrating on the task at hand. To a dog everything has a unique and distinguishable scent and leaves a unique scent trail. The training will start on land with dead game (feather or fur, it makes no difference to the dog.) The game is dragged and the dog is started on the trail. This training then progresses to live, running or swimming game where the dog has to find and then work the trail to make the retrieve. No trailing work should be considered successful if there is no retrieve.

Training a dog to trail can be done alone, but it is far better if you have a partner to lay the trail. The only equipment you need is a standard collar and a long lead with one end that will slide cleanly out from under the collar. The best lead is nylon webbing about an inch wide with one end burned smooth (no loop or snap). You will also need an object to be trailed and a line attached to a pole to separate your partner's scent from the game scent. Actually that is optional as the dog can easily separate the two. Whoever lays the trail should always work on the downwind side. If your partner lays the trail, he should move out of sight of the object beyond and downwind of where he left it and stay there. In later training you will want him there to tell you what happened. Do not let minor things distract you. Remember that the dog is capable of sorting out a multitude of scents and will select the correct one. In early training, however, you should try to eliminate some scents whenever possible to aid in correct performance. You want to start off well so you can get in plenty of praise early.

Training a dog to **Fetch** by trailing will be divided into three stages: (1) Work on lead, (2) Work starting on lead and finishing off lead, and (3) Work off lead to find and follow a trail on land and water.

STAGE I

During this stage the dog works on lead at all times. Only enough restraint is used to keep the dog on the trail, and that restraint will be relaxed as the dog progresses so that he is, in essence, "pulling" you with a slack lead. You start out guiding him -- he ends up guiding you. For all work during this stage you want short cover that allows you to see the trail so that you can help the dog when needed. It will also be helpful if you can see the game at the end of the trail. It is not necessary for the dog to see the game. A few feathers or hairs are pulled from the game and left on the ground to mark the start of the trail and to give the dog a point of concentrated scent. Lay all trails either downwind or crosswind -- *never* into the wind. All game used should be dead and cold.

STEP 1

1. The dead game trail is marked and laid about 40 yards in a straight line and the game left at the end
2. The dog is **Heeled** to about 10 feet upwind of the start of the trail and given a **Whoa** command
3. Calm the dog and caution him -- take as much time as you need
4. With the lead held very short, **Heel** the dog to the start of the trail and direct his attention to the scent
5. When he acknowledges the scent and indicates direction, give a soft calm **Fetch** command
6. As the dog moves along the trail, praise him quietly (keep enough pressure on the lead to keep him from straying)
7. Keep the dog on a short lead all the way to the game
8. Praise the dog as he picks up the game
9. Praise him all the way back to the start
10. Stop, grip the game and check dog's grip
11. Give the **Out** command and *gently* take the game
12. Praise the dog profusely

Review the questions. Repeat the sequence increasing the length of the trail as the dog improves. Keep the dog on a shortened lead for correct repetitions. (See Figures 63 and 64.)

STEP 2

The sequence will be the same as for Step 1 except for item 1. The

Figure 63   Get the dog's attention on feather or fur scent.

Figure 64   Note dog's concentration on trail and dog's pull on lead.

trail will be laid with a gentle bend in it. Vary the bend from side to side so that the dog does not get used to turning the same way each time. Review the questions. Repeat the sequence and as the dog improves, allow him to draw out some lead after he has rounded the bend and settled on the trail. If he strays from the trail shorten the lead again.

STEP 3

The sequence will be the same as in Step 1 except for items 1 and 7. Keep the bend in the trail and as the dog improves, increase the length of that portion of the trail beyond the bend. If the dog makes the bend properly and is on the trail with the lead fully extended, let the lead go as you approach the game and let the dog pull it as he goes in to pick up the game. Repeat the sequence increasing the distance that the dog pulls the lead to about 20 yards. You must be alert to pick up and shorten the lead if the dog strays from the trail.

Questions for Stage I

1. Did you take enough time to calm the dog?
2. Did you direct his attention to the scent?
3. Did the dog acknowledge the scent?
4. Did the dog indicate the direction of the trail?
5. Did you have to show the dog the direction of the trail?
6. Was the **Fetch** command soft and calming?
7. Did the dog stay on the trail or just downwind of it?
8. Did you have to hold the dog on the trail?
9. Did the dog struggle to leave the trail?
10. Did you praise and encourage him on the trail?
11. Did you praise the dog on the pickup and all of the way back to the starting point?
12. Did you and the dog complete the delivery properly?
13. Did the dog take the bend in the trail?
14. Did the dog have trouble on the bend?
15. Did you have to guide him around the bend?
16. Did the dog work well as the lead was lengthened?

Figure 65   Feed the end of the lead (that is to slide) under the collar and back over to your left hand.

17. Did the dog attempt to wander?
18. Did the dog work well while pulling the lead on the ground?

STAGE II

During this stage the dog will be started on lead and released as soon as he is working the trail. Game, both dead and alive, will be used and can be either feathered or furred or a combination. Live birds are easier to handle than live furred game. Most of the work in Steps 4 through 6 can be done with dead game. However, live game should be mixed in from time to time in order to make this phase of training more interesting for the dog. Make sure that the primaries on one wing are pulled or taped so that the bird cannot fly. The trails for Steps 4 and 5 should be laid so that the dog is in sight at all times. Trails laid during Step 6 should be laid so the dog is out of sight part of the time and make sure that he cannot look back and see you when he reaches the game.

Figure 66   Note dog's concentration on the trail, and the loose end of the lead sliding under the dog.

STEP 4

The lead should be coiled and held in your left hand. Take the smooth end and slide it under the dog's collar from back to front. Pull about 3 feet of lead under the collar, bring the end back over the top and grip it with your left hand. (See Figure 65.)

Now all you need do to release the dog is to release the smooth end of the lead and it will slide freely without distracting the dog as he moves off. You can also feed out lead from the coil as needed. The sequence is as follows:

1. The trail is laid with dead game in a straight line about 75 yards
2. The dog is brought about 5 yards upwind of the start and given the **Whoa** command (check the lead to be sure that it will slide free cleanly when you release one end)
3. Calm and caution the dog
4. **Heel** the dog to the pulled feathers or hairs and direct his attention to them by putting your free hand near them
5. When he acknowledges them and indicates direction, give the dog a soft calm **Fetch** command

6. Let the dog take you along the trail (do not restrain the dog unless he tries to leave the trail completely)

7. When you see that the dog is working the scent, release the smooth end of the lead and stop. (See Figure 66.) You must stand right there. You are the dog's reference point. He will look to that spot for help if he needs it. Keep your concentration on the dog, look alert, interested and happy. (Keep your hands off your hips -- that is an intimidating attitude to the dog.)

8. Give the dog leeway here. He may quarter the trail or run on the downwind side. Many dogs will take a quick cast before settling down to work. Speed will vary from dog to dog and, for some, it will be wide open with head high. If the dog is working the trail forward, let him be.

9. The dog works the trail to the game, picks it up and starts back

10. Praise him as he comes in and delivers the game to hand (that will ensure that you look happy)

11. Praise the dog lavishly

Review the questions and repeat the sequence until the dog is getting on the trail quickly and working it to the game quickly.

Caution: If the dog has not started to work the trail by the time you have moved 15 yards and then another 10 yards, do not release him. Give the **Heel** command and take him back and start over. If the dog ignores the trail after he is released, **Whoa** him, go to him, put him on lead and **Heel** him back to the start. Start the sequence at item 2, and at item 5, use a stern low **Fetch** command. If he still ignores the trail, go back to Stage I.

STEP 5

The sequence for this step will be the same as in Step 4 except for item 1. The trail will be laid with a bend (not a sharp turn). The first few bends should be made downwind if the trail is laid crosswind since most dogs will work slightly downwind and handle the bend better. Later on during the dog's training, the trails should be laid in a variety of ways with respect to the direction of the wind. The distance may be increased but keep the bend clearly in sight since you need to know exactly how the dog handles it. Most dogs will overrun the bend and you need to see how quickly he acknowledges the loss of scent, determines the direction to take and gets back on the trail. If the dog does not handle the bend quickly, put him back on lead and work more on Step 2. As the dog progresses make the bends sharper and add a second one. Make sure the dog handles bends well before going to the next step.

Questions for Stage II

Questions 1 through 5 are the same as for Stage I.

1. Did you take enough time to calm the dog?
2. Did you direct his attention to the scent?
3. Did the dog acknowledge the scent?
4. Did the dog indicate the direction of the trail?
5. Did you have to show the dog the direction of the trail?
6. Was the dog working the trail well when released?
7. Should you have kept the dog on the lead for another start?
8. Did the lead slide from under the collar cleanly?
9. Did the dog take a short sidetrack before settling down?
10. Did the dog break and require a **Whoa** command?
11. Was the **Fetch** command given harshly on the restart?
12. How did the dog work the trail? Did he quarter downwind, work close, wide or erratically?
13. Did the dog pick up the game promptly and cleanly?
14. Did you praise the dog all the way back to you?
15. Did the dog drop the game?
16. Did you and the dog complete the delivery properly?
17. How far did the dog overrun the bend?
18. How long did it take him to acknowledge the loss of scent?
19. Did the dog turn in the right direction promptly?
20. How long did it take the dog to pick up the trail again?
21. How long did it take the dog to settle down to work?

STEP 6

This step is more than just an extension of the trailing work. This step will reveal or confirm a lot about your dog concerning temperament, cooperation and how well he has accepted training. It is also the point at which you will make the final reinforcement of the **Fetch** command.

There are several problems that can arise when retrieving by trail while the dog is out of sight. The simplest problem to correct is the dog that gets to the game and leaves it. Usually all it takes to correct this is a sharp **Fetch** command by your training partner who laid the trail and remained relatively close to the game. The next problem may be that the dog picks up the game and does not turn and start back but rather goes away from you. Your training partner can usually handle this by blocking the dog's path while you call the dog to you. If caught early this is not difficult to handle; although it should have been corrected in earlier work. Now go back to marked retrieves and note the dog's action the moment after he picks up the game. Does the dog come immediately or does he take a few too many steps away? The dog's speed and position at pick up will affect his action. What is the commitment? The dog's refusal to return promptly is a lack of cooperation so be sure that the basics are well learned. Dogs that eat, bury, bite, crush or urinate on game have a serious temperament defect as well as a lack of cooperation. The temperament problem will have shown in other areas if you have looked closely enough. Temperament defects cannot be "cured" but may be alleviated. Dogs that do this will never be dependable retrievers.

The dog must work the final part of the trail out of your sight. Your partner should be well off wind of the game, out of sight of the dog, and yet be able to see what the dog does as he reaches and handles the game. Either the natural terrain or cover must block the dog's view of the trainer and his partner. Dead game only should be used for the early work and for the reinforcement sessions.

The sequence will be the same as in Step 4 except for item 1. The trail will be laid 100 yards long with one bend and with the final 20 to 30 yards out of your sight. As the dog progresses, the portion of the trail that is out of sight should be increased as well as the distance. A live bird may also be used on occasions. Increase the length of the trail until the total distance is about 300 yards. **Note:** When you review the questions, check in detail with your partner so that you will know exactly what the dog did near and with the game. You should also check the condition of the game.

Additional Questions for Step 6

1. Was the dog reluctant to go out of sight?
2. Did he stay on the trail while out of your sight?
3. Did he drive straight to and pick up the game promptly?
4. Did he start back promptly?
5. Did he deliver to hand cleanly?
6. Did you check the condition of the game?
7. Did the dog eat, bury, urinate on, ignore, pick up and drop, mutilate, crush with molars, or bite the game with his canines?
8. Did the dog bring live birds back alive? If dead, how did he kill them?

When the dog is working the trail well, it is time to reinforce **Fetch.** Remember, we train by repetitions done correctly until the dog knows exactly what he is to do. We then tempt him to make a mistake in such a manner that we can correct or prevent it. In the case of the trail, we set it up so that he fails on the first attempt and is sent out again and succeeds. Lay the drag in the normal manner, but instead of leaving the game at the end, throw the line over a tree limb about 20 feet up, haul the game up and tie off the line so that it stays there. The dog is then sent to retrieve but of necessity will fail. Your partner must watch the dog carefully so that he can describe his reactions for you. The dog will eventually come back to you -- or at least close enough so that he can see you. Many dogs will obviously be upset and hesitant to come back to you. Do not be upset, this is the dog that knows he is not supposed to come back without the game. This is what you want to see. Use your whistle or a harsh loud **Whoa** command to stop the dog. This will be the signal to your partner to quickly move up and untie the game and drop it at the end of the trail. While this is being done, scold the dog (if you have used plenty of praise, this will indeed upset the dog). Take him back to the start. With the game now on the ground, give the dog a sharp **Fetch** command. He should now retrieve the game. As soon as he comes into view with the game, praise him all the way back in. That's not enough -- praise him lavishly.

You must really get on the dog that shows no persistence in the search, no hesitation or concern and comes in easily. Scold him loudly enough for your training partner to hear you so that he can release the game from the tree. Pick him up, shake him, carry or put him back on lead and take him to the start of the drag. Get his attention on the scent and start him on the trail again with a sharp **Fetch** command and a sharp pinch of his ear. He can and should now make the retrieve. Start praising him as soon as he comes into view with the game and keep it up until he presents the game. Take the game and make a big fuss over him.

Use the following sequence:

1. Lay the trail with the game at the end out of reach of the dog
2. The dog is put on the trail with a **Fetch** command
3. The dog gets to the end of the trail and there is no game
4. The dog searches the area -- nothing. (Your partner must watch the dog closely to see how determined the dog is to find the game and what his attitude is when he cannot.)
5. The dog eventually starts back or takes off hunting
6. When the dog comes into view, watch him closely for a moment (What is his attitude?)
7. Give the **Whoa** command and go to him aggressively
8. Put him on lead
9. Pick the dog up, scold him loudly and shake him
10. Partner drops the game to the ground and hides when he hears you scolding the dog
11. **Heel** the dog to the start
12. Put him on the trail with a harsh **Fetch** command
13. The dog works the trail, picks up the game and starts back
14. As the dog comes into view, praise him effusively all the way to you
15. Take the game and praise the dog generously

Review the questions in detail with your partner. Do not repeat this sequence during this training session. Some dogs show such reluctance to return without the game that a second run is not needed. Very few dogs need three runs at it. If your dog does, you should review your training.

Questions for the Reinforcement Sequence

1. What was the dog's attitude when the game was not there?
2. How hard and how long did he search for it?
3. Was he reluctant to start back?
4. Did he take off hunting?
5. What was his attitude when he saw you?
6. Did he stop and look uncertain?
7. Did he try to come racing to you?
8. Did you stop him and go to him?
9. Did you shake and scold him?
10. Did you calm him before the restart?
11. Was he sent off with a harsh **Fetch** command?
12. Did you praise him effusively as he came back to you with the game?

STAGE III

The dog knows how to retrieve from a trail on which he has been started. Now he must be trained to find the trail, work it out and retrieve in response to one **Fetch** command. This does not mean that he will be inclined to work a trail that he encounters while hunting or carry a low head looking for ground scent. The dog knows the difference between **Hie on (Hunt** command) and **Fetch.** He will not trail healthy game when he has been told to **Fetch** shot game. The dog's nose is well capable of making the distinction.

STEP 7

1. A trail about 100 yards long will be laid with a live bird (wing taped or primaries on one side pulled)
2. The bird will be released at the end of the trail and your partner will move downwind and out of sight to watch the dog as he comes along
3. The dog is heeled toward the trail from upwind and stopped 10 to 15 yards away at a right angle and about 15 yards from one end of the trail

4. The dog is cautioned and calmed
5. The dog is given a line to cross the trail
6. Give a soft calm **Fetch** command
7. As the dog crosses the trail, give **Fetch** command
8. The dog acknowledges the trail and turns to work it; the dog trails the bird and picks it up
9. As soon as you see the dog returning, praise him effusively all the way in
10. The dog delivers the bird to hand cleanly
11. Praise the dog profusely

Review the questions. Repeat the sequence several times and use the second **Fetch** command in item 6 if it is needed. If the dog does not turn promptly on the trail, give a harsh **Fetch** command. Continue repeating the sequence until the dog handles the trail properly and repeatedly with only the initial **Fetch** command.

Questions for Stage III

1. Did you calm him before the start?
2. Did you give him a good line?
3. Did you time the **Fetch** command well as he crossed the trail?
4. Did he acknowledge the scent quickly?
5. Did he turn the correct direction quickly?
6. Did he stay on the trail well?
7. Did he leave the trail?
8. Did he close on the bird quickly?
9. Did he pick it up cleanly?
10. Was the bird dropped enroute back?
11. Was the bird delivered to hand cleanly?
12. Did you praise him as he returned?
13. Did you handle the delivery correctly?
14. Did you praise him after the delivery?
15. Did you check the condition of the bird?
16. Did the dog damage the bird and, if so, how?

STEP 8

You will now need a duck with the primaries pulled or taped on one side so that it cannot fly. You will also need a pond with some emergent growth or shore cover that will hide the duck. It does not take very high cover or emergent growth to hide a duck. Remember, the eyes of a dog swimming are only about 6 inches above the water. If you have a pond to which you can lead the duck to establish a trail, fine; if not, toss the duck so that it lands about 10 to 15 feet out and prevent it from coming to shore. The duck must swim until it will not be visible to the dog as he is brought to the water's edge. As the dog progresses, increase the distance from the shore to the point of trail contact to about 50 yards.

Be very conscious of where the trail is on the water so that you can give the follow-up **Fetch** command whenever the dog crosses it. Know the distance at which your dog can be handled in the water -- this will be an exciting activity for the dog. If the dog has not been well trained on hand signals, you will have to rely on **Whoa** and **Come** as you move along the bank. Do not try to direct the dog to the duck. Try and get him to cross the trail since the trail is the first objective of the training. You are trying to train him to use the trail to get to the duck.

If the dog has done a good job of trailing and finding the duck but cannot possibly catch it, let him force it to dive several times (this will indicate how much desire he has). When the dog is well clear, shoot the duck so that the dog can make the retrieve. That is his true reward. If the dog refuses to close and catch the duck when it is clearly possible, you have missed something in the training or the dog lacks the needed drive and desire. A dog can swim faster than ducks and geese, can catch a duck underwater and can wear down most crippled waterfowl.

Some dogs may need encouragement work before starting this training. Take the dog and a wing-taped duck to the edge of the water. Toss the duck out and give the **Fetch** command as soon as it hits the water. Let the dog chase the duck until it dives. When the dog has relocated the duck and is chasing it, shoot the duck when it is safe to do so.

1. Lay trail or release the duck as outlined above to establish a trail (be sure the primaries on one side are pulled or taped)

2. **Heel** the dog to the water
3. Give the **Whoa** command and calm the dog
4. Give the dog the line to the trail
5. Give soft calm **Fetch** command
6. As the dog crosses the trail, give the **Fetch** command
7. The dog acknowledges the scent and starts to work the trail
8. The dog finds and closes rapidly on the duck
9. Praise the dog
10. The dog catches the duck or forces it to dive
11. If it dives the dog circles, searches and finds the duck (if you can see the duck, give the dog some help)
12. The dog closes rapidly on the duck
13. If the dog cannot possibly catch the duck, shoot it when the dog is well out of the way
14. The dog delivers the duck to hand (praise him generously as he comes to you)
15. Continue to praise him after delivery

Review the questions. Repeat the sequence as often as possible. Each duck will give the dog new experiences and build his confidence

Additional Questions for Step 8

1. Did you give the dog a line that would help him use the wind?
2. Did the dog drive to catch the duck?
3. Did the dog force the duck to dive?
4. Did he stay and search hard for the duck after it dove repeatedly?
5. Were you able to help him?
6. Did he catch the duck alive?
7. Could he have caught the duck alive?
8. Was the duck shot?
9. Did the dog make a clean delivery to hand?
10. Did he drop the duck during delivery?
11. Did you praise him each time the duck dove?
12. Did you praise him as he came in with the duck?
13. After he delivered the duck, did you stand there and praise him

15 | Retrieving Distractions

Once a dog has picked up the object for which he was sent, he must ignore everything else and deliver it to hand. Other game, whether dead or alive, must not interfere with the retrieve. While some dogs are capable of properly carrying more than one bird at a time with no damage to the birds, allowing them to do so will cause more problems than it is worth. Therefore, it is far better to train a dog to ignore all distractions once he has the intended object. There is one exception. If other game is shot while the dog is returning from a retrieve, he should mark the retrieve with as little deviation from the task at hand as possible. That means that the dog should keep moving toward you while turning his head to mark the fall. Clearly, if it falls behind him, he must pause to mark the fall. That can change a difficult blind retrieve into a simple marked retrieve.

The prerequisites for this training are: **Whoa**, Steadiness, **Fetch, Negative** command, and **Come.** Do not even think about it if these elements of training are not well mastered.

This work will be divided into three phases each of which includes land and water work as follows:

Phase I.   Dummy retrieve and dummy distraction.
Phase II.   Dummy retrieve and dead bird distraction.
Phase III.   Dummy retrieve and flown bird shot for distraction.

You will need a partner to throw the dummies and the birds. You will shoot close to all dummies and dead birds while they are in the air. You must do so quickly giving the dog as much time as possible to mark. This exercise will go better if a gunner beside the live bird thrower shoots the bird. As always, your partner should not be visible to the dog. For the first few repetitions during each phase, be sure that the dummy or bird lands downwind of the dog's line to you. After he gets the idea, throw some objects upwind and then throw some objects downwind and vice versa, i.e., mix it up.

PHASE I: Dummy Retrieve and Dummy Distraction

With the dog off lead at **Heel**:

1. Give the **Whoa** command
2. **Mark** command (to dog and thrower)
3. Retrieve dummy thrown
4. You shoot while it is in the air
5. Dog is steady
6. Give the dog the line
7. **Fetch** command and **Line** hand signal given simultaneously
8. Dog goes out, picks up dummy and starts back
9. Distraction dummy thrown to land ahead of and 10 to 15 yards off the dog's line to you
10. You shoot while the dummy is in the air
11. Dog keeps moving toward you but turns his head to mark the fall
12. Dog comes to delivery position and presents the dummy
13. Check dog's grip, give the **Out** command and take the dummy
14. Praise the dog lavishly (this is the place for lavish praise because it is the object of the lesson)
15. **Heel** the dog to face the distraction dummy and give the **Whoa** command
16. Give the **Mark** command and **Line**
17. Give the **Fetch** command and the **Line** hand signal simultaneously
18. The dog retrieves and presents the dummy
19. Check the dog's grip, give the **Out** command and *gently* take the dummy
20. Praise the dog

Review the questions. Repeat the sequence until the dog does not go toward the dummy, but merely turns his head to mark. (See Figure 67.)

Figure 67   Dog's eyes on thrown dummy as he moves to handler. Note happy disposition.

If the dog breaks on the first dummy, go back and teach steadiness. He is not ready for this.

If the dog drops the dummy he is carrying:

1. Give a very harsh **Negative** command followed immediately by a harsh **Whoa** command
2. Put down your shotgun
3. Get to the dog quickly and aggressively
4. Pick him up and drop him roughly at the spot where he dropped the dummy
5. Pick up dummy, give a harsh **Fetch** command and put it roughly into his mouth
6. Walk back to your position and pick up your shotgun
7. Give a stern **Fetch** command
8. Dog delivers and presents dummy. You accept properly
9. Praise the dog briefly
10. Go and pick up the distraction dummy -- do not let him retrieve it

If the dog got to the distraction dummy before you could get to him, take it from him roughly and throw it down -- then start with item 4 above.

If the dog gets to the distraction object at anytime, you have gone too fast or the dog does not know **Whoa.** Review your training and correct the problem. If the dog drops the retrieve dummy, go back and teach him that **Fetch** means hold the object until told to release under all conditions.

If the dog starts toward the distraction dummy while still holding the retrieve dummy, give a hard **Whoa** command using Voice, Whistle or both. When the dog stops, give a very harsh **Negative** command, and when he is looking at you, give a stern **Fetch** command. Finish off the retrieve properly and praise the dog.

When the dog performs flawlessly for several consecutive repetitions, start throwing the dummy to land progressively closer to the dog's line of return. Make sure that the dog only turns his head to mark at each distance. The next step is to throw the dummy to land right in front of the dog. He must mark it and step over or around it. To be sure that you have this well trained, set a long retrieve and distraction. The retrieve dummy should land about 100 yards out and the distraction dummy should land about 70 yards out. When the dog is flawless on this exercise, no matter where the dummy lands, it is time to take him to water.

The sequence at the water will be the same as on land. If the dog switches dummies in the water, it means that you did not teach the distraction thoroughly on land or that you do not have control of the dog in the water. Find out which it is and correct the problem. Work through the sequence until you have flawless work in the water just as you did on land. Do not forget the long retrieve setup.

PHASE II: Dummy Retrieve and Dead Bird Distraction

The dog's eyes are good enough to know the difference between a dummy and a dead bird. The dead bird is much more enticing than the dummy he is carrying -- especially when he gets downwind of it. The sequence is the same in Phase II as in Phase I. All you are doing here is increasing the level of enticement. Be sure that you get flawless work each step of the way and do not forget the long retrieves on both land and water. Review the

Figure 68   Dog's eyes on gun about to be fired. Duck at extreme right.

questions in detail. (See Figure 68.)

PHASE III: Dummy Retrieve and Flown and Bird Shot for Distraction

It does not matter to the dog what type of birds you use. **Caution:** It is your responsibility to make sure that they are legal. Mixing objects may keep the dog's interest higher. There is no doubt that a flying bird dropped in front of a dog is far more enticing than the dummy that he is carrying -- it is the ultimate. If you have properly prepared the dog, voice and/or whistle is all that you will need to control him. The sequence for Phase III is the same as in Phase I. Be sure to get flawless work at each step and do not forget the long retrieve and distraction on both land and water. Review the questions. (See Figure 69.)

Questions

1. Did you give the **Whoa** and **Mark** commands both times?
2. Did you shoot close to the dummy both times quickly?
3. Was the dog steady?
4. Did you give the dog the line and the **Line** signal?
5. Did the dog go to and pick up the bird eagerly or hesitantly?

Figure 69   Dog's eyes on flown, shot and falling bird; dog marking as he moves to handler.

6. Did the dog stop and mark the distraction or the shot?
7. Did the dog start toward the distraction or come straight to you?
8. What did it take to stop the dog from going to the distraction -- caution, negative command, whistle, voice, multiple commands: or could you not stop him?
9. Did the dog finish the retrieve and present the dummy eagerly, calmly, or reluctantly?
10. Did you handle the delivery properly?
11. Did you praise the dog?
12. Did you set the dog up properly for the distraction retrieve?
13. Did the dog retrieve and present the distraction retrieve eagerly, calmly, or reluctantly?
14. Did you handle the delivery properly?
15. Did you praise the dog?
16. Did the dog drop the retrieve and go for the distraction?
17. If so, did you get after him aggressively?
18. Did you show severe displeasure in the correction?
19. Did you prevent him from getting to the distraction?
20. Did you retrieve the distracting object?

16 Come

In order to avoid problems during **Whoa** training, a dog should not be trained to **Come** until he has been trained to **Whoa** to voice, whistle, hand and gunfire. It is much easier to train a dog to **Come** if he knows **Whoa.** Very few dogs are dependable to **Come** when they do not know **Whoa.** Before you start training a dog to **Come**, you must decide what action is required of the dog. Does **Come** mean **Come** to heel, **Come** in front of me and stop, or **Come** to within a few yards? During training it is easier to train the dog to heel or to stop in front of you, then back off. That is, you will then allow the dog to **Come** only close enough to you to find out what you want him to do and to get instructions. This is what you will do during hunting except when it is time to quit. The command **Come** is not needed in retrieving except as a directional signal because the command **Fetch** means go and get it and deliver it to hand.

At this point, the question is, how do I get my dog if he knows neither **Whoa** nor **Come?** You either go and get him or he comes to you. Puppies are easy -- just kneel and clap your hands and they will usually come running. Praise gets dogs up to about a year old to come to you. However, by then they should know **Whoa.** Walk or run down older dogs. In fact it is a good idea to walk down your dog at least once so he will know that you can do it. Do not use the command you plan to use for **Come** because the dog will not obey it most of the time and that will set his training back.

Caution: As with all training, to ensure correct response, the first commands will start with the dog on lead and close enough to feel your presence. Then progress through increments to long distances.

STEP 1

The long lead will be used for the basic work.

1. Give the **Whoa** command
2. Walk out about 5 feet (feeding out the lead)
3. Turn and face the dog
4. Pause and establish eye contact
5. Give an upbeat **Come** command
6. Tap (snap if needed) the lead immediately
7. Dog starts toward you
8. Take up lead slack while maintaining eye contact
9. Praise the dog to where you want him
10. Give the **Whoa** command
11. Praise the dog lavishly

Review the questions. Repeat the sequence until the dog will come to the desired position without guidance. (See Figures 70 and 71.)

Questions

1. Did the dog anticipate the command?
2. How quickly did the dog commit to **Come**?
3. Did the dog avoid eye contact?
4. Did the dog come straight in or veer off **Line**?
5. Did the dog resist guidance to position?
6. Did the dog come to position on his own?
7. Did you praise the dog all the way in and appear happy?
8. Did you praise him on position?

Caution: Do not increase the distance or stop the tap on the lead until you get the final position well taught. If you do, you will have unnecessary trouble later.

When the dog is performing flawlessly for several consecutive repetitions, increase the distance that you walk away in 5-foot increments to the full length of the lead. Repeat the sequence until the dog's performance is flawless for several consecutive repetitions at each distance. When the dog's performance is perfect at the maximum length of the long lead, it is

Figure 70   The dog is on **Whoa**, slack lead.

Figure 71   Lead snapped, dog is paying attention and moving toward handler.

time to eliminate the tap of the lead. As the distance increases, the dog may try to wander or take liberties -- do not allow it. Pop the lead to get his attention back on the job and use a stern **Come**.

STEP 2

The sequence will be the same as in Step 1 items 1-5.

6. Give the **Come** command
7. Do not tap the lead
8. Coil the lead so that the dog comes to you
9. Dog takes final position
10. Praise him generously

If the dog does not start toward you immediately on the command **Come**, snap the lead. Repeat the sequence until he comes to the proper position on voice command only for several consecutive repetitions from the full length of the lead.

STEP 3

When the dog is working well at the length of your long lead, it is time to introduce the whistle command for **Come**. Select the whistle command you intend to use whether it be multiple toots or a trill, it is your decision. You will again start from a short distance -- say 10 feet. With the dog on **Whoa** on lead facing you, the sequence will be:

1. Whistle command
2. Immediate voice command **Come**
3. Dog comes in and takes proper position
4. Praise lavishly

Review the questions. Repeat the sequence perhaps a dozen times then delay the voice command giving the dog time to move on the whistle alone. If he hesitates, use a stern voice cornmand. When he will come to you readily from 10 feet with whistle only, increase the distance between you in 10 feet increments to the length of your long lead. You can now control the dog by voice or whistle on lead -- it is time to take off the lead.

STEP 4

The sequence off lead is as follows:

1. Give the **Whoa** command
2. Walk out 5 feet
3. Turn and face the dog
4. Pause and establish eye contact
5. Give a happy **Come** command
6. Dog starts toward you
7. Praise the dog as he comes
8. Dog comes to wanted position
9. Give the **Whoa** command
10. Praise the dog

Repeat the sequence until the dog is flawless for several consecutive repetitions at 5 feet. Increase the distance to which you walk away in about 5-foot increments. Repeat the sequence at each distance until the dog performs flawlessly for several consecutive repetitions before making the next increase. If at anytime the dog veers off or does not work properly, put him on lead, repeat the same sequence, give a stern **Come** command at the point of error and pop the lead. Take the lead off, and repeat the sequence. If you have trained the dog to a **Negative** command, use it when the dog starts to stray. If he gets unruly, **Whoa** him, go to him and scold him. Repeat the sequence. Do not allow the dog to take liberties such as circling you, wide turns, etc. These actions are his way of avoiding the job. If he persists **Whoa** him. Put him back on the lead and give him a stern **Come** with a pop on the lead. For the next repetition, take off the lead. During this step, whenever he misbehaves put him back on lead, pop or crack the lead, and repeat the sequence. When the dog's performance is perfect through several consecutive repetitions at 60 feet, it is time to start calling him back while he is running free.

STEP 5

All calling up to this point has been done with the dog on whoa looking at you awaiting the command. Now it is time to give the **Come** command with the dog moving. Do not try this from great distances in the beginning.

This is the point at which most people make a big mistake in training a dog to **Come**. You must overcome the excitement of running and whatever else has the dog's attention. How do you ensure that the first **Come** command will be obeyed? Get eye contact before the command. Either select a time when the dog is looking your way or stop him with a **Whoa** command.

With the dog angling toward you:

1. Get eye contact
2. Give the **Come** (voice or whistle) command
3. Keep eye contact and praise the dog as he comes (praise makes it easier to keep eye contact)
4. Give the **Whoa** command when the dog is in the proper position
5. Give praise

Repeat the sequence until you have several consecutive flawless repetitions at about 10 yards. Increase the distance between you and the dog in increments of at least 5 yards or more depending on how the dog responds.

In the event that you have trouble getting eye contact, use the **Whoa** command to stop the dog and get eye contact, then use the sequence described above. There will be many times while working with a young dog, or even an older one, when you will be better off to stop the dog before you call him. The **Come** command will never have the attention getting ability of **Whoa**.

STEP 6

Now that the dog handles **Come** well with eye contact, he must be trained to do so without it. The first few repetitions must be made so that the dog can feel your presence. Therefore, start at about 10 to 15 yards and increase the distance as the dog responds. Watch closely to see how quickly the dog acknowledges the command and commits to obey. With the dog angling away or crossing so that there is no eye contact proceed as follows:

1. The dog is close enough to feel your presence
2. Give the **Come** command

3. The dog turns and starts toward you
4. Praise the dog and show pleasure (clap, smile, have a happy attitude -- coming to you must always be pleasant)
5. Give the **Whoa** command when the dog is in the proper position
6. Praise profusely

Review the questions and repeat the sequence at close range until you have several consecutive good repetitions.

When you start to increase the distance from you to the dog do not try to hammer the **Come** command into him during a few intensive lessons. You do not want the dog looking over his shoulder, so mix the **Come** command in with other work. Continue variations in the training until the dog responds properly when he is out of sight and 100 yards or so away from you. The distance for flushing dogs will be much shorter as it should never be more than 30 yards away while hunting game, and if they are at a great distance while retrieving, they should be stopped before they are called.

There is no point in repeating the **Come** command to a moving dog. If he does not come in immediately, give the **Whoa** command, get his attention, and then call him or go and get him. The strongest command you have should be **Whoa,** therefore, whenever you have to call an excited, headstrong dog, stop him first. If you cannot stop him, he will certainly not come to you.

Whoa -- and wait here for the boss!

17 Going Afield

Going afield means taking a dog to work, whether it be in fields, woods, water or marsh to introduce him to and familiarize him with his work. It exposes the dog to the sights, smells, sounds, feelings and conditions of his working world. It is the complement to table and yard work. Proper introduction to going afield while the table and yard work are progressing is essential to develop the complete dog. It is also relief from table work. It presents an opportunity to evaluate such things as desire, boldness and cooperation (as opposed to desire to please). It is not play-time, although it is fun for both you and the dog. It is development time. Going afield is learning time -- you learn about the dog and the dog learns about you. You must concentrate on the dog at all times. Going afield is his reason for being. It is an essential element of his development.

Going afield is divided into two parts: (1) land activities and (2) introduction to water.

Whether you plan to use your dog for only upland or water work, it is necessary to expose and acclimate him to both. He cannot be a complete dog without exposure to both.

GOING AFIELD ON LAND

Caution: The most important consideration in selecting an area to work a dog is safety.

Find an area where the dog can hunt hard and as wide as his breed demands without being in danger. No dog can develop properly if he must be constantly hacked in an attempt to keep him out of danger. Look for terrain and cover that will be similar to what you plan to hunt. You will need variety, especially for a young dog, so that you do not overwhelm him. Work the dog into situations that are unusual for him slowly.

There is, all too often, a tendency to overwork young dogs and puppies in the field. Keep the sessions short. Think about the dog's attention span, as well as his strength and endurance. The young dog should always be picked up when he is still raring to go. Do not wait for fatigue to set in with its attendant problems. The height and density of the ground cover as well as the temperature and humidity must always be considered in determining the effective length of time that a dog can work -- especially young dogs. Keep in mind how long it will take to work back to the starting point or you may have to carry the dog or walk him back on lead. You are there to prepare the dog to be an effective hunter, not to see how long he can run. Dogs under a year old should never run more than a half hour, often less.

The biggest problem most hunters have with young dogs afield is keeping quiet. They insist on trying to use commands the dog has not been trained to obey and then get angry when the dog does not respond to their satisfaction. Commands such as **Whoa, Come, Heel, Fetch** and others are not taught afield, they are taught elsewhere and then used in the field at the proper time and in the proper place. There are, however, three items that can only be taught afield: (1) a command to Hunt (**Hie on, Find the bird,** etc.), (2) a **Negative** command (**Leave it, Gone**, etc.), and (3) that you can walk him down and catch him. Virtually all a dog should hear in the field is the **Hunt** command and praise. Of course, the flushing dog will hear the **Turn** command (whistle) frequently.

Be aware that constantly talking to a dog will generally tend to make him want to stay closer to you. While this can be beneficial to a flushing dog, do not overdo it with a pointing dog.

If a dog is to have the time needed to hunt properly, you must be conscious of the wind at all times and vary your pace accordingly. To hunt efficiently, a dog must work across the wind and make his turns into the wind at the end of each lateral cast. It is not always possible to hunt into the wind, therefore, sometimes you must hunt downwind, crosswind or at various angles to the wind. The fastest and easiest approach is hunting into the wind.

When hunting a flushing dog downwind, most of your time is spent standing still. When the dog has covered one section of ground and you have sent him out to one side and then downwind, you walk over the ground that he has just covered and stand at the edge of the new ground while the dog hunts back to you. When working a crosswind, you must stand while the dog works across in front of you from downwind to the upwind side of you. You then walk over the ground just hunted while the dog casts back downwind.

With a pointing dog, you will move constantly, but adjust your pace on a downwind hunt so that you cross the ground previously covered just as the dog finishes hunting the new bite and turns to cast back downwind for the next bite. If you walk too slowly, the dog will rework previously hunted ground or get progressively farther and farther away. If you move too fast, you force the dog to miss some ground.

Young dogs should always be worked into the wind. Take the time to get into position for them to work into the wind. Even if that means putting him on lead and skirting the areas that you want the young dog to hunt.

Everyone wants to see the young dog work game, however, everything has its time and place. Do not overdo the game work with young uncontrollable dogs. If you have good proven hunting stock, more problems will be caused than solved by giving young or uncontrolled dogs too much game. While there may possibly be some need to really fire up a young field trial dog to develop the short bursts of energy he needs, it is not needed for the hunter who must sustain a good energy level for an all day hunt. The field trial circuit demands a sprinter; the hunter needs a marathoner. There is little doubt that the young flushing dog should be kept away from game until he is controllable. However, the dog may be worked in an area where there is game scent, but no game. A sniff of game scent can enliven any dog's day. As the pointing dog has more leeway in hunting, occasional contact with game is not a problem as long as he cannot catch it.

A flushing dog's search for game must of necessity be a tightly controlled and disciplined affair. He must not be allowed to hunt for himself. He must hunt the ground in a prescribed manner within gun range. The dog must spend virtually all of his time within 20 yards of you. If the dog is any farther away from you when he scents game, it will be flushed out of gun range. The dog that scents game at 20 yards will probably flush it at about 25 yards, which puts it at least 40 yards out before you can shoot. That is stretching most upland game guns, loads and gunners. To get a perspective on this, get a piece of clothesline 40 yards long and go to the type of terrain and cover you normally hunt. Fold the line in half and lay it on the ground in several locations. Then open it to 40 yards and do the same. Think for a moment about the 20-yard distance, and then ponder the 40-yard shot. If your normal hunting area has much growth over waist high, the 40-yard shot is out of the question --- 20 to 30 yards will be a tough shot. Therefore, before you take a young flushing dog afield for the first time, you should know what 20 yards looks like under all conditions that you plan to hunt. Otherwise you will not know when the dog is out of proper hunting range.

There are only 3 commands that you will be concerned with when you take a young flushing dog afield: (1) **Hunt**, (2) **Turn** and (3) **Negative** (Leave it). The **Hunt and Turn** commands are positive and will be used to control the dog's search pattern. The **Negative** command will only be used when the dog is pottering or sniffing old scent. However, he should hear a lot of praise when he is pleasing you. Do not try and use any other commands. When it is time to leave the field, do one of two things: Kneel, get his attention, clap your hands and sweet talk him until he comes to you; or say nothing and go and get him.

A pointing dog must range out, exercise initiative, use knowledge of game, utilize the wind to find game, and point and hold the game until the hunter arrives. Therefore, the young pointing dog must be given the latitude to develop these abilities.

Proper or desired range cannot be defined in yards without first describing every feature of the terrain and cover hunted, the dog doing the hunting, the type of game hunted and a particular individual's perception of all three. Therefore, a pure definition of proper range is impossible. Range can be defined, however, in terms of maintaining necessary visual contact, efficiency and effectiveness. The dog must maintain sufficient visual contact to hunt in front, to take directions from your movements and let you know where he is generally. That does not mean that he must be within your sight at all times. In fact, the dog may be out of sight more than he is not when hunting some covers. A dog's hunting range is efficient if it allows the dog to hunt the ground thoroughly at a smooth continuous pace without reworking or missing any ground and you do not have to waste a lot of time looking for him when he is on point. The range is effective if the dog holds all game pointed until the hunter arrives. Therein lies a problem; most hunters will not give up the shot and bird while a young dog learns to handle various game birds. Two things happen when a pointing dog is held in too close: (1) His effectiveness and efficiency are greatly diminished and (2) The hunter is often so close that he has made the bird nervous and starts it moving before the dog has a chance to handle it properly. On many wild birds that is disastrous.

A young pointing dog should hear only 3 things from his handler while afield: (1) The **Hunt** command, (2) Praise, and (3) The **Negative** command (**Leave it**) if he starts to potter or snuffle at field mice, etc. He should be allowed to develop his natural hunting range and style with minimum guidance from his handler. When you know what that is and it does not suit your needs, change it. If he works too close, get another dog; if his range is too wide, shorten it.

You can help the young dog to develop a quartering (across the wind) search by quartering the wind yourself and giving the **Hunt** command at the right time. Whenever the dog has gone far enough in one direction, you should turn and quarter the wind away from the dog, give the **Hunt** command and when the dog crosses ahead of you, praise him. Remember to face the direction that you want the dog to hunt when you give the **Hunt** command. Do not use **Come** or any combination of words with **Come** in it. You do not want the dog to come to you; you want him to hunt ahead of you, so use the appropriate command. The **Hunt** command is never inhibiting or negative. The **Come** command is always inhibiting and often negative in connotation.

When the young dog has had a workout and it is time to pick him up, do not give a command. Do one of two things: (1) Kneel down, get his attention, clap your hands, sweet talk him and put a lead on him when he

Figure 72   Handler kneeling, clapping his hands, "smiling" puppy running to him.

comes to you, or (2) Go and get him. He knows that you want him and he does not respond. Say nothing -- walk him down and put a lead on him. Do not scold him when you get to him. Give the **Heel** command in a normal tone. (See Figure 72.)

If the dog's range and pace are too great for your pace and the cover that you want to hunt, shorten his forward carry. The dog must know **Whoa** and hand signals thoroughly before you start to shorten his range. If you merely restrict his forward carry, you force him to stand and wait for you or rework the same ground. The most efficient way to reduce his forward carry is to increase the dog's lateral movement as you decrease the forward carry. Decreasing the forward carry is relatively easy even though it takes quite a few repetitions. When the dog reaches the maximum range at which you want him to work, **Whoa** him. Walk to the dog and send him to hunt with a hand signal that sends him at right angles to your line of hunting, which is straight into the wind. Increasing the lateral movement is more difficult. Each time you stop the dog's forward carry, go to him and give him a hand signal to move out laterally, keep a sharp eye on him. If he tries to turn forward into the wind too soon, stop him and send him out wider with a hand signal and the **Hunt** command. Do not use **Back** or **Over** which are retrieving commands. This exercise will take time but the dog soon learns that he is stopped at a given forward distance, but has considerable lateral freedom. While it is difficult to do, if you have or can set up a situation where you work between distant lateral objectives and direct him to them alternately, it will help get the lesson across. You must not allow him to strike out too far forward for his objectives. If the dog tries to stretch out, stop him, go to him and send him for the lateral objective. When you know that he has learned the lateral hand signal well and openly defies you -- go and get him. This is one reason why you walked him down as a youngster. If you are able, pick him up roughly and shake him all the way back to the point of defiance. If not, put him on lead, handle him roughly and scold him all the way back.

Most tough, bold, fast, hard-working dogs will have to be reminded from time to time, as terrain and cover change, of what proper working range is; you will smile inwardly when you do it.

GOING AFIELD ON WATER

Introducing a dog to water probably causes him more bewilderment than it should. All dogs can swim, some better than others, and a few to the point of hilarity. Any dog will swim if there is sufficient incentive. The amount of incentive required varies greatly from the seemingly negligible need of the water retriever to the almost insurmountable amount needed by some pointing dogs. Therein lies the problem.

Caution: The one thing that the dog does not need is to be forced (thrown) into the water. That is not incentive. It does not work. It only produces panic.

The strongest incentive a dog can have to enter the water is a strong retrieving instinct. If the retrieving instinct is strong enough, the water as a barrier does not exist. It becomes a medium that the dog will use to get to the retrieve object. There are no problems with dogs like that, except for you. Do not work young dogs to the point of exhaustion or boredom.

As the strength of the retrieving instinct diminishes, there comes a point when the dog will not enter the water. Then a second element, temperament, may enter the picture. Fear of the water is a problem for the shy or fearful dog. Uncertainty can also be a problem for a very young puppy. A little more age usually takes care of that. While you cannot change a dog's basic temperament you can, by proper handling, increase his self-confidence as well as his confidence in you.

Find places like small, slow moving streams or ponds where the water is shallow enough so that the dog can wade across. Cross the water and encourage the dog to come with or to you. Use any temptation that you can, including his favorite snacks. Praise him profusely when he comes to you. Above all, do not get angry if he does not come to you. That will only cause more problems. Be happy and encouraging.

If you cannot find water of wading depth to cross and you must stand in the water to entice the dog to you, pick him up and praise him when he comes to you. Carry him to shore every time you pick him up. As his confidence builds, wade back to shore, encouraging him to come with you.

Gradually increase the depth until the dog must swim to cross the water or to get to you standing in the water. The first time or two that he swims to you while you are standing in the water, pick him up and praise him as you walk to shore. You should remain happy, praise him and not get angry.

When the dog will swim to you readily, it is time to get him to go into the water. There is no point in throwing an object into the water for him to go after if he will not go and pounce eagerly on the object on the ground. Encourage him with play retrieving by tossing an object on the ground for him to pounce on and pick up. Work around until you are tossing it close to the water. At the next session start with the object at the water's edge and work it out to wading depth. Do not go into swimming depth water until the dog is working eagerly at wading depth. When the dog works eagerly in wading depth water, toss the object just far enough so that the dog must swim to reach it -- wading depth distance plus 2 or 3 feet of swimming. Increase the distance slowly in small increments; you are trying to build up the dog's self-confidence. Rushing will only set the dog back.

Build the dog's confidence slowly and make the sessions at the water short. Five or six repetitions at each session are enough. Keep the swimming distances short, no more than 10 or 15 feet. That is enough for a nervous or uncertain dog.

Similarly, when training the eager young retriever, do not overdo it. Keep the retrieves short and do not run too many repetitions. Always quit while the dog is still very eager to go again. Do not overwhelm him with a retrieve that is too long. Every young dog has a limit beyond which lies intimidation. No useful purpose is served by pressing until you find out what that limit is. It can in fact set back the dog's development.

If you plan to use force trained retrieving, do not use the command you plan to use for **Fetch** while introducing the dog to or playing with a dog at the water. That command should only be given when it can be enforced; it is not enticement or encouragement.

18 Hunt Command

Decide what command you want to use to send the dog out to hunt and use it only when you want the dog to hunt. It should not be used for anything else. **Hie on** is popular as is **Find the bird** and **Get'em up.** Training the dog to the **Hunt** command is relatively easy -- just use it every time the dog is sent out to hunt and for nothing else. The dog must be taught that the **Hunt** command means to hunt in front of you and not behind you. Anytime you give the command, make sure that he hunts in front of you -- that means the area forward of you. He should not be allowed to cross behind the line that runs at right angles to the direction you are walking. The dog has no business behind you since that ground has already been worked. If the dog tries to go behind you, do not let him. The method that you use to prevent it will be determined by how far along he is in his **Whoa, Hie on** or **Negative** command training. Do not try to use **Whoa** unless you can stop him in his tracks, i.e., do not cause one problem while trying to stop another. If you cannot use **Whoa** to stop him, get his attention, pick up your pace, wave your arm forward and give the **Hunt** command. If he responds to the **Negative** command of displeasure, show displeasure and wave him around and forward with an upbeat **Hunt** command.

If he has not bolted on you, you will rarely have trouble finding a dog hunting in front of you. However, the dog that gets behind you will always cause problems.

Just as a dog can take direction from gunfire, he can also take direction from the projection of your voice. Always face the direction in which you want the dog to hunt before you give the **Hunt** command. Give the **Hunt** command and move forward. The dog will quickly learn to move in front of you and hunt. If the **Hunt** command has been taught properly, a dog that cannot see you and is running in the opposite direction can be sent to hunt in front if you face the direction you want him to hunt and give the **Hunt** command.

19 | Turn Command

It is absolutely essential that a flushing dog obey a command to turn immediately, and most pointing dogs will be called on to respond to a command to turn on occasions. Most flushing dogs are trained to respond to the whistle, while pointing dogs generally do so to a voice command. That's your decision to make, but make it before you start teaching it and before you teach any whistle command. Fortunately, most properly bred spaniels and retrievers are very biddable and cooperative; therefore, they take to the **Turn** command readily.

FLUSHING DOG

Since you want the finish-trained dog to turn at about 20 yards, you must start out training the young dog to turn at about 10 yards. This will also give you the force of presence or closeness generally necessary for controlling the dog. Your movements will be the controlling factor. Therefore, you must concentrate all possible body language to "enforce" the **Turn** command. This is tight control so keep the lessons short, especially for a young dog. Break the **Turn** work into 3 or 4 short sessions per outing. It is essential that you have everything (all body language) in position and motion *before* you give the **Turn** command. You must also maintain that body language until the dog crosses ahead of you. Body language is your lead.

The basic training for the **Turn** should always be done with the dog working into the wind. This approach allows the dog to use his natural quartering instincts to best advantage.

1. Give the **Hunt** command and direction to left
2. The dog bears 10 yards away from you to the left
3. You turn right 45 degrees to the wind
4. Get hand signal in place and head straight in the direction you are going, ready to give **Turn** command
5. Give the **Turn** command
6. Do not turn your head to look at the dog
7. The dog turns and works across
8. The dog crosses to the right
9. Praise the dog as he passes
10. As soon as he passes to your right, you turn straight into the wind

Review the questions quickly as the dog is crossing. (See Figures 73 and 74.) Repeat the sequence until the dog is turning flawlessly and responds immediately at 10 yards. Then increase the distance in small increments until he handles flawlessly at 20 yards.

Anytime the dog does not turn on the command, go and get him, pick him up, take him back to where he should have turned, put him down, give a stern **Turn** command and send him to **Hunt** in the proper direction. When the dog has learned the **Turn** command and is willfully disobeying, go and get him, pick him up roughly, shake him all the way back, put him down roughly, give a stern **Turn** command, stand over him about a minute, and then send him on to hunt in the proper direction.

Your biggest problem will be keeping your concentration on the task at hand and giving the **Turn** command at the correct distance each time. The **Turn** command must be trained thoroughly since this command controls the hunt.

POINTING DOG

While the **Turn** command is essential and precise for the flushing dog, it is not for the pointer. For most hunters, the **Turn** command is used as guidance rather than as a precise command. With the dog hunting ahead of you to one side:

Figure 73   Dog moving to left 10 yds. out. Handler quartering right: hand up to right, looking to right, whistle in mouth. Note: You *must* have all signals in motion before you give **Turn** command.

Figure 74   Dog turned and going right. Handler still looking right, going right and right hand still up to right. Note: You *must* maintain this movement and position until dog crosses beyond you.

1. You turn away from the dog and angle about 45 degrees to the wind
2. Give the **Turn (Hunt)** command
3. As dog turns, give the hand signal in the direction you want the dog to hunt and continue walking
4. As the dog crosses in front of you, praise him
5. After the dog passes by you, turn and walk straight into the wind

Review the questions and repeat the sequence until the dog responds well. If the dog does not turn, go and get him as indicated for flushing dogs.

Questions

1. Were you properly prepared to give the command?
2. Did you turn and look properly before the command?
3. Was the hand signal in place?
4. Did the dog acknowledge the command quickly?
5. Did the dog commit to turn quickly?
6. How quickly did he turn?
7. Did he refuse to turn?
8. When he refused to turn, did you go and get him immediately?

20 Negative Command (Leave It)

There will be many times when working a dog (during both hunting and training) when you will want and need a **Negative** command. It is always given harshly. **Whoa** or **Hup** is not a **Negative** command, it requires a positive action on the dog's part -- he must stop. A **Negative** command tells a dog that you are displeased with what he is doing (pottering around, etc.) and that he should get on about his business; or that he must ignore what he is concentrating on (e.g., wrong retrieve object) and pay attention to the next command.

The training of a **Negative** command is basically taught by actually doing it. The easiest approach to this is to do it while the young dog is working in the field. Any time that he potters over scent or sniffs around in one spot:

1. Give a harsh **Negative** command (remember, when introducing something new, use the most forceful command you have to assure compliance)
2. Move aggressively toward the dog
3. Repeat the harsh **Negative** command
4. Give the **Hunt** command
5. Dog moves out
6. Praise the dog

Repeat the sequence whenever the dog is pottering or snuffling around until he will go on about his business with only the verbal command. If the dog does not stop pottering as you approach giving the **Negative** command, walk through him pushing him out of the area with your legs. Do not kick him -- push him. Keep doing it until he leaves it, then praise him and send him on to hunt.

When this command is well learned, you have taught the dog two things: the **Negative** command and that pottering is not allowed. You also have the ability to break his concentration on something that he thinks is very enticing. It will have many applications during retrieving and steadiness training.

Many people develop an alternate command for the **Negative** command. It's not a whistle nor a recognizable word. It's a harsh guttural sound -- yes, you might call it a growl. It is most effective with dogs that have had a lot of praise.

Questions

1. Was the command given harshly?
2. Did you move aggressively toward the dog?
3. Did the dog leave it and move away?
4. Did you have to repeat the command, push him away with your legs, or put him on a lead and crack it?
5. Did he respond to the **Hunt** command properly?
6. If the dog tried to double back, did you prevent it?
7. Did you praise the dog profusely when he was right?

21 | Walk Him Down

As you may not be able to use **Whoa**, **Come**, **Heel** or any other command to get a dog to come to you or to stop so that you can go to him, how do you pick him up or put a lead on him? Walk him down. All young dogs should be walked down a few times just to prove to them that you can do it and, therefore, catch them whenever you want them -- running away does them no good. While it is difficult to walk or run down a mature dog, it is easy to walk down a youngster. The young dog gives up, both physically and mentally, very quickly. The mature dog can be tough -- it may take a half hour the first time. It will take less each time thereafter.

If you have indicated that you want the dog and he refuses to accept it, say nothing, show displeasure and start walking straight at him. Keep your eyes on him and keep walking at him aggressively. Every time he looks back he will see you coming at him intently. Your silence and attitude will get to the dog quickly and he will stop and wait for you. Do not lunge or grab at him. He must be standing still so you can slowly bend over and snap on the lead. **Heel** him to where you started after him. Do not scold or punish him. Each time you do this the dog will stop in less time than before. You will be pleasantly surprised at how quickly you can walk down an old pro that was walked down as a youngster.

The old lady with two youngsters and
Canada geese in Maryland.

<table>
<tr><td>22</td><td>Pottering</td></tr>
</table>

No dog should potter or snuffle around old scent or around any scent for that matter. Do not allow it and do not let it become a habit. All too often a handler allows it to become a habit by standing around watching the dog potter and hoping he will come up with something. Forget it. If the dog's nose is that bad (very, very few are) get rid of him. The dog must do what he is perfectly capable of doing -- take one sniff and instantly react. The sniff is all that the dog needs and the sniff is about all that wild game will give him. No wild upland game hangs around for a dog to potter over, so if he is pottering it's old game scent or field mice, woodchucks, etc. Be especially alert to this with young dogs and planted birds. Do not stand and let them root around trying to find the bird. Hunt the dog through the area, if he does not find the bird, keep moving and make a big swing before giving him another pass at it. Be sure to check the wind on the next approach.

Anytime the dog starts to potter or snuffle, walk to him quickly, and as you get near him give a harsh **Negative** command such as **Leave It.** If the dog does not move off quickly, walk right through him. That means push him away from whatever he is pottering over with the front of your legs. Do not kick him. Give the **Hunt** command and directional signal as soon as you start pushing him with your legs. If the dog tries to circle back, give the **Negative** command again and force him away with your legs. When you have broken his concentration on the scent, give the **Hunt** command with a directional signal. If he persists put the lead on him, give the **Negative** command harshly and crack the lead. Now take the lead off and give the **Hunt** command and a directional signal away from the scent. Praise the dog when he moves off and starts hunting.

23 | Pointing

Pointing is a basic instinct developed in dogs we call the pointing breeds. Pointing intensity and strength varies greatly within and between the breeds. While a dog with no pointing instinct cannot be taught to point, he can be taught to stand birds. The difference, and it is considerable, is in the dog's attitude. Very few pointing dogs start pointing as puppies and point continuously for the rest of their lives. They generally go through a period, normally in their teenage months, when they appear to lose the instinct to point. Other desires and instincts become dominant.

There are two ways to handle this turn of events: (1) Keep the young dog away from birds that he might catch during this period, and (2) Restrain him in the presence of birds. Keeping the young dog away from birds that he might catch presents only one problem -- your ego. You need to see your dog point birds *now*. Keeping him away from birds at this time does not delay his final training. You can still work him in the field, and by keeping a close eye on him, he will tell you when he is ready to point by his reactions to the scent of planted, previously flown, or wild birds. The advantage to this method becomes apparent now. The dog will make rapid progress in his training as there have been no negatives or discipline imposed for him to overcome while around birds. You have not tried to make a dog point that has temporarily stopped pointing or a dog with very weak pointing instinct point. The major problem in restraining the young dog that has stopped pointing is that it requires a good rapport between dog and handler, a very light touch, and precise reading of the dog by the handler. Unfortunately, what happens all too often is that the dog is not restrained, instead he is jerked around on the end of a check cord or worse. Many good dogs cannot take that punishment and still work birds with intensity and happiness. Many people in this situation think that they have taught the dog to point, but in reality the instinct to point has naturally increased with age as expected.

What you can teach the dog is staunchness once the point has been established. The minimum prerequisites for this is a dog that knows **Whoa** thoroughly to voice, hand and whistle. There are two things that cause a dog to break point and take a bird out: (1) Excitement and a wild urge to get the bird; as seen in virtually all young dogs, and (2) The dog's determination to keep you from getting the bird. This indicates a lack of cooperation and/or a temperament problem. The dog will usually point intensely and remain staunch as long as you remain at the dog's prescribed distance away from the action.

Caution: There is one cardinal rule when working pointing dogs. *No* bird is ever shot that has been flushed by the dog until he is completely steady to wing, shot and fall. *After* the dog is completely steady, you may decide to teach him to flush on command, or shoot birds that he accidently flushed, provided that he stops to flush and does not chase.

The young dog filled with the excitement of a nose full of intoxicating bird scent has only one purpose at the moment -- get that bird. Most young dogs do not have a pointing instinct that is strong enough to anchor them for very long. Therefore, you must help your dog to calm down in the presence of birds. Before you can help the dog you must be calm. Your **Whoa** command, voice or whistle, must be calm. As you approach the dog, the cautionary **Whoa** must be calm and soothing in a tone that conveys that you are pleased with him. *Do not run* to the dog. Walk with a smooth even pace. Do not show your excitement. Your hands on him must convey calmness -- it's hard to do since you're so excited and happy. Calm down and do not convey by your actions a sense that you are competing with him for the bird. Now that you have calmed down, the work can proceed.

What kind of birds to use when working on pointing and staunchness? Use game birds only -- quail, pheasant, chukar etc. Do not use pigeons for this work. Many dogs do not point pigeons naturally. Do you know of anyone, or have you ever heard of anyone taking a dog hunting, expecting him to point pigeons or dove? Then why teach him to point them?

Very few people can train dogs on wild birds, so you have to use pen-raised birds, and that presents a problem. It is difficult, it seems, for most people to let birds that they have purchased get away without trying to shoot or recover them. When the bird has allowed you to teach the object of a particular lesson (in this case staunchness) your money has been well spent. Forget about the bird -- think about the dog.

How do you end the point without giving any negative connotations to the dog? Many fast dogs can and will catch pen-raised birds if they are allowed to chase them. That needs to be prevented, yet the dog is not ready for steadiness work. There are three ways to prevent it: Pick a dog up and carry him away, pick the bird up, or restrain the dog while flushing the bird. Do not, under any circumstances, pull the dog from the bird. By far, the best solution for the dog is to pick him up and carry him away. This allows more time to praise him -- and there is never too much time spent on praise. While you are carrying him, the bird can be flushed out of the area. There are two reasons for this: You do not want the dog to work that bird in that area again, and if you cannot prevent a delayed chase, the bird will be gone when the dog arrives. In order to pick up the bird, you will have to confine or restrain it in some way that is not natural, and the dog will be aware of it. If the dog breaks point before you get there, he is sure to catch the bird or stick his nose onto the bird trap. The least desirable is to restrain the dog while the bird is flushed. The usual occurrence is that the dog (naturally) tries to chase the bird and gets stopped with varying abruptness. Even if you use restraint properly, that lead has to come off eventually and the dog will know when. Yes, there are some dogs that will require this and with these few the restraint must be used.

STEP 1

When you have a dog with enough pointing instinct to establish a solid intense point for a few seconds, it is time to work on extending that point for a useful amount of time. What is a useful amount of time? The time required for you and your partner to get to the dog and/or be in position to shoot. By definition, that cannot be measured in seconds or minutes. The control will be the **Whoa** command (voice or whistle). If you are using planted birds, use cover that is difficult for the dog to penetrate from downwind, yet easy for the bird to get out of upwind. Work the dog so that you are not more than 10 to 15 yards from the dog when he hits the point.

1. The dog points
2. Immediate **Whoa** command (voice or whistle)
3. Walk calmly and promptly to the dog (keep your concentration on him so that you can anticipate any movement and prevent it with another **Whoa** command)
4. Put one hand on his chest or under his neck so that you can block the dog
5. Praise and caution him briefly with a calming **Whoa**
6. Pick the dog up and carry him away praising him all the while
7. Have someone flush or pick up the bird while you are carrying the dog
8. Put him down and praise him
9. Send him on to hunt
10. Do not let the dog delay chase

Review the questions. Repeat the sequence until the dog will stay on point for extended praise without your hand blocking him.

STEP 2

In the event that you are restraining the dog with a lead, it will of necessity have to be trailing behind the dog when he hits the point. If you can walk up and snap it on the dog after he points you don't need it. You must pick up the lead and take up the excess gradually -- no jerks or yanks. When you have control of the lead:

1. Give the **Whoa** command (voice or whistle)
2. Tap or lightly snap the lead
3. Walk calmly to the dog (taking up the excess)
4. Praise the dog for a brief moment
5. Get a firm grip on his collar
6. While you praise him, have someone flush the bird
7. **Heel** the dog in the opposite direction
8. Praise him

9. Send the dog on to hunt
10. Do not let the dog delay chase

Review the questions and repeat the sequence until only the **Whoa** command is needed without a tap. Now work the dog to the off-lead sequence above.

Questions

1. Was the point solid and intense?
2. Are you sure the dog was solid on point before the **Whoa**? Command was given?
3. Were you ready to give the **Whoa** command instantly?
4. How quickly was the **Whoa** command given?
5. Did you walk calmly to the dog?
6. Did you keep your concentration on the dog?
7. Did you see any sign indicating that the dog wanted to break point?
8. Did you anticipate and stop the dog's attempt to break?
9. Did you praise him lavishly?
10. If the lead was used:

    a. Did you take up excess smoothly?

    b. Was the tap or snap given after the **Whoa**?

    c. Was it a tap or a snap, or did you maintain tension on the lead?
11. Were you calm and steadying to the dog throughout the sequence?

When you no longer need a hand on the dog's chest, it is time to tempt him. While you are praising the dog, gently press forward on the dog's back leg while giving the caution **Whoa**. Do not press hard -- just enough so that you can feel the dog resisting. If there is strong resistance, push a little harder. (See Figure 75.) An intense dog will resist so strongly that you can lift his rear right off the ground. The object is to know that the dog will resist strongly with no restraint of any kind. Do not overdo this and remember that you always have an obligation to flush the bird as promptly as you can. Do not show off or clown around with a dog on point. That has nothing to do with hunting.

By definition pointing is an instinct. What triggers it? Many things trigger pointing in different dogs at different ages. The one thing that is common to all pointing dogs is the immediate body scent of a healthy alert upland game bird. That scent invariably produces the most intense point in all dogs and is the only one of value to the upland bird hunter. The dog should not point a bird's track or body scent left on the ground, and he should not point dead or crippled birds. The dog that points these wastes the hunter's time and energy and is a handicap in retrieving.

The field trial idea that once a dog points he is not allowed to move for any reason causes the hunter many problems. It is much easier to break the dog since no movement lends itself to breaking while movement with discretion does not. It is much easier to judge (if he moves pick him up). To make this work, they had to develop the concept of the "nonproductive" point. That is, anytime a dog points and no bird can be found, it is presumed that a bird was there at the time of the point and then walked away. This concept promotes false pointing, which is a fault. It is discouraging to hunt with a dog that is prone to false point. The dog is supposed to point and hold birds for the gun. Granted, it is more difficult to train a dog

Figure 75   Feel the dog's resistance to the pressure. There is no need to lift his rear end.

to go with a moving bird and pin it down than it is to stay anchored -- but it sure adds to the pleasure of the hunt.

Once the dog has shown that he is a dependable pointer, there are some other facets of pointing that you must consider. How do you want your pointing dog to handle game that moves before you get to him? Do you want the dog to stay anchored or move cautiously and reestablish point when the bird stops? If the bird runs when you try to flush it, should the dog stay anchored or move with, but behind you, out of the way, making no attempt to get the bird? The dog must, at some point, learn to relocate and point a bird that has moved after the point was established, especially if he has been required to stay anchored once he had established point. The degree of difficulty that the dog will have doing these things depends on the strength and relative balance of his pointing and retrieving instincts. There is no doubt that a hunter is better served by a pointer that is allowed to stay with moving birds of his own volition. The **Whoa** command is always an option in a given situation if you wish to anchor the dog.

In order to train a dog to handle running birds he must be a staunch pointer who is steady to wing and shot and responds readily to **Whoa** and **Easy.** This approach does not train the dog to track, as the dog is working with the moving bird's body scent -- not its track. It is most difficult to set up situations where the dog points and the bird moves out. Therefore, lessons must take place whenever the occasion arises. It is difficult to set up because you cannot guarantee that the bird will run rather than flush without having a contradictory or unnatural scent pattern. If you pull the primary feathers on one wing, you in effect have a wounded bird, which the dog should retrieve -- not point. If you tape a wing, you have the scent of tape.

STEP 3

The most common occurrence will be the need for relocating the bird. Your dog has pointed and you cannot flush a bird, nor have you seen one. The dog must relocate it. Return to the dog and stand so that he is at **Heel**. Before giving a command to **Hunt,** you must be sure that the dog is no longer pointing. If you give the **Hunt** command while he is still pointing, the dog may not move or if he does, he will lunge out. Therefore, to teach controlled relocation, use the following sequence:

1. Dog in the **Heel** position

2. **Heel** command and take one or two steps in the direction the dog was pointing
3. **Hunt** command given softly and soothingly
4. Immediate **Easy** caution on dog's movement
5. Dog works cautiously
6. Dog locates and points the bird
7. Walk to dog
8. Praise the dog briefly (do not give the bird time to run out again)
9. Flush the bird quickly and if appropriate shoot it
10. Praise the dog and send him to retrieve

Review the questions. Repeat the sequence whenever the opportunity arises. After a few good repetitions, drop the **Heel** command and the steps. When the dog works well with just the **Hunt** command and the **Easy** caution, drop one or the other, whichever suits you better.

Questions

1. Did the dog relax on point?
2. When did the dog relax the point?
    a. Before you got to him?
    b. While you were beside him?
    c. On the **Heel** command?
    d. When you stepped forward?
3. Did you give the **Hunt** command soothingly?
4. Did the dog drive forward?
5. Did the dog work cautiously?
6. How quickly did you give the **Easy** caution?
7. Did the dog react to the **Easy** caution?
8. Was the **Easy** caution given soothingly?
9. Did the dog relocate and point the bird?
10. Did you have to stop and calm him?
11. Did you remain quiet as the dog neared and pointed the bird?
12. Was a command needed to stop the dog from flushing the bird? (Are you sure?)
13. Did you praise the dog generously after the shot?

If at anytime during the sequence above the dog gets too excited or charges too hard, stop him with a stern **Whoa** command (voice or whistle). Walk to him, calm him down, and restart the sequence from the beginning.

STEP 4

Training a dog to move with you as you try to flush a running bird is more a matter of encouragement than anything else. The prerequisites for this are a strong pointer that is steady to wing, shot and fall and knows **Whoa** well. The key is to recognize when the dog is no longer pointing so that you can encourage him to move. The bird is running and you cannot get it to flush:

1. Check the dog to see if he has stopped pointing and is standing
2. The dog has stopped pointing
3. Give **Easy on** or soft **Hunt** command
4. The dog starts forward
5. You turn and try to flush the bird
6. Caution the dog when he comes up beside you -- do not let him pass you
7. Flush the bird. (If you, with the dog, get close enough to the bird, the dog will point giving you a better line on the bird)
8. The dog stops to flush and marks
9. Shoot the bird
10. Praise the dog lavishly
11. Send the dog to retrieve

Review the questions.

If at anytime the dog gets too excited or tries to charge the bird, stop him with an appropriate **Whoa** command. Use a firm command but do not project anger. **Hand** or **Heel** commands are helpful, Step to the dog, calm him down and start the sequence from the beginning.

Questions

1. Are you sure that the bird moved?
2. Did you see the bird?
3. Did it move away or toward the dog?

4. Is the bird upwind or downwind of the dog?
5. When did the dog stop pointing?
6. Did the dog move with you of his own volition?
7. Did the dog move promptly on command?
8. Did the dog stalk the bird?
9. Did the dog stay behind you of his own volition or was only a caution necessary?
10. Did the dog have to be commanded to stay behind?
11. Did the dog point?

Training a dog to move with a pointed bird that moves before you get to the dog really starts with his initial pointing work. All too frequently as soon as a young dog starts to make game or begins to point restraint is applied. This presents a problem, as the dog is trained to point before sufficient or proper scent has fully triggered a natural solid intense point. This causes two problems for the hunter: (1) false pointing and (2) lack of precise location of the bird by the dog. The dog is trained to point as soon as he hits scent of any kind -- not just direct body scent. He is also trained not to move once he hits any scent. By contrast, If the young dog is allowed to work the scent until it is strong enough for him to establish a solid intense point with precise location, he will learn to point only direct body scent. Therefore, when that scent moves, the dog will relax the point and move to reestablish it. Yes, there is no doubt that a young dog will flush a few birds while learning this -- as any dog will when he works a strange species of upland bird. The advantage to the hunter is that he will know immediately when there is a running bird.

STEP 5

During the process of training steadiness to wing, shot and fall, most dogs will be hesitant to move or stop moving with a running bird. The trained dog will normally relax the point when the bird moves. The trained dog that relaxes point can be sent on before you get to him.

1. Dog points
2. The dog relaxes the point before you get to him
3. Short, soft praise ("Good dog")
4. Soft calming **Hunt** or **Easy on** caution

5. Dog works the bird and points
6. Walk to the dog and praise him
7. Flush and shoot the bird

Review the questions and repeat the sequence whenever the opportunity arises. It will not take many repetitions until the dog will move with the bird of his own volition.

If at any time during this sequence the dog gets too excited or tries to charge the bird, use a harsh **Whoa** command, go to him and calm him down. Praise him and send him on to relocate the bird.

Questions

1. Did the dog relax the point before you got to him?
2. Did the dog start to move of his own volition?
3. Did the dog move promptly on your command?
4. Did the dog move cautiously?
5. Did the dog charge forward?
6. Did the dog trail the bird or use air scent?
7. Did the dog have to work into or downwind?
8. Did the dog point the bird again?
9. Did you have to stop the dog because of excitement?
10. Did you calm the dog well before sending him on to relocate?
11. Did you praise the dog generously when he did well?

Sea ducks at Cape Cod Bay.

24 | Flushing

A flushing dog should flush -- not point or try to catch game. His attitude should convey flush. His actions should convey flush. This is especially true of spaniels as they were bred and developed to flush only. They did no retrieving during most of their history. Retrieving is a recent addition. Granted, this is in opposition to current field trial philosophy and training that encourages a dog to catch game. When you introduce a hunting dog to game you must be certain that he does not catch it. The best way to do that is to work the dog on wild game only. Unfortunately, working a dog on wild game only is not usually possible.

To ensure that the dog develops a bold driving flush, you must not restrict his movements in any way (no check cords). No cautions or commands should be used as he approaches the game. He must be free to drive in and flush. If the dog could work wild game, you would have no problem. It is the use of "planted" game that causes so many problems or perhaps it is its misuse.

The biggest problem you will have with planted birds is the flight potential of the birds at the moment of flush. This has two elements: (1) the physical quality and strength of the bird (is it capable of quick strong flight?) and (2) the alertness of the bird at the flush. No bird that has been dizzied, rendered semiconscious or unconscious is capable of quick strong flight. To plant a bird that is not fully alert in front of a flushing dog is asking for trouble. The bird's flight is so weak and unsteady that the dog believes he can catch it in the air -- if he didn't catch it on the ground.

A quick high rising bird is essential to good hunting dog training. If the bird is to be flushed off the ground by the dog, pigeons cannot be used effectively because they must be dizzied or put to sleep, or worse yet, put in a bird trap. Quail are easy to plant fully alert but, as a rule, do not fly very high so the dog believes that he can catch them. The cover in which they are planted, therefore, must obscure the dog's view of the bird's flight. That leaves pheasant and chukar as the best choices. The best way to plant them is to tuck the head under a wing and lay the bird gently on its side with head side down. As soon as you feel the bird relax move away quickly. Yes, occasionally a bird will get up and fly but that is a small price to pay for an alert quick flying bird. Never work a young dog toward a bird that cannot get up and away quickly and cleanly. The rewards will be well worth the cost.

You must eliminate the dog's ability to follow the planter's trail to the bird. Both you and the planter must be aware of the wind and the direction from which the dog will approach the bird. If the dog picks up the planter's scent trail, he will follow it right to the bird and approach from the wrong direction. Dogs learn this very fast. In addition, you do not want the dog to learn that human scent leads to birds. In the event he picks up the human scent trail, get between the dog and the bird quickly. Pick him up and do not let him work that bird. Allowing the dog to continue to work that bird will only hurt his future work.

The selection of cover to plant the bird is very critical, The cover must offer resistance to the dog's attempt to flush the bird, yet allow the bird to get out and airborne quickly. The bird should be planted on the opposite side from which the dog will approach. For young dogs, the bird should always be planted on the upwind side of the cover. The young dog should always approach from the downwind side. If he tries to circle the cover, get on him quickly, pick him up roughly, take him to a position straight downwind of the bird and put him down roughly. He goes straight in to flush or he goes nowhere. If he persists in circling the cover, take him away. Do not let him work or flush the bird.

During all flushing work, you must keep a sharp eye on the dog for signs that he is trying to catch the bird. Attempts to catch the bird must not be allowed. He should not be praised if he flushes the bird while trying to catch it. When a dog is trying to flush he forces his way through the cover.

Figure 76   Dog flushing. Note the attitude of the dog.

He does not circle the cover trying to find a way to catch the bird. He does not sneak up on, stalk, or attempt to pounce on the bird. He does not go in snapping at the bird or leap into the air after the bird. (See Figure 76.)

Occasionally a flushing dog will be inclined to point or stand birds. This should not be encouraged. Those who believe that the point was developed from the pause that precedes the pounce of the predator consider a pointing attitude by a flushing dog an attempt to catch the bird. Others consider it tantamount to blinking or a lack of interest in the bird. The real clue is the attitude of the dog when commanded to flush. Yes, the dog should always flush the bird. He is a flushing dog not a pointer. Therefore, you should encourage the dog to flush as you approach. Get excited and urge him to flush. Use any word, except **Fetch.** You do not want him to retrieve -- you want him to flush. Praise the dog for all good, clean, eager flushes. Do not start training a young dog with a tendency to point to stop when he is getting out of range on the trail of a running bird. Hold off that work until he becomes a dependable quick flusher.

When he has the desire and ability to flush game quickly, stop working the dog on birds. Do not work the dog on birds again until you have sufficient control over the dog to ensure that he will work the bird as you planned. Two or three birds are enough for any one training session. Do not stop hunting immediately after the last bird has been worked.

Questions

1. Did the dog flush the bird quickly and cleanly?
2. Did the dog hesitate before the flush?
3. Did the dog point?
4. Did the dog stalk the bird?
5. Did the dog sneak up on the bird?
6. Did the dog circle the cover?
7. Did the dog try to catch the bird on the ground or in the air?

25 | Steadiness

There are many reasons why a dog should be steady to wing, shot and fall. The most important reason is safety -- his and yours. That alone makes the effort completely worthwhile. There are numerous other reasons for teaching a dog steadiness. He will not cost you a shot; he will not flush game when you have an empty gun; he can mark fallen game better and, therefore, retrieve it quicker; he can hunt with other dogs and not cause trouble; and he can be trained to honor his bracemate's finds and retrieves. Then there is a thing called class -- which only a completely steady dog can exhibit.

Many people want a dog that is steady to the shot but breaks to retrieve immediately after the shot. That can never be achieved if the dog is not first completely trained steady to wing, shot and fall. If the dog breaks on the shot, he has no way of knowing if the bird was hit. He may flush game you are not prepared to shoot, cannot mark well, and worst of all, may get shot as a second shot is taken. Unsteady dogs do get shot.

A prominent national organization that does not require steadiness held an invitational trial of regional champions and two dogs were called back to determine the championship -- one broke and was shot. A writer for one of the major hunting magazines killed his dog while shooting at a second grouse when the dog broke for the first one he shot (his young son saw it all). A friend of one of the authors called him to say that he had just killed his dog when the dog broke for the first duck and he swung and shot at a second duck. Six months before we had discussed the need for steadiness until well after midnight. He didn't think steadiness training was necessary. He does now.

When teaching a dog to be steady on game, you must make every effort to keep him as calm as possible. Work only a few birds at one training session. Most inexperienced dogs cannot handle a lot of game in a short period of time without getting overly excited. Do not let him retrieve every bird shot -- if you do, the "falling bird" will become the **Fetch** command and you will have taught the dog an alternate command for **Fetch.** You must stay calm and walk at all times (unless you are running him down for misbehaving). Never give any command but **Whoa** unless you are standing beside him. Whenever the dog does anything right, praise him and show him that you are happy. This training for steadiness is a tough time for him.

There has been much discussion about whether it is easier to teach a flushing dog or a pointing dog steadiness. If the flushing dog has been taught that **Whoa** means sit, teaching steadiness at your side is easier than teaching a pointing dog that **Whoa** means stand. Esthetics necessitates teaching a pointing dog to stop and stand on **Whoa**, as not many hunters in this hemisphere want a pointer to sit or drop before or at the flush. On the other hand, a pointing dog is stationary at the flush, which makes the job relatively easy. In contrast, a flushing dog must drive the bird into the air, stop and remain steady. It is probably more difficult to teach complete steadiness to a flushing dog -- but not by much.

There is one milestone that must be reached before an attempt is made to teach a dog steadiness. **Whoa** must be thoroughly learned to voice, hand, whistle, and shotgun. Without this, the dog cannot be trained to be steady; he can only be "broke steady" with all the problems that ensue. Therefore, we must break this training down into its basic elements so that each progressive step can be controlled to ensure correct repetitions. This training will involve two phases. First, the dog must be taught steadiness to dummy and game without scent. The dog must then be taught steadiness with scent prior to the flush.

PHASE I: Without Scent

The basic elements are as follows:

1. Steady at your side to thrown dummy
2. Steady at your side to thrown dummy with shot (shotgun)

3. Steady at your side to flown bird
4. Steady at your side to flown and shot bird
5. Stop and steady to thrown dummy while hunting
6. Stop and steady to thrown dummy and shot while hunting
7. Stop and steady to flown bird while hunting
8. Stop and steady to flown bird and shot while hunting

When the dog is steady, the bird should be shot. The bird should not be shot if the dog is moving.

PHASE II: With Scent

Pointing dog owners may ask why they should teach their dog the next two steps. All pointing dogs should stop to flush and this is the logical place to teach it.

The basic elements are as follows:

1. Stop and steady to a bird that is thrown on the ground a few yards ahead of the dog while hunting. (The bird is thrown so that it can fly immediately on hitting the ground. Use strong pigeons.)
2. Stop and steady to a bird that is thrown on the ground and then shot when it flies
3. a. Flushing dog: stop and steady to bird that dog finds and flushes

    b. Pointing dog: steady to bird that dog finds and points (handler flushes)
4. Steady to wing, shot and fall of bird that dog produces

Note: Shoot all birds on which the dog is steady. Do *not* shoot at *any* bird that the dog is chasing.

Caution: The purpose of this lesson is to teach steadiness. Do not let retrieving cause you problems with steadiness. If the **Fetch** training is not far enough advanced that the dog can handle a particular retrieve quickly and cleanly, you must retrieve the object. Even if he retrieves well, do not allow him to retrieve all items -- about half is enough. Under *no* circumstance should he be allowed to retrieve unless he is completely steady. He must also be completely steady as you walk to him, praise him and send him to retrieve.

For the purposes of training, we must define steadiness so that you or anyone working with you can recognize when a dog is completely steady as well as the nuances that tell you he is not. Not only does the completely steady dog not chase, he must remain stationary, relaxed and alert. The flushing dog must put his rump on the ground immediately and keep it there, relax, follow the flight with his eyes without inclining forward and he should not stand. The pointing dog must stand where he was at the time of the flush, relax the point, remain alert, and follow the flight with his eyes and head without taking a single step forward. As a dog may on occasion point in an awkward position, he may be allowed to assume a comfortable posture but no more. As he progresses, he should be allowed to move to mark the flight and fall of the bird if his view is obstructed but no more. This will not be a problem for the flushing dog.

PHASE I

You can handle the first two steps of Phase I alone. However, it is much better if you have someone else throw the dummy. During the other steps, you will need someone else to throw the object or the bird. There is no way to efficiently train a dog steady to wing, shot or fall independent of each other. There are too many things to do and see all at once. The thrower should be out and away from the dog and handler. During this work it is imperative that the thrower watch the dog carefully so that he can tell the handler exactly what happens -- good or bad. Steps 1 and 2 may have been well taught during **Fetch** training. If you are sure, go to Step 3.

STEP I

The dog is steady at your side to a thrown dummy.

With the dog at **Heel** on lead begin the sequence:
   1. Give the **Whoa** command
   2. **Mark** command (the signal for the dummy to be thrown)
   3. The dummy lands about 30 yards in front of the dog
   4. Dog steady

Figure 77   Note dog's alertness; yet he is relaxed.

5. Praise the dog
6. Retrieve dummy as applicable (you or dog)
7. Praise the dog

Review questions at the end of Step 4 with the thrower before the next repetition. (See Figure 77.)

Repeat the sequence and if the dog moves in any way, immediately give the appropriate **Whoa** command and snap or pop the lead as needed. Whenever you must use the lead, do not let him retrieve. When you have several consecutive flawless repetitions without using the lead, take the lead off. Repeat the sequence until you have several consecutive flawless repetitions off lead.

Now that the dog is steady with the dummy landing 30 yards out, it is time to throw it closer to the dog. Do not move the thrower closer; let him throw the dummy toward the dog. Work the dummy closer to the dog in decrements of 5 yards. Make sure that the dog is performing flawlessly at each stage before shortening the distance. Watch the dog closely so that you can anticipate any problems. If the dog gets too eager, use a stronger command or the lead if necessary. When the sequence is flawless at 5 yards for several consecutive repetitions, it is time to go to Step 2.

STEP 2

The dog is steady at your side to thrown dummy and a shot.

Whenever you are going to shoot over a dog, it should be done with a shotgun pointed at the target object. It will help the dog learn to mark by the direction the gun is pointed and by the sound of the shot. Blank pistols cannot do this, but blank shotgun loads can. The handler should do the shooting.

With the dog at **Heel** on lead:

1. Give the **Whoa** command
2. Give the **Mark** command
3. Dummy thrown
4. Shot fired
5. Dummy lands about 30 yards out
6. Dog is steady
7. Praise lavishly
8. You or dog retrieve, as applicable
9. Praise the dog

Review questions at end of Step 4 with thrower. Repeat the sequence and if the dog moves in any way, use the lead as noted in Step 1. When you have several consecutive flawless repetitions without the use of the lead, remove it. Repeat the sequence without the lead until you have several consecutive flawless performances. (See Figure 78.)

Now start throwing the dummy closer to the dog as described in Step 1. When the dog performs flawlessly with the dummy landing 5 yards away,

Figure 78   Fully alert, yet relaxed after shot and fall.

it is time to start Step 3.

STEP 3

The dog steady at your side to flown bird.

Because the dog will not smell the bird, it does not matter what type of bird you use. Pigeons work very well and are usually much cheaper. Place the bird thrower on the same line with you and the dog, about 5 to 10 yards away. You should not be between the dog and the thrower. When the **Mark** command is given, the bird should be thrown so that it angles out ahead of the dog. It normally takes only a few birds for this step. If the dog is not steady to the flown bird, there is no way he will be steady to a shot bird.

With the dog on lead at **Heel**:

1. Give the **Whoa** command
2. Give the **Mark** command
3. Bird thrown
4. Dog is steady

5. Praise the dog lavishly
6. Give the **Negative** command
7. Give the **Heel** command
8. Walk dog around a bit and set up in a different place for the next sequence

Review the questions at end of Step 4 with the bird thrower and repeat the sequence. Use the lead as outlined in Step 1 if the dog moves or breaks. If he breaks, crack the lead and take a moment to review Steps 1 and 2. Work the dog on lead until he is steady with no active use of the lead. Remove the lead and repeat the sequence. When the dog's performance is flawless through several consecutive repetitions, move on to Step 4. Review the questions with the thrower and be sure that the dog is performing perfectly.

STEP 4

The dog steady at your side to flown and shot bird.

Both you and the bird thrower should have shotguns. A gun may be needed to safely shoot the bird. In other respects, the setup is the same as in Step 3. With the dog at **Heel** on lead:

1. Give the **Whoa** command
2. Give the **Mark** command
3. Bird thrown
4. Both you and thrower check dog
5. If he looks too eager, give a **Whoa** command
6. Dog steady
7. Shoot bird
8. Dog steady
9. Praise the dog generously
10. Retrieve bird as applicable
11. Praise the dog
12. **Heel** command and walk dog to a new position for next sequence

Repeat the sequence until the dog is performing flawlessly for several repetitions on lead. Remove the lead and repeat the sequence until the dog is flawless for several consecutive repetitions.

If the dog moves or breaks, give the **Whoa** command and pop or crack the lead. Work back through the **Whoa** commands and lead actions until the dog is steady without lead action. Remove the lead and use the sequence above. When the dog is flawless through several consecutive repetitions, it is time for Step 5.

Note: The dog is now at the stage where he can profit from pass shooting wild birds such as pigeons or crows. Most farmers consider pigeons a nuisance and welcome responsible hunters who want to shoot them. It is great experience and fun for both you and the dog and pigeons make good eating.

Questions for Steps 1- 4

1. Did the dog become "alert" to the **Mark** command?
2. Did the dog look up and out or at you?
3. Was the dog steady?
4. Did he stand (flusher)? Did he prance (pointer)?
5. Did the dog inch forward?
6. Did the dog step forward?
7. Did the dog break?
8. Did the dog chase?
9. Could voice or whistle stop the dog?
10. Was the lead required to stop the dog?
11. Was the praise generous?

You have now taught the dog standing beside you to be steady when game is shot and falls. You must now teach a moving dog to stop at the sight of flying game. You now know from the previous four steps that he will be steady if you can stop him. To reinforce stop to flush or flight you must walk to him and praise him every time he stops to a flying dummy or bird during this training. Actually, what you are teaching is another command for **Whoa** -- the flying bird. Therefore, you must be prepared to use your strongest **Whoa** command immediately when the dog sees the flying object. For control, we will start with a dummy and progress to birds.

STEP 5

The dog must stop and remain steady to thrown dummy while hunting.

You may want to start Step 5 by throwing the dummy yourself; however, you will need help later on. It is important that whoever throws the dummy not twirl it around where the dog can see it. That gives him too much time to anticipate the command and he will commit to stop before the dummy is in the air. The dummy must be thrown with a minimum of arm movement during the early work and from out of the dog's sight as you progress. In order to ensure a correct response, you will want all the help you can get -- your strongest **Whoa** command, eye contact, hand signal, and physical presence (closeness).

With the dog hunting the field ahead of you, pick a time when he is about 20 yards away approaching or checking in with you so that you have eye contact.

1. Establish eye contact
2. Dummy thrown
3. Immediate **Whoa** command
4. Simultaneous hand **Whoa**
5. Dog commits to stop
6. Dog stops
7. Walk to dog (body language must project happiness)
8. Praise the dog
9. Retrieve dummy as applicable (you or dog)
10. Dog at **Heel**
11. Praise the dog
12. Give the **Hunt** command

(See Figure 79.) Review the questions after Step 8 before the next repetition. **Caution:** Do *not* repeat the sequence too frequently. Separate the throws by 2 or 3 minutes. Repeat the sequence about 5 times and go on to something else. Do not permit the dog to start looking for and anticipating the throw. Come back to it at another session later in the day or the next time out. Repeat the sequence until you get several consecutive flawless responses.

Figure 79   Stop to thrown dummy with **Whoa**. Note dog's commitment to stop and rump on the way down.

It is now time to start eliminating controls. Be sure you have several flaw-less responses to each control before you eliminate the next one. Elimi-nate controls in this order: hand signal, eye contact, presence (closeness), and finally eliminate the **Whoa** command. You will now delay the **Whoa** command allowing the dog time to commit to stop immediately. If he doesn't, give the Whoa command.

1. Dummy thrown into dog's line of sight
2. Delay **Whoa** command giving the dog time to commit to stop
3. Dog stops
4. Walk to dog
5. Praise him
6. Cautionary **Whoa**
7. Pick up dummy
8. Return to dog
9. Praise him
10. Send him on to **Hunt**

Before you go to the next step, be sure that the dog is stopping to the thrown dummy only. If the dog does not commit to stop immediately, go to the dog, pick him up, carry him back to the point where he should have made the commitment, put him down roughly and give a stern **Whoa** command. Whenever the dog refuses to commit to stop to flight immediately, get after him. Work the dog in such a manner that the thrower will be completely hidden from the dog. You may need a **Whoa** command the first time or two you try this. When you have several consecutive flawless responses to the thrown dummy only, it is time to go to Step 6.

STEP 6

The dog must stop and remain steady to thrown dummy and shot while hunting.

For the first run through of this step have the dog hunting across in front of you and throw the dummy before he is straight out from you. You want the commands, thrown bird and **Whoa** in front of the dog, so to speak, rather than have the **Whoa** command behind him. Do not shoot if the dog does not stop.

1. Dummy thrown
2. Dog commits to stop
3. Dog stops
4. Gun fired
5. Give the **Whoa** command
6. Dog steady as you walk to him
7. Praise the dog lavishly
8. Retrieve dummy as applicable (you or dog)
9. Dog at **Heel**
10. Praise him
11. Give the **Hunt** command

Review questions at the end of Step 8 with thrower. (See Figure 80.)

Repeat the sequence until the dog is performing flawlessly with the **Whoa** command. Now run the sequence without the **Whoa** command until it is flawless. Make sure that the thrower is hidden for some of these. Any time the dog moves or breaks after the shot, go to him quickly (do not run),

Figure 80   Stop to thrown dummy, steady to shot. Note intensity and concentration on the dummy.

pick him up roughly, take him back to where he should have stopped before the shot and put him down roughly with a harsh **Whoa** command. The dog must perform flawlessly in this sequence since the next step presents the ultimate temptation -- a flying bird with the dog running free.

Do not use too many birds in any one session -- three or four should be enough. Give the dog at least a half hour between sessions. Repeat the sequence until the dog handles a complete session cleanly.

STEP 7

Stop and steady to flying bird while hunting.

During this step, you will need a partner to fly the birds. Strong pigeons will do. Mix the work up so that the dog cannot see the person who flies the bird. With the dog hunting in front of you:

1. A bird is flown
2. Give the **Whoa** command
3. Dog commits to stop

4. Dog stops
5. Dog is steady while you walk to him
6. Praise the dog lavishly
7. Dog at **Heel**
8. Review questions
9. Give the **Negative** command
10. Walk him away from the direction in which the bird has flown and send him on to hunt

Review questions at the end of Step 8 with thrower.

Note: Do not let the dog hunt back in the direction that the bird flew. That is a delayed chase and should be prevented. It will be easier to stop now without scent than it will be later when he has a nose full.

Repeat the sequence until you have several consecutive flawless repetitions, then drop the **Whoa** command and repeat the sequence. Watch the dog carefully as the bird flies and be ready to give a stern **Whoa** command if needed. If he moves, get to him quickly, pick him up roughly, take him back and put him down roughly with a harsh **Whoa** command. Repeat the sequence until his performance is flawless without the **Whoa** command.

There is no doubt that teaching a dog to stop on the flight, shot and fall of a bird without a training partner or helper is very difficult if not impossible even for a professional trainer. Knowledgeable help will make the job much easier; therefore, make every effort to get help. Ideally, two helpers are best -- one to throw the bird and the other to shoot it. The type of bird used is immaterial since the dog does not point or flush the bird and only scents it when retrieving.

STEP 8

Stop and steady to flown and shot bird while hunting.

No birds are to be shot if the dog is moving. Make a real effort to shoot all birds the dog handles properly. Both you and the bird thrower should have a shotgun. The second gun may be needed to safely shoot the bird. Since there is no scent involved, pigeons will do very well for this work.

Use your stronger **Whoa** (voice or whistle) command. You actually will be using three **Whoa** commands: (1) Sight of flying bird, (2) Shot, and (3) Voice or whistle. Therefore, if the dog breaks, he has disobeyed three commands and it's time to get on him. Make sure that some of the birds are flown when the dog cannot see the release.

With the dog hunting in front of you:

1. A bird is flown so the dog can see it
2. Dog commits to stop
3. Dog stops
4. Bird shot
5. Immediate **Whoa** command
6. Dog steady while you walk to him
7. Praise the dog profusely
8. Retrieve bird as applicable (you or dog)
9. Praise the dog
10. Review the questions with partner
11. Send dog on to hunt

Repeat the sequence until the dog's performance is flawless for several consecutive repetitions.

Now it is time to drop the voice or whistle (whichever you used) command. Repeat the sequence and keep an eye on the dog at the shot so that you can anticipate any movement and prevent it with a timely **Whoa** command. When the dog remains steady, sweet talk him as you walk up and praise him. Repeat the sequence until he is steady, relaxed and alert for several consecutive repetitions.

If the dog breaks at shot, put your gun down, give a harsh **Negative** command and get to him quickly. Do not let him come to you. If the dog got to the bird before you or your partner did, give a stern **Out** (or whatever you use) command, take the bird and drop it on the ground. Pick him up roughly, take him back to the spot from which he broke, put him down roughly and give a very harsh **Whoa** command. You or your partner will pick up the bird. Give the dog a harsh **Heel** command, walk him opposite to where the bird fell and send him on to hunt. Do not, under any circumstances, let him go back to the area where the bird fell. Do not let him retrieve the next two or three birds. Repeat the sequence and be sure that he has completely stopped before you shoot the bird. If he cannot be stopped with the **Whoa** command after the shot, go back and review his work in Steps 6 and 7. Is he completely steady in both? Work through several flawless repetitions of these and then bring him back to Step 8.

Questions for Steps 5-8

1. Did you have eye contact with the dog?
2. How close was the dog?
3. How quickly after dummy was airborne and seen by the dog did you give the **Whoa** command or **Hand** command?
4. After the dog saw the dummy or bird and heard the **Whoa** command:
   a. How quickly did he commit to stop on command?
   b. How quickly did he stop on command?
   c. How quickly did he commit to stop on sight?
   d. How quickly did he stop on sight?
5. Did the dog remain steady?
6. Did the dog move as you approached?
7. Did the dog chase?
8. How many commands were needed to stop the dog?
9. Did the dog get to the dummy or bird?
10. Did the dog move at the shot?
11. Was the dog steady after the shot?
12. Was the dog steady to fallen bird as you approached?
13. Did the dog try to delay chase?
14. How difficult was it to prevent the delay chase?

PHASE II

You now come to the work that is the most exciting and enticing for the dog -- the intoxicating scent of game birds on the ground at close range. The scent of game is also the ultimate in pleasure and temptation. Because we are going to require the dog to exercise complete self-control under these overwhelming temptations, it was necessary to lay the groundwork in detail so that voice or whistle alone will provide the control you need. It is obviously not fair to bring a dog to this with no control other than the neck-breaking punishment of a check cord or shock collar. Take a moment to review the control you have established. The dog has been taught three audible **Whoa** commands: voice, whistle and shotgun fire; three visual **Whoa** commands: hand signal, thrown dummy and flying birds. He has been taught to be steady at your side to a thrown dummy, a flying bird, and a shot and fallen bird. He knows to stop at the sight of a thrown dummy and a flying bird as well as to stay there until you come to him. He has never seen a bird shot that he was chasing. You do not have to train him to be steady to wing, shot and fall; you need only transfer the training to scent and birds the dog produces, so finish the job with style!

Many trainers make a big mistake here. They quit and walk out of the field as soon as the last bird has been produced. How often does that happen hunting wild birds? They quit whether they put out only one or two birds as soon as the last one is produced. Don't do this in training especially with a young inexperienced dog. Keep on working for a reasonable period of time. Maintain a hunting attitude and concentrate on the dog and his work.

STEP 1

The dog must stop to a bird thrown on the ground ahead of him.

You will need a partner to help you with this. The object is to throw the bird so that it hits the ground and immediately flies off. Strong flying pigeons are best for the first few repetitions -- in the event that the dog decides to really take off, he will not be able to catch the bird. When you have control, you may want to use game birds. The first sequence should be run with the dog no more than 10 yards ahead of you at the time the bird is thrown. You want to be close enough so that the dog can feel your presence and the **Whoa** command can nail him to the ground. As the dog progresses, increase the distance between you and the dog. You should also have the thrower out of sight.

With the dog working in front of you:

1. A bird is thrown on the ground about 5 yards ahead of the dog
2. The bird flies immediately

3. Give the **Whoa** (your strongest) command
4. Dog commits to stop (watch closely for this)
5. Dog stops
6. Dog steady while you walk to him
7. Praise the dog lavishly
8. Review the questions with your partner
9. **Heel** the dog in a direction away from the flight of the bird and send him on to hunt
10. He will try to go after the bird (delayed chase) -- do not let him

Review the questions and repeat the sequence until the dog does several consecutive repetitions flawlessly. (See Figure 81.)

If the dog does not stop on **Whoa,** give a harsh **Negative** command and go get him. Say nothing, just go at him aggressively. Catch the dog and carry or haul him back, scolding him all the while and put him down roughly with a harsh **Whoa.** Let him stay there while you make plans for the next bird. When you send him on to hunt, do not let the dog go in the direction that the bird flew.

Many dogs can be very sneaky when it comes to a delayed chase. You must keep an eye on him. The moment he turns his head in the direction of the flown bird, stop him. Do not let him move one step toward the bird, i.e., he goes away from the flown bird or he goes nowhere. The dog is easy to stop the moment he turns his head. In contrast, he is hard to stop if he has gone 30 or 40 yards toward the bird and has gotten up a full head of steam.

If the dog stops and then breaks to chase as you approach, give a strong **Whoa** command. If that does not stop him, go and get him. This is one time you'll be glad you walked him down as a youngster.

It is now time to drop the **Whoa** command. If you have been watching the "commitment to stop" closely, the dog may have already told you that he is ready. Repeat the sequence but delay the **Whoa** command at Step 3 and watch for the commitment to stop. If the dog does not commit immediately, give a harsh **Whoa** command. Repeat the sequence until you get several consecutive flawless repetitions without the **Whoa** command. If the dog chases the bird after the **Whoa** command, get on him. Give a

Figure 81   Dog moving, thrown bird close to ground.

harsh **Negative** command and go get him. Pick the dog up roughly, carry him back to where he should have stopped and put him down roughly with a harsh **Whoa** command. If you cannot pick him up, put a lead on him and haul him back. At the point where he should have stopped, crack the lead and give a harsh **Whoa** command. Let him stand there while you review the questions with your partner. Praise the dog and send him on to hunt. Do not let him work in the direction the bird flew, and if he breaks a second time, go back to Phase I as far as needed to find your problem.

Questions for Steps 1 and 2

1. When did the dog commit to stop?
   a. At the throw of the bird?
   b. At the landing of the bird?
   c. At the flight of the bird?
   d. At the **Whoa** command?
   e. After the command?
2. How quickly did the dog stop?
   a. As quickly as possible?
   b. A few steps later?

      c. At his leisure?

      d. Did not stop? Chased?

3. Could you stop the chase or did the dog just give it up?

4. Was the dog steady as you walked to him?

5. Did you praise him profusely?

6. When sent to hunt, did the dog delay chase?

7. How difficult was it to stop the delay chase?

8. Was the dog steady after the shot?

9. How much did he move after the shot?

      a. Fidget?

      b. Lift his rump?

      c. Edged forward?

      d. Walked forward?

      e. Break?

STEP 2

The dog must stop and remain steady to bird thrown to ground, flown and shot.

Again there should be two guns available for safe shooting. No bird is to be shot if the dog is not steady. The setup is the same as it was for Step 1. Use either game birds or pigeons, whichever you choose. The dog is not allowed to retrieve any bird on which he was not completely steady.

With the dog working ahead of you:

1. A bird is thrown on the ground ahead of the dog

2. Bird flies immediately

3. Dog commits to stop

4. Dog stops

5. Dog is steady

6. Bird is shot

7. Give the **Whoa** command

8. Dog is steady as you walk to him

9. Praise him lavishly

10. Retrieve bird as applicable (you or dog)

11. Praise the dog
12. Review questions with partner
13. Send the dog on to hunt

Repeat the sequence until the dog is flawless for several consecutive repetitions.

Now repeat the sequence but drop the **Whoa** command. If you have watched the dog closely, you will probably have noticed that the **Whoa** command is already unnecessary. Repeat the sequence through several consecutive flawless repetitions.

If the dog breaks after the shot, get on him -- he knows better. He disobeyed two audible **Whoa** commands: the shot and the whistle or voice. When you get near him, scold him. Roughly pick him up and put him back where he should have been steady and give a harsh **Whoa** command. Go and retrieve the bird yourself. Praise him and send him on to hunt. Do not let him hunt toward where the bird fell. If he breaks again, back up and review his training. You have missed something.

STEP 3A

Flushing Dog: Stop and steady to bird that the dog finds and flushes.

For this work game birds only should be used and pheasant are probably the best choice. The birds should be placed in cover that is difficult for the dog to penetrate from the downwind side but easy for the bird to get out of on the upwind side. Do not put the bird to sleep. It is too easy for the dog to catch a groggy or sleeping bird. With pheasant, tuck the head under the wing, set it down and leave. With quail, just throw them in backwards and leave. Yes, you will lose an occasional bird, but it is a small price to pay for having birds react well for the dog. The person who puts the bird out should approach the cover from upwind, plant the bird and leave going back upwind. This will prevent the dog from picking up his trail and following it to the bird. This step should not take more than about 10 birds.

As the dog works toward the cover, you want to be close behind him -- no more than 10 to 15 yards away at the flush. This puts you close enough to read the dog well and keep him out of trouble. The primary problem will be the dog's attempt to catch the bird rather than flush it. He will indicate this most often in one of two ways: (1) Attempting to work under the cover as opposed to bounding or slapping at it, and (2) Circling the cover to try and find an easy way in to the bird. You have to be close enough to see this developing and stop it. In either case stop him, bring him downwind of the bird, hold him for a moment and then turn him loose. With a nose full of scent, he will normally bound straight into the cover.

As the dog works in front of you:

1. The dog flushes the bird
2. Immediate **Whoa** command (do not let him get started after the bird)
3. Dog commits to stop
4. Dog stops
5. Dog steady while you walk to him (i.e., his rump stays on the ground)
6. Praise the dog lavishly
7. Review questions with your partner
8. Praise the dog and send him on to hunt. Do not allow him to delay chase the bird

Repeat the sequence until the dog is flawless through several consecutive repetitions. (See Figure 82.)

Now drop the **Whoa** command, item 2. The dog may have already told you that he can handle this if you have been closely watching the commitment to stop. Run the sequence and delay the **Whoa** command to see how quickly the dog commits to stop. That will tell you how forceful or soft any **Whoa** command must be. Repeat the sequence until the dog's performance is flawless through several consecutive repetitions.

If the dog breaks, get after him in a hurry and scold him severely. Pick him up and shake him if you are able. If you have been praising him appropriately, this scolding will be like a bolt of lighting to him. Put him down roughly with a harsh **Whoa.** If he breaks a second time, back up and find out where the problem is.

Figure 82   Note that the dog is completely steady as bird flies away.

STEP 3B

Pointing Dog: Steady to bird that dog finds and points, you flush.

There is no reason whatsoever for trying to steady a pointing dog if he does not point staunchly. Therefore, a prerequisite for this work is a staunch pointing dog. If he isn't staunch on point, wait until he is before starting to work on steadiness.

The bulk of the work on steadiness should be done with quail, but you might want to throw in a pheasant or chukar from time to time for variety. Quail are much easier to put out. (Just throw them in backwards and leave.) This step should not take more than a half a dozen birds.

Be quick but careful when you flush the bird. Do not stomp around or kick at the cover. You may injure or kill the bird. Shuffle quickly through the cover. If the bird is running, stomp your foot beside it. Flush the bird as you would while hunting. The use of flushing whips or leads, backing toward the bird while looking at the dog and commanding **Whoa,** or holding up your hand are not allowed. Wild birds won't let you do those things, and if they do, they won't give you a decent shot.

Let the dog hunt before you and establish a point. As you near him, sweet talk him a little and let him know that you appreciate his work. Stop beside him and locate the bird as best you can from his attitude.

1. Give your strongest **Whoa** command
2. Flush the bird quickly but smoothly with minimum excitement
3. Dog remains steady
4. Walk back to dog
5. Praise the dog
6. Review the questions with your partner
7. Give the **Negative** command
8. **Heel** dog away from the flight of the bird
9. Send him on to hunt
10. Do not let the dog hunt back to the flown bird

Repeat the sequence. When the dog is performing flawlessly, it is time to drop the **Whoa** command, item 1. Repeat the sequence until the dog is steady with no command for several consecutive repetitions. (See Figures 83 and 84.)

Some dogs may require a second **Whoa** command after the bird is flushed. If so, work back until only one **Whoa** is needed and, finally, until no command is needed.

If the dog breaks and chases, get on him quickly. Pick him up and shake him. Put him down roughly with a harsh **Whoa** command. If the dog breaks a second time, review the training -- something has been missed.

STEP 4A

Flushing Dog: Steady to wing, shot and fall *of bird produced by dog.*

The setup is the same as used in Step 3A, except that you and your partner will be carrying shotguns. Actually, you would be better off with two gunners so that you can concentrate on the dog. Again, you want to be in close (10 to 15 yards) to the dog when the first bird is shot. You do not want a bird shot if the dog is not sitting. Therefore, the gunners must

Figure 83   Dog on point, handler giving strong **Whoa** whistle in ear, hand in face.   Be sure dog shows reaction to the **Whoa**.

Figure 84   Dog marking, handler ahead, bird flying.

delay the shooting to give you time to make the decision to shoot or not. Because any upbeat signal by you to the gunners may cause the dog to break, the gunners will shoot after the delay unless they hear your **Whoa** command. Be sure to tell them whether the **Whoa** command will be voice or whistle. This approach will allow you to stop both the dog and gunners.

As the dog works in front of you:

1. The dog flushes the bird
2. Dog commits to stop
3. Dog stops
4. Gunners delay
5. Bird is shot
6. Immediate **Whoa** command
7. Dog is steady as you walk to him
8. Praise him lavishly
9. Retrieve the bird as applicable
10. Praise the dog
11. Review the questions with your partner
12. Praise the dog and send him on to hunt

Repeat the sequence until you get several flawless repetitions consecutively.

It is now time to drop the **Whoa** command, item 6. Repeat the sequence. When the shot is fired, you must be ready with the **Whoa** command in case it is needed. The key is to be ready so that you can anticipate any movement by the dog and prevent it. Keep a close eye on his rump and make sure it stays on the ground, not half raised.

If the dog breaks after the shot, get on him in a hurry. If he has the bird, take it and drop it. Pick up the dog and shake him. Scold him all the way back to where he broke. Put him down roughly with a harsh **Whoa** command. Retrieve the bird. Review the questions with your partner.

Praise the dog and send him on to hunt. Do not let him work another bird. You have missed something somewhere in the training. Review the steps that involve shooting: Phase I, Steps 2, 4, 6 and 8 and in Phase II, Step 2. Also review stop to shot. Find and correct the problem, then bring the dog back to Step 4.

STEP 4B

Pointing Dog: Steady to wing, shot and fall *of bird produced by dog.*

The setup is the same as in Step 3B except that you will be carrying a gun. Because you will be in front of the dog flushing the bird, your partner will stand a few yards behind the pointing dog and observe. If you have others to gun, that is fine too. After the bird is flushed, you will delay the shooting to give your partner time to be sure that the dog is steady. Be sure that you and your gunners have your signals straight to stop the shooting if the dog moves. You do not want to have to turn and look at the dog to see if he is steady. The first bird worked should be shot at but missed so that you can get a good reading of the dog. In fact, a bird should be missed on occasion so that you can work on preventing a delayed chase. How a dog handles a missed bird is a strong indication of his steadiness.

With the dog staunchly on point, sweet talk him as you walk to him and take time to locate the bird from the dog's attitude.

1. Give your strongest **Whoa** command
2. Flush the bird quickly and smoothly
3. Delay the shot
4. Dog steady
5. Shot fired
6. Immediate **Whoa** command
7. Bird hit or missed as agreed upon
8. Dog steady
9. Praise the dog as you walk to him
10. Praise him as you stand beside him
11. Send the dog to retrieve it if appropriate
12. Send the dog on to hunt

Review the questions with everyone involved. It will be especially important for your partner to tell you if the **Whoa** command after the shot was needed. Repeat the sequence but do not work more than two or three birds in a session. However, you may want to have two or three sessions in a day. Be sure and separate the sessions by an hour or so.

When the dog is fully steady with the use of the two **Whoa** commands, it is time to drop the command after the shot. Run the sequence as above and eliminate the **Whoa** command after the shot. Praise the dog and send him on to hunt. If the dog breaks for the bird:

1. Give a strong **Negative** command
2. Go get him
3. Pick him up and scold him all the way back to where he should have remained steady
4. Put him down roughly and give a harsh **Whoa** command

Review the questions with all concerned and repeat the sequence until the dog is flawless without the **Whoa** command after the shot.

Now eliminate the **Whoa** command before the shot.

1. The dog is beside you staunchly on point
2. Locate the bird as best you can
3. Move forward to flush the bird
4. You may want to use a cautionary hand signal as you do
5. Flush the bird
6. Dog steady
7. Bird shot at and hit or missed as agreed
8. Dog steady
9. Praise the dog as you walk to him
10. Praise him lavishly when you get to him
11. Send him to retrieve or not as the situation dictates
12. Send the dog on to hunt

Review the questions with all concerned and repeat the sequence until the dog is dependable.

Whenever the dog breaks for the bird, go and get him as outlined above. He should not be allowed to get to the bird. Do not let him retrieve that bird -- ever. Do not throw it for him later; do not send him for it after you bring him back. If you cannot find the bird, get another dog to retrieve it. Getting the bird is what he wants, therefore, he cannot be allowed to misbehave and then be rewarded.

Questions for Steps 3 and 4

Flushing Dog

1. Was the dog steady before the shot (rump down)?
2. If not, why was the shot fired?
3. Was the dog steady after the shot and **Whoa** command?
4. Did the dog keep his rump on the ground, stand up or move?
5. Was the dog steady to shot only with no **Whoa** command?
6. Did the dog keep his rump down, stand up or move?
7. Was he completely steady as you walked to him?
8. Did you praise him when you got beside him?
9. Did the dog try to delay chase when sent on to hunt?
10. How difficult was it to stop the delay chase?

Pointing Dog

1. Was the dog on point staunchly before the shot?
2. Were his movements intensely controlled before the shot?
3. Was the dog steady after the flush?
4. If not, why was the shot fired?
5. Was the dog steady to the shot and **Whoa** command?
6. Was the dog completely steady while you walked to his side?
7 Did you lavish praise on the dog when you got to him?
8. Was the dog steady to shot only with no **Whoa** command?
9. Was he completely steady as you walked to his side?
10. Did you praise him when you got to his side?
11. Did the dog try to delay chase when sent on to hunt?
12. How difficult was it to stop the delay chase?

This may seem like a long drawn-out procedure; however, it is not. The pace accelerates as you progress through the steps. This method has repeatedly produced many dogs that are steady to wing, shot and fall well before their third birthday and some before their second birthday. It is also much easier to maintain that steadiness because the control is the **Whoa** command in its various forms. There is no need for any paraphernalia such as check cords, pinch collars or shock collars. A dog broken with any of those items always knows when they come off and reacts accordingly. To maintain or reinforce steadiness, a "broke" dog requires the reapplication of the same tools that were used to "break" him in the first place. Contrast that with a few sharp blasts of a whistle, harsh **Whoa** commands or, at worst, a good shaking.

The actual time (days, weeks, months) necessary to train a dog to be completely steady basically depends on five things:

1. How well does the dog know **Whoa?**
2. How fast can the dog absorb training -- temperament?
3. How much self-discipline do you have -- temperament?
4. How frequently will you take the dog out for training?
5. How much good training help will you get? It cannot be done alone.

By the time the dog is a year old, you should know enough about him and how he responds to training to set a realistic time schedule. Anyone who expects a dog under two years of age to be completely steady to wing, shot and fall, is not being realistic. Yes, there are combinations of dog and trainer that can do it, but only a very few.

There has never been a hunting dog trained or broken steady to wing, shot and fall, nor had game shot over him and remained steady on every bird for the rest of his life. We must all face that fact. Whenever the dog slips backwards in his training, you must correct him and from time to time refresh his memory. That correction must take place immediately at the time of the infraction.

26 | Hunting From A Blind

Most hunting from a blind is done for waterfowl, which generally means shooting multiple heavy loads with more than one gun being fired. Therefore, it is imperative that no dog, that has not been thoroughly tested for reaction to gunfire, be taken into a blind. The dog must have shown only positive reactions to gunfire regardless of his age. Be very careful with young dogs. Ideally no dog should go into a blind until he is steady to passing birds, shot, fall, duck calls, and knows what retrieving is all about. This will never happen. The question then is how do you use the partially trained dog so that he profits from the experience so that his future training is not made more difficult.

You must honestly evaluate the dog's abilities and training and decide what retrieves he can be reasonably expected to handle. You must have the self-discipline not to send or allow the dog any other retrieves. Your hunting partners must also agree and accept the limitations, and if a problem arises unavoidably, you must make the retrieve. Do not browbeat the dog if he cannot make the retrieve.

There are four areas of training to be considered: **Whoa,** steadiness, retrieving and hand signals. If the dog is not thoroughly **Whoa** trained, he must be leashed in the blind so that he is not visible when he moves. This also holds true for the dog that is not steady to flying birds, calls, shot and fall. This is for safety, both yours and his, and it will also prevent flaring birds. If the dog is being forced-trained to retrieve, do not use the **Fetch** command unless the training has advanced to where the dog is making water retrieves. Do not command the dog to do something for which he has not been trained. Allow him to use only his instinct to retrieve and accept the results gracefully. The most critical part of evaluating hand signal training is to be aware of the distance at which the dog will obey the signal. Remember, you will be trying to handle a keyed-up dog. If the dog is not trained well enough to make a given retrieve, do not browbeat him; you go and get the bird.

Introduce the dog to blind work during training by taking him out and setting up a simple blind (or no blind) and train him to stay quietly with you. Yes, it's boring but it will sure make the first few hunts with the dog a lot more pleasant for both you and the dog. Get up and fire the gun from time to time. If you can set up and shoot pigeons, they provide excellent training for both blind work and retrieving.

If the dog's **Whoa** training is thorough, then he can be trained to stay off lead in the blind or outside in a designated place. When you approach a land blind, let the dog off lead so that he can check everything out and relieve himself while you are getting set up. This lets him satisfy his curiosity and he will be more willing to accept restraint.

1. Select the best place for the dog in the blind
2. **Heel** the dog there. (If he knows the kennel command, give it and point to the place)
3. Give the **Whoa** command
4. Praise the dog
5. Repeat the **Whoa** command
6. Dog remains in place
7. Check on him from time to time
8. When he gets restless, go to him. If possible let him off **Whoa** for a few minutes
9. Praise him
10. Give the **Whoa** command

Review the questions. If the dog starts to move, give a harsh **Negative** command and a stern **Whoa** command to prevent the mistake. These commands do not need to be loud -- your tone and attitude is what counts. Repeat these commands as needed. What you are trying to establish is self-restraint in the dog -- that is, he must learn that he is not free to move around. Of course, the dog will get bored at times, so call him to you on occasion or let him out of the blind if hunting permits it.

You will notice that there was no **Down** or **Sit** command. The dog that has been thoroughly trained to **Whoa** has long since learned that on prolonged **Whoa,** he is free to make himself comfortable. Therefore, the dog trained to **Whoa** standing will sit or lie down, and the dog trained to **Whoa** sitting will lie down when he knows that there is nothing happening. That is the action that tells you that he plans to stay where he is.

Questions

1. Did you give the dog both a voice and a hand **Whoa** command?
2. Did you praise the dog?
3. Did you reinforce the **Whoa** command'?
4. Did you check on him and go to him occasionally?
5. Did you praise him and reinforce the **Whoa** command?

When the dog has accepted his role in the blind, it is time to put him outside (which is his true position) if conditions permit. The real advantage to this approach is that the dog can mark the falls much better. Although the dog can mark the fall by the line of gunfire and hear the bird hit the water or land (if he is steady), sight is still by far the best mark. Before the dog can be put outside, he must be completely steady. Select the place you want him to be and then use the sequence above. Be sure to check him at times and praise him when he is doing well. When he gets bored, he will undoubtedly come to you. As the dog gains experience and your confidence in him increases, let him pick the place. The dog will accept that better. A dog that is calm outside a blind facing the water will not flare birds.

Woodcock in New Brunswick

<table>
<tr><td>27</td><td># Hunting From
Boats And Canoes</td></tr>
</table>

A dog hunted around or on the water must know how to behave in a boat or canoe. There is really no difference between a boat and a canoe except size and stability, and they overlap. A properly prepared dog will handle both without causing the hunter any problems. Be sure the dog works water well before you introduce him to boats. There are three areas of work to consider: (1) getting into the boat, (2) behavior in the boat, and (3) getting out of the boat.

GETTING INTO A BOAT

Getting into a boat might be required in two situations: (1) from land or a dock and (2) from swimming-depth water. The command **Kennel** is a prerequisite. If the dog knows the command **Kennel** well, the job from land is easy. You point to a spot in the boat and give the command **Kennel**. The dog jumps in and you praise him. (See Figure 85.) Be sure the spot you point to is where you want him to stay, otherwise, he may have to climb over gear to get there. Also have the dog jump in the boat a time or two from shallow water. When he jumps in with no problem go to a dock.

Jumping down into a boat from a dock will cause many dogs a little trouble the first time or two. Be sure there is a good spot for the dog to land and that it is not slippery. The first attempt may require you to get off the dock and into the boat before commanding the dog to **Kennel**. Use **Kennel** not **Come**. Be sure to point to the spot where you want the dog to land. You must be patient. Do not make the transition from a dock to a boat in the dark -- prepare the dog beforehand. Practice a few times so that the

Figure 85   Handler pointing into boat --- dog going in. Note that dog has gotten where handler is pointing.

dog is comfortable making the jump. Use reason in selecting the drop distance and make the early ones no more than a foot over the gunwale.

Getting a dog back into the boat or canoe is not as difficult as most people make it seem. There are two possible conditions: (1) the dog can reach up and hook his front feet over the gunwale or (2) the dog cannot reach the gunwale. All dogs that return will try to get back into the boat.

STEP 1

The Dog Can Reach the Gunwale.

If you watch a dog that is having trouble trying to get into a boat, you will notice that as he makes the effort to get his rear end up, his head goes up and back with the muzzle pointing straight up or slightly back. The muscles and ligaments from the croup to the back of the skull cause this to happen. Therefore, if you brace the dog's head (that is, press down hard enough on the top of his head to keep it level), he will have a solid anchor to work against. The dog's muscles will lift the rear end, push the dog forward and let him hook his back feet over the gunwale. In preparation for this, you will be in the center of the canoe with your weight slightly to the off side.

1. You prepare
2. Dog hooks front feet over the gunwale
3. Dog stretches his head and neck forward
4. Reach over and put your hand on his head
5. Brace the dog's head as he contracts his muscles
6. Dog lifts and hooks his hind feet over gunwale
7. Dog jumps into the canoe
8. Praise the dog lavishly while he shakes

Review the questions and practice getting the dog into the boat until you both are comfortable before you go hunting. (See Figures 86 and 87.)

STEP 2

Dog Cannot Reach the Gunwale.

You may have a canoe or boat with gunwales so high that the dog cannot reach them or there may be decking and cowling that prevent a dog from hooking his front feet over anything. You do not have to lift the dog's total weight. You only have to supply enough lift for him to hook his front feet over the gunwales or railing. The dog will be working with his hind legs and part of his body will be supported by the water's buoyancy.

1. You get set
2. Grasp the dog by the scruff of the neck
3. Lift the dog so he can hook his front feet over the gunwale or suitable object
4. Let go of the scruff and brace the dog's head
5. Dog lifts and hooks hind feet over gunwale
6. Dog jumps into the boat
7. Praise the dog as he shakes

Practice this sequence until you and the dog are both comfortable before you go hunting.

Questions

1. Did you get prepared before the dog got to the boat?
2. Did you have to supply lift for the dog to hook gunwales?
3. Did the dog hook his front feet over gunwales? •

Figure 86   Dog getting in, handler's hand on dog's head bracing. Note handler in center of canoe bracing dog.

Figure 87   Dog getting in, handler's hand bracing dog's head. Note handler in center of canoe bracing dog's head with free hand on same gunwale as dog.

4. Did you brace the dog's head?
5. Did the dog jump into the boat immediately?
6. Did you praise the dog while he shook?

There are some boats (because of design or rigging) that a dog cannot get into by either of the above methods. In most cases of this type, the best solution is to rig a platform at or near the water surface. The dog gets on the platform and then into the boat. Practice getting the dog onto the platform and into the boat before you go hunting.

BEHAVIOR IN A BOAT

STEP 3

Traveling in the Boat.

It is pointless to take an uncontrollable dog into a boat and try to hunt waterfowl. The dog must know **Whoa** thoroughly just to travel in the boat. Before he can be an asset, he must be steady to flying birds. Otherwise, the dog will flare birds and rock the boat causing missed shots. To be fully effective, he must be steady to wing, shot, fall and to duck or goose calls.

The most stable position for a dog while traveling in a boat is sitting (as opposed to standing or lying). Even though he will want to stand in the bow or as far forward as possible or lean out to the side, for his own safety and yours, he should be made to remain sitting on the floor as near the center as possible. There is no way to do this unless he knows **Whoa** thoroughly to voice or whistle. Practice the following sequence:

1. **Kennel** command and point to the spot he is to occupy
2. Dog goes there
3. Reinforce the command with a stern **Whoa** (voice or whistle) and hand signal
4. Short praise
5. **Whoa** hand signal

Review the questions. If the dog tries to move, give both a harsh **Negative** sound plus a harsh **Whoa** command. There will not be room to use leads or other corrections nor would it be safe. Take the dog out in a boat before hunting season and settle the issue of control while traveling. It's too late when you are hunting.

Questions

1. Did you pick a good spot for the dog?
2. Did you give a stern **Kennel** command and a clear point?
3. Did the dog go there promptly?
4. Did you give a stern **Whoa** command?
5. Did you praise the dog?
6. Did you reinforce the **Whoa** command?

When you are hunting waterfowl from a boat used as the blind, the dog must be steady to calls, wing, shot, and fall. These should be taught first on land (refer to Chapter 26, Hunting from a Blind) and then transferred to a boat. A boat is no place to teach steadiness. This transfer work should be done well before the hunting season starts (say midsummer). Pigeons can be flown by the boat to finish off the training and if he moves, he does not get to retrieve the bird.

GETTING OUT OF A BOAT

STEP 4

Leaving the Boat.

Many good waterfowl dogs will be hesitant to jump out of a boat the first time for a variety of reasons. It may, perhaps, be a question of stability or unsure footing -- don't lose your temper. Do not throw the dog overboard under any circumstance (unless you want more trouble). There is undoubtedly a lack of confidence; throwing the dog in will certainly not build confidence. Be sure the dog has good footing as opposed to a slippery surface. If he is on the bottom of the boat, he must get enough thrust to go up and over the gunwale far enough to avoid banging his hind legs on the gunwale as he drops into the water. If he is on the seat or decking, his weight will in all probability be on the gunwale or edge of the boat making it very unstable. Therefore, use a wide boat with low gunwales if possible for the first attempts at having the dog jump out. The boat will be far more stable if the dog jumps from the bottom of the boat.

The desire to retrieve is going to be the stimulus that gets the dog out of the boat whether it be natural or force trained. In either event be sure the dog is a willing water retriever before you start this training. Use whatever object most excites the dog to retrieve for the first attempts at getting him out of the boat. Give the dog a few simple water retrieves so that you can give him plenty of praise before going out for his first try at getting out of the boat the first few times. This will be much easier if you have someone to handle the boat and throw the retrieve object. Before you start this work, decide whether you are going to take the object from the dog while he is in the water or after he gets in the boat. The dog can get into the boat with game in his mouth without biting it if he wants to do so.

Get in the boat and move a short distance off shore. Turn so that you and the dog are facing the shore with the retrieve object to be tossed between you and the near shore, This will be less intimidating to the dog. Practice the sequence that follows from the boat:

1. Give the **Mark** command to alert the dog
2. Object thrown to land in the water about 5 yards from the boat
3. Immediately give an upbeat **Fetch** command
4. Dog jumps out of the boat
5. Praise him lavishly
6. Dog retrieves the object
7. Praise him profusely as he comes to the boat
8. Get the dog in the boat
9. Praise the dog as he shakes

Repeat the sequence 3 or 4 times and call it quits for this session and review the questions. Do not overdo it to the point of no interest or diminished desire. Take a break and come back later for another session. As the dog develops confidence, change the conditions (face a large body of open water, set up longer retrieves, delay the **Fetch** command, etc.).

If the dog hesitates give encouragement, toss a rock beside the object, but do not spend a lot of time. If the dog has refused a retrieve, row the boat to the object and pick it up. Take the boat to shore and beach it so that it is stable. Get in the boat with the dog. Stand at one end of the boat, toss a dummy to the other and send the dog to retrieve it. Do this several times with plenty of praise. With you and the dog in the beached boat:

1. Give the **Mark** command
2. Toss the object on the shore to land about 5 feet from the boat
3. Immediately give an upbeat **Fetch** command
4. Dog jumps out of the boat
5. Praise the dog lavishly
6. Dog retrieves the object
7. Praise him as he returns
8. Get the dog into the boat
9. Praise him generously

Review the questions and repeat the sequence until he leaves the boat willingly. (See Figure 88.)

When the dog will leave the beached boat willingly, set it up so that when he jumps out of the boat he lands in the water even though the boat is still beached. When he does that willingly take the boat off shore a few yards and use the original sequence. Work under different conditions until the dog goes eagerly. (See Figure 89.)

Questions

1. Did the dog jump out quickly?
2. Did the dog hesitate before jumping?
3. Did the dog run fore and aft in the boat before jumping?
4. Did the dog whine or bark before jumping?
5. Could the dog be coaxed out?
6. Did you throw a rock and did it help?
7. Did the dog refuse to leave the boat?
8. How far out was the retrieve object?
9. Did the dog retrieve the object?
10. Did the dog return to the boat, go ashore or swim around?

With the boat beached:

11. Did the dog retrieve quickly in the boat?
12. Did the dog jump out of the boat toward the object?
13. Did the dog jump so as to be on land?
14. Did the dog jump into shallow water or deep water?
15. Did the dog deliberately go away from the object to jump on the

Figure 88 Boat beached, dummy on land, dog leaving boat. Note canoe held steady as dog leaves.

Figure 89 Notice the two dogs: one leaving eagerly and the other is steady.

land?

16. Did the dog stand in the boat and whine or bark?
17. Did the dog refuse to leave the boat?

28 Call Off Retrieve

There are times when a dog is in close pursuit of live game when he must be called off primarily for the dog's safety.

The prerequisites for training this are: (1) **Whoa**, (2) **Negative** command, (3) **Hand signals,** (4) **Come** and (5) **Fetch** (thoroughly trained under all conditions). Without **Whoa**, you cannot stop the dog's pursuit. The **Negative** command is needed to break his concentration and to tell him, in no uncertain terms, that he must leave the game. **Hand signals** have prepared him to leave one object he wants and to go to another. **Come** is the best command to use to get him away from the game after you have his attention. **Fetch** must be thoroughly learned so the dog does not have trouble in other retrieving situations.

The setup requires the dog to be chasing game in response to a **Fetch** command -- a duck swimming ahead of him. On the first few sequences, do not try it with the dog too close to the duck nor too far from you (you want him to feel your presence if possible). If for some reason the dog is too close to the duck, let the dog force it to dive. When it comes up there will be a greater distance between the dog and the duck. As soon as the dog is in eager pursuit at about 15 to 20 yards from the duck, it is time to stop him. The whistle is better than voice for the first **Whoa** command. To prevent loss of retrieving enthusiasm, always shoot the duck after the call off and send the dog to retrieve. If the prerequisites have been well trained, it will not take as many repetitions as you may think.

With the dog in pursuit of the duck, the sequence will be:

1. Give the **Whoa** command

2. Dog looks at you as though you are nuts
3. Dog looks back toward the duck
4. Give a very harsh **Negative** command
5. **Whoa** command (lay on that whistle and as soon as he looks at you, give a harsh voice **Whoa** command and a hand command)
6. Repeat the harsh **Negative** command every time he looks at the duck
7. Repeat the **Whoa** command until the dog looks at you and accepts the command
8. Give upbeat happy **Come** command
9. Dog comes to you
10. Praise him lavishly as he nears you
11. If you are on land, give **Heel** command
12. Praise the dog
13. Shoot the duck
14. Send the dog to retrieve
15. Praise him generously when he delivers the duck properly

Review the questions. Run no more than two sequences in one training session and separate them by some easy retrieving.

Note: Do not get angry if he does not obey the **Whoa** command. Go and get him -- wade, swim or use a boat -- but go and get him. Grab him by the scruff of the neck, shake him and give a full blast of the whistle. Now that you have his attention, give a **Come** or **Heel** command and head for shore.

Repeat the sequence until only one **Whoa** command, one **Negative** command, and one **Come** command are needed to call the dog off the duck when they are only about 5 feet apart.

Questions

1. Did the dog know all the prerequisites well?
2. How close was the dog to the duck on the **Whoa** command?
3. How close was the dog to you on the **Whoa** command?
4. On the **Whoa** command did the dog turn and start toward you;

turn and stop; turn his head to look at you and keep going; or ignore you?

5. On the **Negative** command, did the dog stop; turn and look at you; or turn, look and continue to ignore you?

6. On the **Come** command did the dog start toward you and keep coming; start toward you and then turn toward the duck; or ignore you completely?

7. Did you praise him lavishly as he approached you and at the **Heel** position?

8. Was he steady at **Heel** as the duck was shot?

9. Did he retrieve properly and did you take the duck properly?

10. Did you praise the dog well?

11. Did you have to go after him?

12. Did you shake him well and really blast that whistle?

Look carefully. He is carrying two Canada geese
clear of the ground.

29 Flush On Command

There are situations when a pointing dog must flush the bird on command if there is to be any chance for a shot. The real advantage to it is that the pointing dog never faces a negative action after a point. The dog is never pulled off a bird nor commanded to leave it. Furthermore, he never flushes the bird improperly. You and your partner get better shooting and "all is right with the world." These situations develop in all types of upland bird hunting from alder thickets to briar patches to running birds in the open.

There are four prerequisites for training flush on command and if they are well trained the job is fairly easy. They are: (1) a staunch pointer, (2) steady to wing shot and fall, (3) stop to flush, and (4) the **Whoa** command. Do not try to start this training too early. Be sure that the dog has the experience to handle birds well. That will take at least a couple of full seasons. In setting up the training lesson be sure the birds are strong, alert, standing and ready to fly (or wild if you are that fortunate). Be sure the dog faces more difficulty getting to the bird than the bird has getting away. Decide what you will use for the flushing command. The command should convey a sense of excitement and urgency.

Send the dog out to hunt and when he points:

1. Walk to the dog
2. Praise him (good dog)
3. Give the **Flush** command excitedly. (Very few dogs will relax the point and flush the bird on the first command.)

If you have used a tap on the head to release the dog, use it along with the **Flush** command. Coax him -- repeat the command excitedly (no anger) and tap his head. Use the word that releases him from all work. Be patient and encouraging, as this is contradictory to all his training and instincts. Do not lose your temper. Keep your voice happy and excited. When he looks at you as though you are nuts, laugh and say "Yes."

4. Dog flushes the bird
5. Give the **Whoa** command (upbeat not stern)
6. Dog stops
7. Partner shoots the bird
8. Walk to the dog
9. Kneel beside the dog and praise him lavishly
10. Send the dog to retrieve

Review the questions. Repeat the sequence until the dog will flush the bird on a single or, at most, two commands. Do not do a lot of consecutive repetitions. Mix in some normal work -- that is, you flush the bird.

Before the dog is trained to **Flush** on command consistently, he should be stopping to flush without the **Whoa** command. Watch out for this and drop the **Whoa** command from the sequence.

Questions

1. How many commands did it take to get the dog to relax the point?
2. How many commands did it take to get the dog to flush the bird?
3. What cornmand or combination was most effective?
4. With what attitude did the dog flush?
5. When did the dog commit to stop: before the **Whoa**, on the **Whoa**, after the **Whoa?**
6. Did you praise the dog enough?

30 | Stop In Mid-Charge

There will be many times when a dog is well within gun range, and there will be no shot possible if the dog flushes. Therefore, you must be able to stop a dog that has started his drive to flush the bird. This is no problem in open country or over low cover. It is a frequent problem in alder thickets and heavily wooded areas.

The prerequisites for this training are: (1) an experienced hunting dog, (2) a quick forceful flusher, (3) a steady dog, (4) **Whoa** thoroughly learned. The dog needs to be wholly confident in his work and you need to be able to read your dog very well.

In setting this up with planted birds, the selection of cover is critical. You must be able to see the dog's change of attitude as he picks up the bird's scent and starts to drive in for the flush. The combination of the distance from the bird and the cover's resistance to the dog must give you time to give the **Whoa** command and the dog time to stop before he flushes the bird. The bird must be fully alert and free to fly.

Note: Be sure you are as close to the dog as possible the first time you run this sequence. If he does not stop to the command the first time, get closer to him on the next try.

With the dog hunting in front of you and nearing the point where he will pick up scent:

1. You get ready to give the **Whoa** command
2. Dog picks up bird scent
3. Dog starts drive to flush

4.   You give the **Whoa** command
5.   Dog stops
6.   Praise the dog as you position gunners
7.   Position gunners for the shot
8.   Send the dog to flush
9.   Dog flushes the bird
10.   Dog stops
11.   Gunners shoot the bird
12.   Dog retrieves the bird to hand
13.   Praise the dog lavishly

Review the questions. Do not make continuous repetitions of this. Mix in some normal hunt and flush work. Repeat the sequence until the dog handles several consecutive repetitions flawlessly. This does not mean run the sequence consecutively. You still want to alternate between normal hunting and flushing work.

If the dog does not stop instantly to **Whoa,** give a harsh **Negative** command and get after him. Pick him up roughly and shake him while you take him back to where he should have stopped. Put him down roughly with a harsh **Whoa.** Let him sit there awhile before you send him on to hunt. If he did not stop on command, run the **Stop** sequence on the next bird contact.

Questions

1.   Were you ready before the dog picked up bird scent?
2.   Were you aware the instant the dog made his move to flush the bird?
3.   Did you give a clear sharp **Whoa** immediately?
4.   Did the dog have time to stop without flushing the bird?
5.   Did the dog flush the bird?
6.   Did the dog react instantly to **Whoa?**
7.   Did you praise him while you set the gunners?
8.   Did the dog ignore the **Whoa?**
9.   How far from the dog were you at the **Whoa?**
10.   Did you give a prompt **Negative** command?

11. Did you discipline him and put him down roughly where he should have stopped?

The end of a good day in North Dakota ---
sharptail grouse and Hungarian partridge.

An outstanding day hunting sharptail grouse in North Dakota.

31 | Honoring

Unless you hunt alone or take only one dog afield at a time, your dog should be trained to honor its bracemate's work. Few things are more thrilling to watch in dog work than outstanding honoring by your dog. Done without commands or cautions, it demonstrates the ultimate in fine dog work and manners, Taking out a bracemate's pointed bird is most discouraging; almost as much as having your dog chase a steady bracemate's flush. Worse yet is having two dogs trying to retrieve the same bird. A damaged bird is the least you may get and damaged dogs are very likely.

There is no reason to even think about or consider training a dog to honor another's work unless he is completely steady to wing, shot and fall and waits until told to retrieve. The second prerequisite is that **Whoa** be thoroughly trained. The third is that the **Negative** command be well understood. This work goes better if honoring retrieve is taught before point and flush.

HONOR RETRIEVE

Training a dog to honor a retrieve is easy if the above prerequisites have been met. He has already been taught steadiness. All you are doing is adding one more temptation. Granted, it is a tough one, especially for dominant dogs. This requires a bracemate and it will be helpful if the bracemate is steady, but not absolutely essential. Put him on lead when it is your dog's turn to retrieve. It matters not whether you start over land or water, but you should work both.

STEP 1

Beside Dog with Whoa.

Start with the handlers standing a few feet apart with their dogs at **Heel**.

1. **Whoa**
2. **Mark**
3. Dummy thrown
4. Gun shot
5. Short pause
6. Bracemate sent to retrieve
7. Your dog steady
8. Bracemate delivers dummy
9. Praise your dog lavishly
10. Turn and send your dog for a short romp
11. Do not let him go to the mark (delay chase) (See Figure 90.)

Review the questions and repeat the sequence until you get several consecutive flawless repetitions. Be sure to alternate as to which dog gets the retrieve. Your dog should never get the retrieve if he takes even one step forward or lifts his rump off the ground.

If your dog breaks on the throw, quit. Go back and teach him steadiness. If he breaks with his bracemate, give a harsh **Whoa**. Go to him, pick him up roughly and put him back where he was with a harsh **Negative** command.

Questions

1. Was the dog steady on the throw?
2. Did the dog break on the throw?
3. Was the dog steady to his bracemate leaving?
4. Did the dog break with his bracemate?
5. Could you stop the dog?
6. Was the dog steady throughout the retrieve?
7. Did he have to be cautioned?
8. Did you praise the dog after the retrieve when he was steady?

Figure 90   No lead, but you are right by the dog so he feels your presence.

STEP 2

Beside Dog Without Whoa.

Now that the dog is steady on **Whoa** in Step 1, it is time to eliminate it. The dog may have already indicated that it is not needed. The sequence will be the same as in Step 1 starting with the **Mark.** Watch him carefully and be ready to stop him if he indicates that he is going to move. Becoming alert is fine, movement is not. Judge what is needed to anchor or stop him and use it accordingly. The **Negative** command is preferable to the **Whoa.** It tells the dog that what he is about to do is wrong. When the dog handles several consecutive repetitions flawlessly with no commands or cautions, it is time to go to Step 3.

STEP 3

Out of Dog's Sight.

This step is to prepare the dog to be out of your sight as he would be outside of the blind while waterfowl hunting. He can mark a lot better if he is outside.

1. **Whoa**
2. Step about 5 yards away in sight
3. **Mark** by partner
4. Dummy thrown
5. Shot fired
6. Short pause
7. Bracemate sent to retrieve
8. Your dog steady
9. Bracemate delivers dummy
10. Step to your dog
11. Praise him profusely
12. Turn and send your dog for a short romp
13. Do not let him go to the mark

Review the questions. Repeat the sequence at this distance until the dog handles several consecutive repetitions flawlessly. Then start to increase the distance in small increments. Be sure that his performance is flawless at each distance and when he can handle a separation of about 25 yards, it is time to step out of sight. (See Figure 91.) Start at the shortest distance you can arrange. Always go to him and praise him after the retrieve. Remember to mix in some retrieves for your dog.

Anytime your dog makes any movement toward the dummy, give a **Negative** or **Whoa** command, whichever is needed. If he breaks, go and get him and shake him up on the way back. If you see he is getting edgy, use a **Negative** command that tells him to forget about it.

Now that the dog is honoring all retrieves with the dummy, go through each of the three steps with flown and shot birds. Throw double dummies or more and mix up the order of the retrieves. When he handles all of this, send him to retrieve while you are out of sight.

HONOR POINT

In addition to steadiness, **Whoa** and the **Negative** command, the dog should honor retrieve before he is trained to honor point. Otherwise, he may break to his bracemate's retrieve and the sequence will end on a negative rather than a positive note. The dog must honor point on sight

Figure 91   Your dog is alone, steady and honoring retrieve while you are out of sight.

alone. To differentiate this training the word "honor" will be used to denote no scent involved, while "back" will denote scent is involved. While some dogs seem to honor instinctively or at least learn very rapidly, there are others that try to avoid the situation. Then there are the outlaws that steal the point, or worse, deliberately flush the bird.

If at all possible, use a dog that points intensely and is steady until sent to retrieve. If a steady pointer is not possible, restrain the pointer before the bird is flushed and shot. You want as much calmness in the pointer as possible.

STEP 1

Back Point.

Dogs that have the inclination to honor can be readily trained to back. All you need are a few **Whoa**'s to teach him that a pointing dog is an alternate command for **Whoa**. To prevent boredom, mix in some pointing for your dog along with the backing.

With the bracemate on point and clearly visible to the dog approaching the bird from downwind:

1. **Whoa** the instant the dog is in the bird's scent zone and sees the pointer
2. Dog commits to stop
3. Dog stops properly
4. Move calmly to your dog
5. Praise the dog
6. Gently try to push your dog forward as you did in pointing
7. Praise the dog as he resists
8. Caution him if he lessens resistance
9. Have your partner flush the bird
10. If both dogs are steady, shoot the bird
11. Alternately send your dog and the bracemate to retrieve
12. Dog delivers bird
13. Praise your dog
14. Send the dog on to hunt but do not let him delay chase

Review the questions. Repeat the sequence until the dog is performing flawlessly for several consecutive repetitions. Then delay the **Whoa** to give the dog a chance to back on his own. Be ready with the **Whoa** or **Negative** command if needed. When the dog is flawless on his own with no caution or command through several consecutive repetitions, go to Step 2.

Questions

1. Did the dog commit to stop before the command?
2. Did the dog commit to stop immediately on command?
3. Did the dog stop promptly on command?
4. Did the dog stop promptly on his own?
5. Did the dog try to steal the point?
6. Did the dog try to avoid the back?
7. Did the dog flush the bird?
8. Was the back intense?
9. Did the dog resist the push?

10. Did you praise the dog before the flush?
11. Did the dog honor the retrieve?
12. Did you praise the dog after the retrieve?
13. Did the dog try to delay chase?
14. Did you stop him if he tried to delay chase?

STEP 2

Honor Point with Command.

Now the dog must learn to honor point on sight alone when there is no possible chance of help from prior bird scent. The dog must work downwind or crosswind above the pointer with the bracemate on point clearly visible to your dog as he approaches.

1. **Whoa** the instant the dog sees the pointer
2. Dog commits to stop instantly
3. Dog stops promptly. (See Figure 92.)
4. Move calmly to your dog
5. Praise the dog profusely
6. Gently try to push the dog forward
7. Praise him as he resists
8. Have your partner flush the bird
9. If both dogs are steady, shoot the bird
10. Dog steady
11. Praise the dog
12. Send a dog to retrieve
13. Praise your dog after the delivery no matter which dog retrieved

Review the questions and repeat the sequence until you get several consecutive flawless repetitions.

STEP 3

Honor Point without Command.

The sequence will be the same as in Step 2 except that you will delay the **Whoa** to give the dog time to commit and stop on his own. If the dog gives indications of stopping but does not stop promptly, a mild **Negative**

Figure 92   The honoring dog must not have bird scent. Honor is by sight alone.

may be all that is needed. If the dog is willful, use a harsh **Negative** followed by **Whoa;** then get after him. Pick him up and scold him back to where he should have stopped. Put him down roughly and let him stand there a while before the bird is flushed. He does not get a chance to retrieve unless he performs flawlessly. Review the questions and repeat the sequence until the dog stops promptly the instant he sees the pointer.

If you have one of those dogs that, for whatever reason, does not want to back or honor, you will have to bear down on him and force him to honor. He must be trained in detail to stop whenever he sees a dog on point. He must learn that he stops at the sight of a pointer or he does nothing. Unless you have unlimited birds and an enduring partner, you may want to use a "Judas," painted silhouette, dog. Pop-up "Judas" dogs are available commercially or can be made. Set the silhouette up so that the dog comes upon it quickly, such as around a corner, or over the brow of a hill. If you have the manual pop-up, be sure that you get your signals straight with your partner so that he knows when to pop it. Move the silhouette frequently to prevent anticipation.

STEP 4

Dog at Heel.

With the dog at Heel the sequence will be:

1. The dog suddenly sees the silhouette
2. **Whoa**
3. Dog stops (See Figure 93.)
4. Praise the dog
5. Gently push him toward the silhouette
6. Dog resists the push, praise him
7. Dog does not resist, harsh **Negative**
8. Go to the silhouette and collapse it
9. **Heel** him back away from the silhouette

Review the questions and repeat the sequence about 10 times.

Now try the sequence but delay the **Whoa** giving the dog time to stop on his own. When he does, praise him profusely. If he does not, give a harsh

Figure 93 Do not give the dog room to deny the silhouette. Give the **Whoa** the instant it pops up.

Figure 94   Be sure you are close enough that the dog knows he must obey the **Whoa**.

Whoa. On the next repetition put him on lead at **Heel.** As soon as he sees the silhouette, give a stern **Whoa** and pop the lead. Take the lead off for the next repetition. When the dog stops instantly on seeing the silhouette with no command or caution for several consecutive repetitions, go to Step 5.

STEP 5

Back Silhouette and Bird.

It is now time to bring birds into the training. Set up the silhouette and plant a bird appropriately near it. The dog should be brought in from downwind so that he can get scent. Still he must back on sight and not get close enough to trigger a normal point. You want the scent to generate interest not trigger the point. Do not let him crowd the silhouette.

1. Dog sees silhouette and stops promptly (See Figure 94.)
2. Walk to the dog
3. Praise him

   4. Push him gently forward
   5. Praise the dog as he resists
   6. Walk forward, flush and shoot the bird
   7. Collapse the silhouette
   8. Walk back to the dog
   9. Praise him
   10. Send him to retrieve
   11. Praise him after the delivery

Review the questions.

If the dog tries to crowd the silhouette, use a **Negative** as strong as is needed to stop him. You want him to know you are displeased with his actions. Repeat the sequence until the dog's performance is flawless for several consecutive repetitions. Then go to Step 6.

STEP 6

Honor Silhouette and Bird.

The sequence will be the same as in Step 5 except that the dog will approach from upwind or crosswind above the bird's scent. Repeat the sequence until the dog is performing flawlessly through a number of consecutive repetitions.

Questions

   1. Did the pop of the silhouette startle him?
   2. Did the dog commit to stop the instant he saw the silhouette?
   3. Did the dog stop properly out of pointing range?
   4. Are you sure there was no scent involved?
   5. Was the dog intense?
   6. Did the dog resist the push?
   7. Did you praise him profusely?
   8. Did the dog move on the flush, shot or fall?
   9. Did you collapse the silhouette before you walked back to him?
   10. Did the dog retrieve properly?
   11. Did you praise him after the retrieve?

12. Did the dog move at any time so that he interfered with the bird, pointer or entered the scent cone?

You now know that the dog understands that he is supposed to stop and not move when he sees a pointing dog. He also knows that if he does there will be a bird flushed and shot and he can retrieve. It is time for the real thing. Be sure that the pointer you use points with great intensity and is steady. To keep your dog's interest high, you will want him to make some of the retrieves on which he backed or honored. Now go back to Step 1, Back Point.

HONOR FLUSH

If the flushing dog is truly steady to wing, shot and fall and waits to be sent to retrieve, training him to honor a flush is not difficult. The prerequisites are steadiness, **Whoa, Negative** and **Turn**, all well trained. The **Turn** must be quick and sharp so that the dog will be working in the right direction to see the bird the moment it flushes. There is no point in trying to train a dog to honor flush if both of the dogs are not well trained and experienced in the fundamentals of searching. If a command is needed to stop the dog, he is not honoring. He is obeying the **Whoa** command.

STEP 1

Stop to Command.

With the dogs working ahead and the bracemate approaching the bird:

1. **Turn** your dog if needed so that he is working in the direction of the flushing bird
2. Bracemate flushes and stops
3. **Whoa**
4. If both dogs are steady the bird is shot
5. Walk to your dog
6. Praise him profusely and step away
7. Alternate sending bracemate and your dog to retrieve
8. Dog delivers bird
9. Praise your dog
10. Send him on to hunt

11. If he was not sent to retrieve, do not let him go to the mark of the downed bird

Review the questions. Repeat the sequence until you get several consecutive flawless repetitions. Watch the dog to see how quickly he commits to stop. If he commits to stop very quickly, go to Step 2.

If the dog does not commit to stop instantly on the **Whoa** give a harsh **Negative** and go get him. Pick him up roughly, scold him all the way back to where he should have made the commitment. Put him down roughly with a harsh **Whoa** -- he should know better. If you have to go get him more than once you have missed something in his earlier training. Go back to Step 1 in steadiness and work forward until you find it.

STEP 2

Honor Flush.

The sequence for Step 2 is the same as for Step 1 except that you will delay the **Whoa** command to give the dog time to commit to stop and to stop properly, You must be as close to the dog as possible on the first sequence. You want him to feel your presence. If a command is needed, use a harsh **Negative** command to show your displeasure. Go to him aggressively, pick him up roughly and take him to the spot where he should have committed to stop. Put him down roughly with a harsh **Whoa.** Repeat the sequence until the dog commits to stop instantly without a command or caution and then stops properly. Review the questions and make sure that you get several consecutive flawless repetitions.

Questions

1. Did the flush occur within the dog's view?
2. Did the dog commit to stop on his own?
3. Did the dog stop properly on his own?
4. Did the dog chase?
5. Did his bracemate work the bird properly?
6. Did the dog remain steady to wing, shot and fall?
7. Did you go to him and praise him before the retrieve?
8. Did the dog honor the retrieve?

9. Did you praise the dog after the retrieve?
10. Did the dog try to go to the mark after the retrieve?
11. Did you stop him if he did?

32 | Sit

The command **Sit** is superfluous for a retriever or flushing dog since the **Whoa** command means stop and sit; it is of little value to a pointing dog except as an intermediate step if you plan to train the dog to the command **Down**. To train a dog to sit, refer to **Whoa** for a flushing dog, Step 1B. The time to train a pointing dog to sit is after he is "steady" since some dogs who are unsure of themselves will sit while being taught steadiness. You may find, as many do with pointing dogs, that the **Sit** command is unnecessary if **Whoa** is well trained.

German wirehaired pointer and rabbits
in Michigan snow.

33	Down

Very few dogs who have been thoroughly taught that **Whoa** means stop, stand or sit, and who do not move until told to do so, need to be trained to **Down.** About the only hunting situation would be lying in the decoys while waterfowl hunting in fields. Most people who want to use it do so as a substitute for the well trained **Whoa.** To be effective it must be trained with a negative attitude as the dog must take and maintain a subservient position. Virtually no praise can be used as the dog would be confused by being praised and forced to maintain a servile position simultaneously. Therefore, make these sessions short, only three or four repetitions. Then do something that allows a lot of praise.

The **Down** position requires the dog to rest on his chest and stomach; his hind legs bent with his paws, metatarsus and hock joint flat on the ground; his front legs from the elbow to the pads flat on the ground and his head on the ground between his front legs. The critical aspect of **Down** is that his head must stay on the ground at all times -- between the legs not on one leg.

The prerequisites for training **Down** are **Whoa** and **Sit**. In addition to a training collar and lead, you will need a long stick. The stick should be about 6 feet long and stiff enough to deliver a firm *tap* on the dog's head. The stick may be a cane pole, long dowel, sapling or a metal tube.

STEP 1

With the dog on **Whoa**, at **Sit** or standing on the table:

1. Reach behind and past the right front leg and grasp the dog's left

pastern
2. Place your left hand high on the dog's withers
3. Give a stern **Down** command
4. Immediately move your right hand and arm to the right, moving the dog's legs forward
5. Simultaneously push down on the withers forcing the dog's chest to the table. (As the rump must move in one smooth continuous motion in the **Sit**, so must the chest in the **Down.**)
6. As the dog's chest touches the table, release your grasp on his leg and force his head down flat on the table
7. As his head touches the table, give another stern **Down** command
8. Hold the dog there until he accepts the restraint
9. Immediately give the **Heel** command
10. Step out and praise while he heels.

Review the questions. Repeat the sequence until the dog goes down in one smooth motion with no resistance to the downward push on his withers or his head. (See Figures 95, 96, 97 and 98.)

STEP 2

When the dog accepts the **Down** command with no resistance, it is time to start training duration while you have full control of the down motion. Without duration while down, you may have trouble maintaining control as you train the dog to **Down** on voice alone. Be sure to enforce a precise **Down** position while training duration. With the dog on **Whoa**, at **Sit** or standing on the table:

1. Reach behind and past the right front leg and grasp the dog's left pastern
2. Place your left hand high on the dog's withers
3. Give a stern **Down** command
4. Immediately move your right hand and arm to the right, moving the dog's legs forward
5. Simultaneously push down on the withers forcing the dog's chest to the table. (As the rump must move in one smooth continuous motion in the **Sit**, so must the chest in the **Down**)
6. As the dog's chest touches the table, release your grasp on his leg

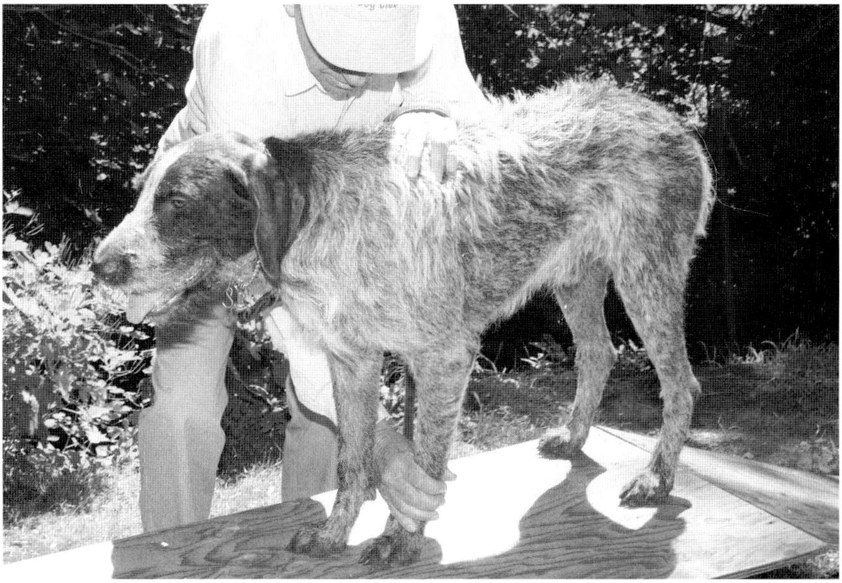

Figure 95   Firm grip on dog's left leg.

Figure 96 Note as right hand moves forward it forces right leg up and out.

Figure 97   Dog's chest on the table.

Figure 98   Note head flat on the table between the paws.

and force his head down flat on the table

7. As his head touches the table, give another stern **Down** command
8. Hold the dog there until he accepts the restraint
9. Keep pressure on the dog for 5 to 10 seconds. (If he struggles, give a harsh **Down** command followed immediately by firm pressure with both hands and start the count over.)
10. Dog remains still for 5 to 10 seconds
11. Give the **Heel** command
12. Step out and praise while he heels.

Review the questions and repeat the sequence until you have several consecutive flawless repetitions.

STEP 3

At this point the dog must be trained to remain on **Down** without your hands holding him down. With the dog in the **Down** position as in Step 2:

1. Give the **Down** command
2. Lift your hands straight above the dog about 6 inches. (That position will let you come down on the dog quickly if he tries to move.)
3. Pause just a few seconds
4. Keep an eye on the dog so that you can prevent any movement. (If it is necessary to correct him, give a harsh **Down** command and come down fast and hard with your hand -- make him feel it. Do not use cautionary action as you do with **Whoa** -- always act harshly.)
5. When the dog has remained still for 5 seconds or more, put your hands on him gently
6. Give the **Heel** command
7. Step out and praise while he heels.

Repeat the sequence until you have several consecutive flawless 5 to 10-second long repetitions. Continue the sequence increasing the pause until the dog will remain motionless for at least one minute. (See Figure 99.)

STEP 4

Now that the dog will stay **Down** without your hands on him, it is time to

Figure 99   Be ready to prevent any movement.

train him to go **Down** on voice alone. With the dog on **Whoa**, at **Sit** or standing on the table:

1. Put your right hand and arm behind the dog's front legs and your left hand a few inches above his withers
2. Give the **Down** command
3. Delay hand movement
4. Dog goes down smoothly and properly. (If the dog hesitates, swing your right hand out knocking his front feet out forward and simultaneously drive your left hand down on his withers forcing him to the table. Bring your right hand over and force his head down 10 to 15 seconds.)
5. Give the **Heel** command
6. Step out and praise profusely while dog is heeling.

Review the questions and repeat the sequence until the dog will **Down** quickly, smoothly and properly to voice alone.

STEP 5

It is now time to move away from the dog while he remains **Down**. Lay the stick lengthwise on the table so that it will be between you and the dog when he sits. With the dog on **Whoa** on the table, pick up the stick and the sequence will be:

1. Give the **Down** command
2. Dog **Downs**
3. Rest stick on the dog's head
4. Give **Down** command and step forward turning as you do so you face the dog (keep the stick on his head)
5. Pause a few seconds. (If the dog starts to move or lift his head, give a harsh **Down** command and tap him smartly on the head.)
6. Step back to the dog
7. Give the **Heel** command
8. Step out and praise profusely while dog heels.

Review the questions. Repeat the sequence until the dog is performing flawlessly with the stick touching his head very lightly. Continue the sequence and remove the stick from his head. When the dog's performance is flawless without the stick touching him go to Step 6. (See Figure 100.)

STEP 6

Now the dog must be trained to remain on **Down** no matter what you do. Walk around, stand and chat or even go out of sight. With the dog in the **Down** position on the table:

1. Give the **Down** command
2. Step out 5 feet or so in front of the dog and turn to face him
3. Keep your eye on him so that you can anticipate any movement and take a few steps. (If the dog attempts to move, tap him on the head with the stick.)
4. Step back to the dog
5. Give the **Heel** command
6. Step out and praise profusely while dog heels.

Repeat the sequence until the dog's performance is perfect through several consecutive repetitions. Now that the dog is doing well with you in front of him, it is time to move to the sides and behind him. Repeat the sequence but step out to sides alternately during item 2. When he is flawless then, step behind him. Do not stay behind him too long the first time or

Figure 100   Keep the dog's head flat on the table.

two. He will want to turn his head to look at you (as he did with **Whoa**). Be alert -- if he starts to move his head, tap the dog's head with the stick. Here is where many trainers get in trouble. As you get farther away from the dog, it will take you time to get close enough to tap him. By then he will be still with his head glued to the ground. Hit him -- he must know that if he moves he gets hit. Remember, his head must stay on the ground.

You will need help to train a dog to stay **Down** when he is out of your sight. For the first few repetitions set them up so that you go out of sight quickly, so that you can get back to him quickly when he moves. Do not let your partner stand between you and the dog or close to the dog. It is best if the dog cannot see him. Caution your partner that any movement including lifting the head is wrong and must be corrected.

Run the dog through all of the Steps 1-6 on the ground. If the work has been done well on the table, it will go rapidly on the ground.

Questions

1. Did the dog resist the action on his front legs?
2. Did the dog resist the pressure on his withers?
3. Did the dog resist the pressure on his head?

4. Did you push him all the way down in one smooth continuous motion?
5. Did the dog try to raise his rump?
6. Did the dog try to raise his head?
7. Did the dog struggle to get up?
8. Did the dog try to lie on his side?
9. Did the dog stay tense?
10. Did the dog relax and accept the restraint?
11. Did the dog **Down** in one smooth continuous motion on voice command only?
12. Is there a hesitation or hitch in the **Down** motion?
13. Did the dog creep or slide along in the **Down** position when left for some time?
14. When you had to hit the dog on the head, did you hit hard enough to get the desired results?

Quail Hunting in North Carolina
A young wirehaired pointer is relaxed but alert after the shot.

34 | Housebreaking

There is little or no doubt that the best dog-handler rapport is established when the dog lives in the home rather than in an outside kennel -- even though the dog needs an outside kennel. The dog becomes people socialized much quicker, especially if there are children around. Another plus is the added protection a dog in the house provides. That happy, friendly greeting you get when you come through the door isn't too hard to take.

The biggest concern most people have with a dog in the house is that he be housebroken -- that is, he will not relieve himself in the house. A dog with a basically sound temperament can be housebroken fairly easily. No dog wants to mess his sleeping or resting area -- take advantage of that. Whenever and at whatever age a dog is brought into the home with the intention that he will live there, he should be immediately put in a crate (travel crate, kennel, etc.). If you have a large crate and a small dog, block it off with a board so that if the dog messes it he cannot lie down without lying in his soil.

Before you start housebreaking the dog, you must decide how you will handle him outside. No! He cannot be let out the back door no matter how big the yard is. That mistake kills many hunting dogs every year. The dog needs an outside kennel in which to relieve himself. It must be set up so the dog cannot dig out or climb out. You must give some thought to where it is placed. Every time the dog is let out, you have to put him in the kennel. There are several ways to handle this but the two easiest methods are: (1) have a flap door that opens directly into the kennel, or (2) place the kennel so that you can raise and lower a guillotine door from the house. If you use the flap door, be sure to put the dog out through it when you are housebreaking him. You will be amazed how it shakes up people who think the dog is out in the kennel and suddenly he is at the door. They become very careful.

The alternative to an outside kennel is a running wire or long lead or chain attached to the house, When it is time for the dog to go out, he is attached to the lead.

Puppies must be given special consideration. They cannot go all day without relief. If you will be gone for several hours, put the pup in the outside kennel. Do not force him to make a mistake. If you take a puppy out of the crate to play with him, stop -- immediately take him outside to relieve himself. That one minute of play or cuddling can be disastrous. Do not play with him every time you take the pup out to relieve himself. You decide when it's time to play, not the dog.

Any normal dog in a closely confined area like a crate, will start to fidget or pace nervously (puppies will also whine) when he has to relieve himself.

1.   Go to the dog
2.   Open the crate
3.   Snap on his lead (pick up puppies)
4.   **Heel** the dog to the outside kennel
5.   Give the **Kennel** command (see Chapter 36) and put the dog in the kennel
6.   Leave him there for a while (whether you stay or go about your business is up to you)
7.   Put him on lead and **Heel** him back to the crate
8.   Give the **Kennel** command and put him in the crate
9.   Praise the dog

A puppy should not be put on lead -- that gives him too much leeway for error. Pick him up and take him quickly outside to the kennel. You may want to stay and be sure that the puppy relieves himself. Continue the sequence until you clearly see that the dog is asking to go out when necessary. Keep track of how long he can go before he needs relief. This will let you know how long he can be left in his crate if you leave. When you leave a puppy, put him out for relief just before you go. No dog should be allowed free run of the house at less than 3 months of age and then only if he has proven beyond a doubt that he will ask to go out when necessary.

The use of the crate in housebreaking the dog will be helpful in many other ways.

1. It can become his bed with the door open
2. It becomes his resting place and security
3. It becomes his traveling home, he is content wherever it is put -- car, airplane, garage, motel, etc.
4. It is his first lesson in accepting restraint

Summertime and the living is easy.

35 Children And Dogs

One of the greatest things that can happen to a dog is a child. They go together so well that the words are almost synonymous. No adult can socialize a dog the way a child can. One of life's real joys is watching two youngsters, one human and one canine, frolicking in the yard or rolling on the floor in the house. That is happiness in action.

The only thing that children must understand is that they do not use the commands you are training the dog to obey until the command is well learned and you have given them permission to use it. To help the child, take the dog and child through the training steps with the child handling the lead and giving the commands. Remember to teach the child to use a commanding tone of voice -- not pleading or screaming. That does not mean the child cannot command the dog, but rather must use different words. Instead of **Fetch,** have the child use **Get It**; instead of **Come**, the child uses **Here** or whatever. No child really needs to call a dog, he or she just kneels, says the dog's name and claps his or her hands. No dog can resist.

One caution -- children can exhaust a puppy or young dog. Limit play or roughhouse time somewhat. If the crate door is left open and the dog comes and goes at will, do not let the children call or take the puppy out of the crate if he went in on his own. The dog may well be tired and will come out when he is ready for more.

Sharptail grouse and Hungarian partridge
in North Dakota

36 | Kennel Command

The command **Kennel** may seem of little importance but it has many uses in hunting as well as around the house. It will progressively mean go into the kennel; go to the kennel and remain quiet; and to go anywhere indicated and remain there quietly. The voice command **Kennel** along with a point of the hand is all that is needed to put the dog in a crate, blind, boat, car, corner, on a mat, vet's scale or anywhere you want him. As with any other command, it is to be obeyed until the next command is given. The necessity for the dog to stay in the kennel location is primarily one of safety. The dog that bolts from a crate could be in great danger if the crate is in your car parked beside a busy road.

STEP 1

The sequence for training the dog to **Kennel** is very short:

1. Stand directly in front of the kennel about a step away with a grip on the dog's collar.
2. Give the **Kennel** command and simultaneously point at the kennel with your free hand
3. Push the dog forward by the collar into the kennel (taking a half step forward makes this easier)
4. Release the dog
5. Close the kennel
6. Praise the dog profusely

Review the questions. Repeat the sequence every time you put the dog in a kennel or a crate. It will not take many repetitions before the push with the collar is not needed. (See Figure 101.)

Questions

    1. Did you give the **Kennel** command before you pointed or pushed?

    2. Did you praise the dog?

When the dog enters readily on command from a step away, start working your way back by increments until you can send him into the kennel from 10 yards or so. Make sure that he is performing flawlessly at each incremental increase. Each time the dog enters properly, walk to the crate or kennel and praise him lavishly. By the way, be sure that the door is open. (See Figure 102.)

STEP 2

Training the dog to stay in the kennel until he is told to come out is not difficult if controlled at the beginning. If you let the dog develop the habit of bolting, then you have a problem. The command to come out of a kennel or crate should be **Heel**. **Heel** is a control command and requires the dog to assume the heel position. He is trained from the start that an open door or gate means come with me -- not take off at will. Once the dog is at **Heel**, you then tell him what to do.

    For a puppy or young dog with no training:

    1.   Open the kennel or crate

    2.   Reach in and hold the dog

    3.   Attach his lead and hold him there a moment

    4.   Praise him

    5.   Pick up a puppy -- **Heel** command and lead out an older dog

Repeat the sequence every time you take the dog out of his kennel or crate.

Do not try to use the **Whoa** command with puppies and young dogs with no training -- you cannot enforce the command or prevent the dog from disobeying. (See Figure 103.)

Figure 101   Keep control until the dog is in the crate.

Figure 102   Be sure he goes in promptly.

Figure 103   Until dog knows Heel flawlessly off lead, always attach lead while the dog is in the crate.

Questions

1. Did the dog try to run out?
2. Did you stop him and attach the lead?
3. Did you make him stand relaxed for a few moments?
4. If the dog is a puppy, did you pick him up?
5. Did you clearly give the **Heel** command before you moved?
6. Did you praise the dog?

STEP 3

For a dog with enough **Whoa** training to stand still for a few moments while you open the kennel and attach the lead:

1. Give the **Whoa** command
2. Open the kennel
3. Attach the lead
4. Praise the dog lavishly
5. Give the **Heel** command

6. Dog comes out to **Heel**
7. Give the **Whoa** command
8. Praise the dog

Repeat the sequence every time you take the dog out of the kennel. When you see that the dog is standing calmly and waiting for you, drop the **Whoa** command, but be ready to use the voice or hand command if needed. Until the dog is trained well to not come out, be sure that you always go into the kennel or reach into the crate to attach the lead. (See Figure 104.)

Questions

1. Did the dog move forward when you opened the kennel?
2. Did the dog remain still while you attached the lead?
3. Did the dog move forward before the **Heel** command?
4. Did you praise the dog?

STEP 4

For the dog that has developed the habit of bolting out of the kennel and

Figure 104   Train the dog to wait for you to step in the kennel to attach the lead.

the **Whoa** command will not keep him, harsher treatment is needed. Very few dogs will stand their ground if you go at them aggressively with an angry attitude and sound.

1. Approach the kennel or crate aggressively with an angry attitude and harsh sound
2. The dog backs off
3. Open kennel, step in and close it -- open the crate, block it and get set
4. Attach the lead
5. If the dog tries to bolt from the kennel, crack the lead; from the crate, slam him back in or slam the door in his face
6. Make him stand and wait
7. Praise the dog lavishly as he stands
8. Give the **Heel** command and move him out

Review the questions. Repeat the sequence every time you go in the kennel or take the dog out of his crate. When he makes no attempt to get out when the gate or door is opened, drop the aggressive, angry and harsh approach. Walk to him normally. Repeat the sequence until you can walk up open the kennel or crate and the dog makes no move to get out.

Questions

1. Did the dog react with uncertainty at your approach?
2. Did the dog back away and stand still?
3. Did the dog remain still when you opened the kennel or crate?
4. Did the dog move forward or backward?
5. Did the dog remain still while you attached the lead?
6. Did you delay a few moments before giving the **Heel** command?
7. Did you praise the dog lavishly while you both stood?

STEP 5

There is no valid reason to ever leave the gate of an outside kennel open. A crate in the house, however, is a different story. It can be left open once the dog is completely housebroken, and it must be, if it is to serve as his bed and/or rest area. Before it is left open, the dog should be taught to stay in it until called out if he were sent to the crate. The well-learned

Whoa command is a prerequisite for training the dog to go in and stay in an open crate on the command **Kennel**.

1. Give the **Kennel** command
2. Dog goes in the crate
3. Leave door open
4. Give the **Whoa** command
5. Step away from the crate a short distance
6. Dog stays in the crate
7. Step to the crate
8. Praise the dog while he is still in the crate
9. Give the **Heel** command
10. Dog steps out and you attach his lead
11. Praise the dog

Repeat the sequence increasing the time you stay away from the crate. Turn your back on the dog -- this will indicate to him that no other command is imminent. As you turn your back and increase time away, you want to pay strict attention to see when the dog relaxes and tells you he has settled down and is going to stay there until given another command. When the dog lies down, you have it made. On the next sequence eliminate the **Whoa** command, but watch him so that you can stop the dog if he tries to leave the crate. Repeat the sequence until he lies down in the crate with only the **Kennel** command.

Questions

1. Did the dog go into the crate promptly?
2. Did the dog try to come out before the Whoa command?
3. Did the dog start to move when you stepped away?
4. What was needed to stop him -- voice or hand, caution or command?
5. Did the dog stand tense, relaxed or cowed?
6. Did the dog move when you stepped back to the crate?
7. Did the dog try to come out when you praised him?
8. During the extended wait, did the dog remain standing, sitting or lying?

The dog knows that the command **Kennel** means go into the crate and stay there. You can now train him to go and stay wherever you point with the command **Kennel**. The dog's bed area (if it is not a crate) or a corner with a pad make an excellent place to start this work. Where and how you use a dog will determine the places you will want the dog to **Kennel**. The sequence to train the dog will be the same as in Step 5.

A note of **Caution**: No dog should be allowed to enter a car, van, truck or other vehicle except on a specific command. This is mentioned here because it is all too easy to get careless and let the dog jump into a car without a command when you are going somewhere. If allowed to, the dog can easily get into the habit of jumping into any open car door. You may even want to use a different command than **Kennel** to put the dog into his crate in the car. It would be relatively easy to do as it is only an alternate command. The main reason for this is that a dog that will jump into any open car door is very easy to steal. Another reason is the inconvenience of having to clean your dog's muddy footprints off someone else's car seat.

37 Whining, Barking, And Howling

A dog that barks, whines or howls (they are all the same -- just a matter of degree) when he is left in a kennel, staked out, in the car, at your side, in a blind or boat hunting is a nuisance to everyone within hearing range. He is wasting energy. It is not a sign of desire to work -- it is idiocy. It tells you one very important thing about his training -- the dog has not accepted the basic principle of restraint, which is to remain in position quietly. Barking is a protest against and a refusal to accept restraint. Like any bad habit, it is easier to prevent than to correct after it is well established.

Young puppies offer a unique problem when you take them from familiar surroundings and litter mates and bring them home to strange surroundings and isolation. As long as someone holds the puppy or is near him, he is usually content. When everyone leaves, for whatever reason, and he is left alone, he naturally tunes up. Be sure before you leave him that he was put out to relieve himself. There is one thing you must do -- hold your temper and let him howl (maybe cry is a better word). The pup will eventually stop crying and go to sleep. There is nothing you can do to help him. The pup has to be left alone for the first time sooner or later. Do not go to the puppy until after he has stopped crying and gone to sleep. If you go to him too soon, he has won round one. You may find it easier on all concerned if your spouse and children go visit relatives or neighbors for the weekend.

Once the puppy has gotten over the shock of his arrival, it is time to be conscious of how he accepts the restraint of the kennel. The pup has the choice of accepting the restraint quietly or fighting it by howling. You will know the difference between the nervous fidgeting and whimper of the pup that needs to relieve himself and the whine of protest against restraint. Get after the protest immediately; do not let it become a habit. To physically punish a puppy is unfair and unnecessary. A show of displeasure (his dam growled at him) and a quiet **Negative** command is often adequate. If not, pick him up by the scruff of his neck and shake him lightly (which is what his dam did to chastise him). If he is really tuned up, give the **Negative** command and rattle and/or bang his crate. He will get the message quickly.

In dealing with a somewhat older dog that starts to bark on restraint, you must get after him no matter where you are or where he is.

1. You hear the dog bark
2. Get to him quickly and aggressively
3. **Negative** command given harshly
4. Appropriate reinforcement (show displeasure, pick him up and shake him, put him down roughly, rattle his crate
5. Dog is quiet. (If you took him out of his crate to shake him, put him back in and close the door.)
6. Walk away

Repeat the sequence every time you hear the dog whine, bark or howl. If this is done every time you hear a noise from the dog, he will learn fast that it is more pleasant if he stays quiet. Even the slightest whine is a protest against the restraint -- get after him. Every time you return to the dog and he has been quiet, praise him generously.

Questions

1. Did you get after him immediately upon hearing him?
2. Do you get after the dog every time?
3. What was required to stop the noise-voice, your approach or crate shaking?
4. If quiet, do you praise the dog every time you go to him?

To stop an older dog that has really developed the habit of sounding off is difficult but well worth the time and effort. The dog has to learn that it is more pleasant for him to be quiet than to sound off. The key to stopping the noise is that every time -- and that means *every time* -- the dog starts up, you (or whoever is closest) have to get after him forcefully. Show vehement displeasure: pick him up roughly, shake him hard and put him down or in his crate roughly. Bang and rattle his crate aggressively. No matter how far away you are or what you are doing, drop everything and run back to him -- every time. Of course, after the first time or two, he will stop the noise as soon as he realizes that you are after him. If you start toward him, go to him and give him the treatment. He must learn that one bark is too many. The dog must be quiet. The habitual barker can be corrected in a short period of time if he is nailed every time he barks.

The sequence to correct the problem will be:

1. The dog whines, barks or howls
2. You get to the dog as fast and as aggressively as you can
3. Very harsh **Negative** command
4. Reinforcement as outlined above, scolding all the time
5. Walk away

Review the questions previously given. Repeat the sequence every time you hear any noise from the dog.

Any time you return to the dog and he has been quiet, praise him lavishly.

This approach will not prevent the dog from barking to protect things and people he is supposed to protect.

Anticipation

38 | Fighting

There is nothing worse than a dog that wants to fight rather than hunt, work or stand quietly with you when told to do so. He is a danger to other dogs and to himself. He is a downright nuisance. Everyone is on edge when he is around. Everyone has an obligation to be sure his dog will not start a fight. If your dog starts a fight, you have to accept *whatever* the owner of the other dog does to stop it and, of course, you are responsible for all veterinary bills for the other dog.

While all dogs have an instinct to be pack leaders and a willingness to fight to prove it (in varying degrees in breeds and dogs within a breed), that instinct must be curbed. This does not mean that the dog does not have a right to defend himself if attacked. He does and he will. It means that he will not start the fight. The dog must be broken of the inclination to start a fight. Yes, broken. It is the only way that this can be handled.

This work will appear to be out of line with and in contradiction to the philosophy expressed and fervently believed in as outlined in Chapter 1, Comments on Training. In all training for hunting, you have time to develop the control needed to ensure correct performance. Nothing is lost or in danger while the training progresses. That is not true when a dog wants to fight. Any and every dog in a fight is subject to severe injury or death. People trying to break up the fight are exposed to severe injury.

Therefore, the dog must be broken of the penchant to start a fight immediately. The longer it is put off the harder the job.

The job will be much easier if it is done the first time the dog makes an aggressive move or sound toward another dog. The first aggressive indication will probably come during his teenage months but may come anytime. Whatever is taking place must stop and the matter should be settled right then and there. To do this properly, you need someone with a dog that will not start a fight. You also need either a riding crop, heavy leather lead or a knotted rope.

With the two dogs on good leads, bring them together and when your dog growls or makes an aggressive move, pull him away and whip him until he *yelps once* -- only *once*. This routine is kept up until the other dog can walk all around yours and even rubbing against him without any indication of aggression. Each time your dog growls he is whipped until he yelps *once*. You will see your dog start trying to avoid the other dog by turning his head away or moving away. When he no longer growls or makes any aggressive move while the other dog rubs against him, it is time for the next step. However, do not make this a separate session. It is all one continuous session. In essence, he has gotten the idea at this point and now you ram it home and reinforce it. Lay your dog down and let the other dog walk over him. If your dog growls, whip him until he yelps *once*. When he accepts the walkover, lay him down and have the other dog lie on top of him. If your dog growls or makes an aggressive move, whip him until he yelps *once*. Repeat this until your dog accepts the other dog on top of him without a growl for several consecutive repetitions. Do this properly and thoroughly and rarely will it have to be done again. Do not stop half way or back off -- finish it.

You will note that you whip the dog until he yelps *once*. That one yelp says, "Okay, I get the message." Anymore licks after that one yelp has a negative effect. The dog submitted and you did not stop -- now he must do something to protect himself. However, do not stop the whipping until the dog gives that one yelp. If you do, he has not submitted and has won that round. Granted, this is rough treatment, some will say brutal, but it is nothing compared to what two dogs that want to fight can do to one another.

In no way does this break a dog's spirit for hunting, nor will he sulk over it later. In fact, he will go right out and hunt as if it never happened. Equally important, however, is that it does not prevent him from defending himself if he is attacked. When two dominant males, who have been through this routine, confront each other, they take a dominant stance and then slightly turn their heads away. In that situation a **Negative** sound from either owner ends the confrontation.